Before Busing

D1565617

ZEBULON VANCE MILETSKY

Before Busing
A History of Boston's Long
Black Freedom Struggle

The University of North Carolina Press *Chapel Hill*

This book was published with the assistance of the Thornton H. Brooks Fund of the University of North Carolina Press.

© 2022 Zebulon Vance Miletsky
All rights reserved
Set in Arno Pro by Westchester Publishing Services
Manufactured in the United States of America

Library of Congress Cataloging-in-Publication Data
Names: Miletsky, Zebulon Vance, author.
Title: Before busing : a history of Boston's long Black freedom struggle / Zebulon Vance Miletsky.
Description: Chapel Hill : The University of North Carolina Press, 2022. | Includes bibliographical references and index.
Identifiers: LCCN 2022020611 | ISBN 9781469662763 (cloth ; alk. paper) | ISBN 9781469662770 (pbk. ; alk. paper) | ISBN 9781469662787 (ebook)
Subjects: LCSH: School integration—Massachusetts—Boston—History—20th century. | African Americans—Education—Massachusetts—Boston. | African Americans—Political activity—Massachusetts—Boston—History—20th century. | Boston (Mass.)—Race relations—History—20th century.
Classification: LCC LC214.23.B67 M55 2022 | DDC 379.2/630974461—dc23/eng/20220608
LC record available at https://lccn.loc.gov/2022020611

Cover illustrations: *Top*, Martin Luther King Jr. leading march in Boston (Entertainment Pictures/Alamy Stock Photo); *bottom*, Rice School, 1949 (author's personal collection); *title block*, paper texture courtesy Freepik.com.

To my father, Marc Alan Miletsky,
who passed away during the completion of this book

Contents

Illustrations

Preface

The Arc of the Moral Universe in Boston

The year 2022 marks fifty years since fourteen Black families and forty-four children in Boston found the courage to file a lawsuit—with the help of the National Association for the Advancement of Colored People (NAACP)—against the City of Boston in federal district court contesting school segregation. Unlike the somewhat inauspicious anniversary of the resulting court order in 1974, perhaps a better case can be made for the recognition of 1972 as a year worthy of recognition. After all, it is hardly worth celebrating an anniversary that so many people found to be painful. Bostonians suffer from an incomplete story. How many of them know that in 1972, Black parents in Boston, Massachusetts, enlisted the help of lawyers from the Harvard University Center for Law and Education (including a young Tom Atkins, who was a student at Harvard Law School) to sue the city's school committee, arguing that Boston was maintaining two separate school systems?

This is a much different narrative from the one that has dominated over the last fifty years. That this was a unilateral decision, which felt more like an edict to some, from a power-hungry federal judge who didn't live in Boston and whose own children attended schools in Wellesley is how many Bostonians remember the decision to implement busing. In this case, the source of pain and strife that appeared to come as a bolt from the blue was actually initiated by a legitimately aggrieved group of parents and children who had been treated unjustly. Like all Bostonians, these parents paid local taxes and were entitled to a quality education for their children from its public school system—a constitutional right—something which they had been denied. The federal court was literally, as Tom Atkins called it, "the court of last resort." In the case of an absolutely defiant and intransigent school committee, after almost nine years of protest—the founding of Freedom Schools, Black independent schools, Operation Exodus, METCO, and many other creative ways of gaining a better education for their beloved children—the somewhat reluctant plaintiffs agreed to file suit against the school committee. After years of warring with Louise Day Hicks (whom Noel Day, the executive director of the St. Mark's Social Center and co-organizer of the "Stay Out for Freedom" movement, called the Sheriff Jim Clark of Boston), the parents would finally see their day in court. The trial took two years to decide. Few realized what was in store for Boston.

The case was *Morgan v. Hennigan*, named for the lead plaintiff, Tallulah Morgan, who—with the help of the NAACP, Freedom House, and other Black community groups—filed a federal suit against the Boston School Committee (whose president at the time was James Hennigan), charging discrimination in school assignments; staffing; and allocation of resources, facilities, and transportation. Legal precedents in Denver and Detroit supported the plaintiffs' case.[1] One of the questions that needs to be asked (which this book seeks to do) is whether Boston is a better city for these changes. Boston has been very fiscally successful, making it one of the most expensive U.S. cities to live in. Has Boston thrived financially from dealing with its racial problems? If that is the case, then why is so little known about the courageous men, women, and children who saw a better future for Boston, and set about to bring it to fruition? Why do so few people know about the lawsuit, and the struggle itself, which brought about a better Boston? Why does so much rancor still exist about school desegregation?

Although there are still many problems, Boston has made progress. At the time of this writing, a Black woman, Kim Janey, was serving as acting mayor and making history in the process. In addition to being both the first woman and the first Black person in the history of the city to occupy the mayor's office, she was also one of the children who rode the buses during school desegregation. Janey comes from a family with important and respected roots in Boston. As was stated on her campaign website, Kim's late great-grandfather, Daniel Benjamin Janey, was an active member of the Twelfth Baptist Church. Her father, Cliff Janey, grew up in the Orchard Park projects and was one of only eight Black students to graduate from the Boston Latin School in 1964. He later attended UMass Amherst, where he was instrumental in bringing about social change.[2]

Janey attended the New School for Children, an independent community school in Roxbury, one of several that were founded to address the grievances being raised by the Black educational movement in Boston. At eleven years of age, she attended the Edwards Middle School in Charlestown. She later became a student in METCO (Metropolitan Council for Educational Opportunity), attending school in Reading, Massachusetts.[3] As president of the Boston City Council, she was next in line to serve when Mayor Marty Walsh was selected by President Joseph Biden to serve as labor secretary. With her swearing in on March 24, 2021, she came the closest to breaking the barrier that thwarted so many Black candidates during the years under study in this book. When a Black candidate is finally elected to the position, they will have to credit people like Kim Janey, Mel King, and Tito Jackson, whose historic campaigns have paved the way to breaking the long-standing bar. (Janey did throw her hat in the ring in the 2021 campaign but was unsuccessful in making it to the final run-off.) Because of the perception of Boston as a city with race problems, her elevation to the acting position drew headlines and national media coverage, bringing more attention to issues of equity.

Boston has been in the news a lot in the past few years. In March 2017, *Saturday Night Live* cast member Michael Che claimed in the popular "Weekend Update" sketch that Boston was "the most racist city I've ever been to." This comment touched off an important discussion about the legacy of racism in Boston. Che refused to back off from his comments, and then Marty Walsh invited Che to sit down to discuss race in Boston. Although the sit-down with the then mayor never took place, Renée Graham of the *Boston Globe* penned a response titled "Yes, Boston, You Are Racist," in which she argued, among other things: "For all its sophistication, Boston is a very parochial city."[4] On May 1, 2017, Baltimore Orioles center fielder Adam Jones had a bag of peanuts thrown at him by a Boston Red Sox fan during a game in which Jones was also called the "N-word" multiple times. The *Boston Globe* undertook a Spotlight series on race in Boston. A study was completed by the Boston Federal Reserve, which determined that the median net worth of white households in Boston stood at $247,000, while the median net worth for Black households was only $8.00 (yes, eight dollars) and the median net worth for Latinx households was $28.60. In the 2020 Democratic debates, the issue of busing was raised by current vice president Kamala Harris when she said, "That little girl was me," turning the nation's attention once again to this largely unresolved problem in American life and culture.

The tension between these antebellum and late modern narratives still exists today as Boston has found itself in a current reckoning with not only its antislavery tradition but its own traditions of slavery. For instance, there has been an ongoing debate for the last several years about Faneuil Hall, which was named after a slaveholder. In 2018, then mayor Marty Walsh supported a proposed memorial by then artist-in-residence Steve Locke, which would consist of a bronze plate representing a slave auction block. The plate would be maintained at the temperature of 98.6 degrees, no matter the climate or weather outside, to represent the humans being sold as property at the time. The artist eventually pulled out of the project following pushback from the local branch of the NAACP. The issue still remains unresolved, perhaps for a future mayor to deal with. Indeed, the question of memorials and how we remember the past has been a pressing issue for the nation as a whole.

In October 2020, the Middle Passage and Port Marker Boston Partnership installed a permanent marker on Long Wharf, which juts out into Boston Harbor, to acknowledge that Boston was a port of entry for enslaved Africans. According to the website of the Boston Middle Passage Project, the port "recognizes the vital role that Africans and their descendants played in the development of the Massachusetts Bay Colony, the Commonwealth of Massachusetts, and the United States of America."[5] The dedication of the port marker took place on August 29, 2021, commemorating an extraordinary development.

King Boston has been working to build a memorial to Martin Luther King Jr. in Boston. The title of the resultant and winning proposal, *The Embrace*, will be anchored on the Boston Common, where in 1965 Dr. King spoke to the masses of Boston in a thrilling April visit that is still emblazoned on the minds of many Bostonians. Having worked on this book for almost ten years, watching the city confront many of the issues that I was researching and writing about has been an exciting experience. I marveled in wonder as these debates—which I had been longing to see for years, decades even—finally began to blossom and bloom. They reflected my own desire to know these hidden histories of Boston. It felt like I was not writing alone—or in vain. There were others who were also interested in these issues, those who saw the value in understanding the backstory of Boston's history.[6]

All the while, it made me think of one of King's most famous quotes—"The arc of the moral universe is long, but it bends toward justice"—and how that prophecy has manifested itself in Boston.[7] These words were in fact a paraphrasing of the words of another theologian, the Reverend Theodore Parker of Boston, who in one of his sermons published in 1854 wrote, "I do not pretend to understand the moral universe, the arc is a long one, my eye reaches but little ways. I cannot calculate the curve and complete the figure by experience of sight; I can divine it by conscience. But from what I see I am sure it bends towards justice."[8] It may have special meaning in a place like Boston, with its centrality in the creation of Jim Crow. The long Black freedom struggle in Boston may contain the clues to the entire question of Black freedom in America.

Considering all that we have witnessed in terms of activism, especially with the arrival of the Black Lives Matter movement in 2013, it is only natural that these issues would also find an outlet in Boston. Alongside the rise of abolition movements, a worldwide pandemic, the killing of George Floyd, and what seemed like the entire world chanting "Black Lives Matter"—all of which was playing out as the sun rose and fell outside the doldrums of my various writing spaces—Boston remained an unsolved mystery. Ushering in an increased desire to confront the true roots of racism in the United States—and a modern-day civil rights movement unfolding—increased inequality, and resegregation of our schools, it felt like history repeating itself. In the midst of so much social change taking place, there must, and will, be a reckoning with the issue of race in Boston.

When we consider the anger, the hatred, and the violence that accompanied school desegregation in Boston—all the things that make Boston a racist city in people's minds—if such a thing as justice exists, one can hardly make a clearer case than Boston as the place where it should happen. We are watching the arc of the moral universe bend toward justice in Boston, with its capacity for both bad and good. There is a chance for restorative justice for the many who were wronged.

Finally, there was an article that appeared in the *Boston Globe* on April 14, 2021, about Tito Jackson, who had served as a city councilor from Roxbury and also ran unsuccessfully for mayor against Marty Walsh. He was vocal about being adopted and mentioned it from time to time at events, especially those in which the question of family was at issue.[9] Tito Jackson was born in 1975 to Rachel E. Twymon—then a thirteen-year-old middle-schooler who was bused to Charlestown—who gave him up for adoption due to the shame accompanied with having been impregnated through rape at such a young age. She was a member of the Black family (referred to as pathological by so many critics) chronicled in J. Anthony Lukas's Pulitzer Prize–winning book, *Common Ground: A Turbulent Decade in the Lives of Three American Families.* Jackson began speaking publicly about this new revelation—a new twist in the long and difficult story of race in Boston. The arc of the moral universe in Boston is long, but it bends toward justice.

There is still a tremendous need for healing in the city of Boston on all sides. There is also a need for truth and reconciliation. Perhaps with a more accurate retelling of the past, we may find ourselves closer to finding such things. So many of the names that fill the pages of this book have sought to bring about a better city—a more equitable one—and are the handmaidens of a more just Boston.

But there is much work yet to do. The state of Massachusetts continues to disproportionately profile, prosecute, and incarcerate Black community members. When funding is cut for social services, Black communities are still hit the hardest. In 2017, forty-nine Boston public schools sustained significant budget cuts predominantly affecting children of color.[10] In Roxbury, the median income for Black and Latinx families in 2015 was $30,000.[11] Black residents in Massachusetts are incarcerated at a rate six times higher than their white counterparts. There are still many Black Lives Matters protesters who are facing various charges for their activism during these years, including blocking traffic on I-93. Due to the years of redlining, segregation, and economic exploitation, the median net worth for Black households is still only eight dollars. Boston's legacy of confronting Jim Crow endures.

Before Busing

Introduction

Boston, that "city upon a hill" as dreamed of by John Winthrop, perches upon twilight—between the long night of northern slavery, the dawn of Jim Crow, and the dusk of freedom. It is a complicated place that has been scrubbed clean by its founders and the many generations that revered it as the "cradle of liberty." Popular narratives of Boston tend to cordon off this early period from later associations with racial discrimination and white backlash. In this telling, Boston's central role in the nation's founding marks it as the birthplace of freedom and equality. This association continues through the Civil War period, during which Boston served as a hotbed of abolitionist sentiment and activism. It was not until the 1970s that white supremacy is thought to have first reared its ugly head in the form of angry white parents who violently opposed integration, attacking school buses carrying Black children. Since then, the busing crisis has featured prominently in discussions of the civil rights era in Boston. Dozens of books, articles, and documentaries have focused on the topic. For many, busing appears as the sole major conflict in the city with regard to race during this period, leaving other areas unmentioned.[1] This narrative quickly unravels when we look more closely at the century-long struggles over race in Boston. For many scholars, the designation of Boston as "the Deep North" has been more exact.[2]

Before Busing offers a new history of Boston, one that undermines the myth of Boston as a city devoid of racial tensions by revealing the ways in which Black self-assertion and white supremacy have long coexisted as major drivers of economic, social, and political life throughout the city's history. These tensions were front and center in Boston's infamous busing crisis. During the crisis, in which busing was ordered as a means to achieve racial balance in the schools by a federal judge in 1974, Boston became the site of some of the era's most acrimonious protests and white recalcitrance. Jonathon Kozol's *Death at an Early Age* describes the problem the busing order sought to fix in great detail. Schools in Black neighborhoods were underfunded, falling down, and in a general state of disrepair. By issuing the federal order, district court judge W. Arthur Garrity essentially ruled in favor of Black parents and families who had brought suit against the Boston School Committee. In so doing, the court found the committee guilty of violating the Fourteenth

Amendment's equal protection clause. White Bostonians who opposed busing organized demonstrations, boycotts, and protests, and both Black and white parents feared for their children's safety.

Yet as previously mentioned, Boston's racial tensions predated and went beyond the narrow focus on busing. Accordingly, *Before Busing* goes further, situating the struggles over education within a broader context of racial justice activism in the city that also targeted employment and housing discrimination, police brutality, access to public welfare benefits, social equality, cultural autonomy, and more over the course of two centuries.

It is perhaps unsurprising that the struggle for racial justice in Boston centered on education. Education is the place where hopes and dreams reside for the future. It is the place that holds possibilities for advancement. It is also a potent symbol of America—the schoolhouse, with its American flag and the potential for shaping the future that it represents for the little people who enter its doors. *They* have not been infected by the scourge of racism yet. *They* can still be shaped and molded to change the future. It also represents the last *sacred space* where change is possible. In a society in which hatred reigns, where injustice snarls, a society's struggle to find social justice will inevitably find its way to the schoolhouse. The schoolroom becomes a microcosm of what's going on in a society—a place where those struggles will ultimately play themselves out—mirroring the larger society and carving out a space and time for youth to work through those issues in the same way that the (National Association for the Advancement of Colored People) NAACP's long legal strategy would trigger the social revolution that would transform the South and bury Jim Crow.

Between a rock and a hard place, when bodies are being lynched, when hopes are dimmed for the future, the schoolhouse holds the potential for the next generation to "do better." And it is the thing that connects all of us in its universality. We want our children to do better than we have done. It is where we *should* be able to find common ground. The children represent hope and the possibility of tomorrow. Like America, Boston finds its civil rights struggle—its own effort to break the back of Jim Crow—starting as a fight in the schoolhouses.

Though the retellings of Boston's history that ignore the city's history of racism and antiracist organizing are mistaken, it is nevertheless true that Boston has its own distinctive dynamics that set it apart. As a city founded by those in search of religious tolerance, a critical site in the struggle for American independence, and the home of abolitionism, Boston has long enjoyed a reputation as a special place. It has been called "the city upon a hill," "the hub of the universe," "the Athens of America," and so forth. Yet the city's unique white ethnic makeup has also meant that it has long been a place where ethnic rivalries were exploited by the ruling class—the so-called Boston Brahmins—to the detriment of many. The historic tensions between the English and the Irish combined to create a strange alchemy regarding whiteness in Boston, playing a major role in the suppression of other white ethnic groups, such as Italian Americans and eastern Europeans, and the small but growing Black community.[3]

As Lily Geismer writes in *Don't Blame Us*, "Dating back to the nineteenth century, the tension between the Boston Brahmin elite and working-class white ethnic groups, especially the Irish, structured the political culture of Massachusetts."[4] Black Americans had to vie for their own equality within these sharply delineated and hotly contested racial realities.

The era of independence and later the abolitionist period fostered the emergence of a small but significant Black political leadership that fought to press abstract notions of liberty and democracy into meaningful concrete realities for Black Bostonians, with some success. Just as white elites sometimes sought to use Black residents as pawns in their wider political efforts, so too did Black leaders and community organizations seek to exploit these cleavages for their own advantage—a complicated political calculus between constituencies that did not enjoy equal power. Yet by the late nineteenth and early twentieth centuries, the curtain of a new regime of white supremacy, "the Jim Crow North," fell across the city, reversing some of the gains of the earlier period and erecting new challenges to Black freedom and equality.

Within this context, Boston again became an important proving ground for Black political leaders seeking to develop new strategies to topple an unjust racial regime—strategies that most often hinged on education. Here, Booker T. Washington, W. E. B. Du Bois, and William Monroe Trotter fought for influence over Black Bostonians as part of a broader national battle to win adherents. Education was a cornerstone for ideas about "Black empowerment" for all three. As the first Black American to receive a doctorate from Harvard University, Du Bois was a beacon and an example of the power of education to uplift. Booker T. Washington, a teacher first and foremost, certainly was as well, founding a Black college that became a model and had implications for all Black education. Trotter, a Harvard-trained "race man," railed against any curtailment of education for Black Americans. Years later, as a result of a community-led effort, the Boston Public Schools named the first post-busing model school for integration in the Boston neighborhood of Roxbury after him. Similarly, organizations like the National Association for the Advancement of Colored People, the Urban League, the National Equal Rights League, the Universal Negro Improvement Association, and Black women's clubs all flourished in Boston. In many ways, the ideological and tactical lines established during this period continued to shape campaigns for racial equality in Boston and throughout the United States well into the twentieth century.

In the decades leading up to the Second World War, new political possibilities emerged in Boston as labor activism, political radicalism, and struggles for economic justice in the Depression-era dovetailed with civil rights campaigns. As in other cities, Black Bostonians attempted to leverage wartime military service to uncover new possibilities in the city's manufacturing base, port-related industries, and service economy. Yet as was often the case, class-based solidarity regularly broke on the rocky shoals of persistent racism. In this political moment, educational struggles moved to the periphery as immediate bread-and-butter issues of economic security dominated.

In the post–World War II period, Black leaders in Boston drew lessons from their predecessors' waves of civil rights activism, hoping to shape a new politics of Black freedom in line with the growing national movement for racial equality in the United States. Among the range of issues Boston activists pursued, education again emerged as a central focus. During the late 1940s and early 1950s, middle-class Black leaders created intergenerational (and often interracial) spaces for the development of new political ideas and organizing, particularly around educational opportunity and equality. Building on the historic victory in *Brown v. Board of Education*, Black parents and Boston civil rights leaders pushed to apply the historic ruling to local circumstances. These efforts included attempts to support Black teachers, a campaign to open up space for Black children in schools outside the segregated Black community, and tutoring programs for inner-city kids. They also supported a historic lawsuit brought forth by the NAACP on behalf of Tallulah Morgan and fourteen other families of Black schoolchildren in Boston charging that Boston public schools were systematically discriminatory. The *Morgan v. Hennigan* case (1972) was one of the most controversial trials in Boston's history, Boston's *Brown v. Board of Education*.[5] Like that landmark case, it took a great deal of legal wrangling and was accused of setting social policy, and, though largely under the protection of *Brown*, it was also bolstered and made possible by an umbrella of other cases on school desegregation writ large—one of which ruled that de facto segregation could be ruled unconstitutional. *Brown*'s legal protection was limited, as it applied only to de jure segregation. Most experts agreed that the northern brand of school segregation resulted from geography—neighborhoods where people chose to live. For many northern cities, that meant ethnic enclaves and fiercely defended neighborhood borders. This was considered de facto segregation. The Warren court, which decided on *Brown*, was very careful to limit its ruling to de jure segregation for various reasons, which are discussed in later chapters. In a footnote to the 1954 decision, Warren wrote: "In the North segregation in public education has persisted in some communities until recent years. It is apparent that such segregation has long been a nationwide problem, not merely one of sectional concern."[6] As Lukas has noted:

> That remark would have surprised the black plaintiffs in *Morgan v. Hennigan* and the white liberals who had drafted the Racial Imbalance Act eight years earlier. To be sure, Warren had been writing still earlier, before the wave of black emigration from the South had intensified the imbalance in Boston's ghetto schools. But in any case, the Chief Justice felt bound by the Court's long-established position that the equal protection clause only prohibited discrimination by the state, not by private practices. Thus, Brown applied only to separation imposed by racially explicit statutes, what became known as de jure segregation, not that which stemmed from social conditions, or de facto segregation.[7]

As Jeanne Theoharis has written regarding her work, which has intentionally focused on the northern struggle:

> Focusing on the North also makes clear that there was nothing accidental or "de facto" (or simply, in fact) about Northern segregation. As historian Matthew Lassiter documents, the framework of "de facto" segregation (as compared to "de jure," or by law) was created to appeal to Northern sensibilities, to make a distinction between the segregation so evident in many Northern cities from the segregation many Northerners decried in the South. Thus Northern "de facto" segregation was cast outside the law, despite the many government policies that supported and legalized these practices (and judges from Boston to California would find intentional segregation in these school districts as well). Many scholars and journalists since the 1960s have clung to this false distinction between a Southern "de jure" segregation and a Northern "de facto" segregation, making Northern segregation more innocent and missing the various ways such segregation was supported and maintained through the law and political process.[8]

As Judge Julian Houston, a faithful chronicler of these events, has written, "*Morgan v. Hennigan*, unquestionably the most important civil rights case in twentieth-century Boston, reverberates throughout the city to this day. But we know little about the historical context behind *Morgan v. Hennigan,* which could not have reached the courts without those who had already challenged entrenched power and privilege in both public and private institutions."[9]

Efforts to secure quality education for Black Bostonians coincided with protests targeting a host of other issues. Local civil rights activists staged rent strikes against absentee landlords, protested housing discrimination, picketed downtown businesses that refused to hire Black employees, fought urban renewal projects that they believed would harm existing Black neighborhoods, and developed support structures for activists involved in the southern movement. But as local campaigns for racial justice accelerated, so too did white resistance.

These forces came to a head during the late 1960s and early 1970s. As activists continued to fight for change on a host of issues, civil order broke down in 1967 in Boston's predominately Black Roxbury neighborhood in what has come to be known as the "welfare riot" following a sit-in of mostly Black mothers in the welfare office.[10] Many of the participants of that particular action would be prominent names in the school desegregation fight to come. The next year, in the days after Martin Luther King Jr.'s tragic assassination, Boston managed to avoid the kind of dramatic race rebellion that took place in cities like Baltimore, Trenton, and Washington, DC. The anger of Black Bostonians was nevertheless palpable.[11] The *Boston Record American* reported that Black neighborhoods "seethed with emotion and tension ... [and] angry bands of Negro youths stoned cars and buses traversing Blue Hill Ave. screaming their vengeance and pathos."[12] As Black demands for liberation became more militant during the Black Power era, white resistance became further entrenched, epitomized by the national call for law and order.

It was in this racially polarized environment that the Boston busing crisis of 1974–76 erupted. The stage was set in 1965 when the state legislature in Massachusetts passed the Racial Imbalance Act, a pioneering measure outlawing segregation in public schools and a direct result of Martin Luther King's visit to Boston that same year.[13] Behind the leadership of school committee and city council member Louise Day Hicks, Boston school officials refused to develop or implement a desegregation plan to achieve integration, defying orders from the state board of education to do so. In response, the NAACP, with the help of Harvard University and other groups, filed a lawsuit on behalf of fourteen Black families in 1972 against segregation in the Boston public schools.[14] Two years later, district court judge W. Arthur Garrity held in favor of the plaintiffs and ordered the implementation of a busing plan to achieve desegregation in all Boston public schools that were more than 50 percent nonwhite.

This triumph for civil rights activists was met with a furious backlash. Garrity's decision provoked a vociferous response from many white Bostonians who expressed their opposition to the plan in a variety of ways, including political organizing, nonviolent protests, racial taunting, withdrawing their children from public schools, and several incidents of outright violence— which at times provoked retaliatory violence by Black teenagers. As an irate John J. McDonough, the head of the Boston School Committee, told the press following Judge Garrity's decision in 1974, "Reconstruction has finally come to the North, with a vengeance."[15] According to a pamphlet put out by the Proletarian Unity League, "McDonough chose his reference carefully. For the white supporters of the anti-busing movement and segregated schools, the allusion to Reconstruction was designed to conjure up the image of carpetbagging suburbanites, backed by what the white anti-busing organization Restore Our Alienated Rights (ROAR) called 'judicial tyranny,' all conspiring to promote a cruel 'Black rule' throughout Boston."[16]

Federally enforced busing lasted thirteen years in Boston, and the ultimate impacts of the plan remain contested and unclear more than four decades later, particularly in light of large-scale economic and demographic shifts. Nevertheless, the media images created in those early years of implementation ingrained a particular view of Boston race relations into the national consciousness that has been hard to shake. *Before Busing* shows that the history of race relations and campaigns for racial justice in Boston are considerably more complicated than this static image suggests. Delving into that more complex—and paradoxical—history is crucial not only to grasp the turbulent Boston busing crisis of the 1970s but also to explain the enduring urban inequalities that still plague the city today.

Movements Outside the South

This book joins a body of work that over the past decade and a half has emerged to explore the complicated dynamics of the Black freedom movement beyond the South. The signal shot in this new wave of scholarship was Jeanne Theoharis and Komozi Woodard's 2003 edited volume *Freedom North: Black Freedom Struggles Outside the South, 1940–1980*. In an introductory essay that reads as a scholarly call to arms, Theoharis argues, "Foregrounding the South has constricted popular understandings of race and racism in the United States during and after WWII," making it seem "as if the

South was the only part of the country that needed a movement, as if Blacks in the rest of the country only became energized to fight after their Southern brothers and sisters did, as if Southern racism was more malignant than the strains found in the rest of the country, as if social activism produced substantive change only in the South."[17]

Similarly, in a special 2012 issue of the *Magazine of History* that focused on new directions in movement history "beyond Dixie," Thomas Sugrue, author of the landmark survey of the northern movement *Sweet Land of Liberty: The Forgotten Struggle for Civil Rights in the North* (2009), declared, "Our histories—and our collective memories—of the civil rights era do not reflect the national scope of racial inequality and the breadth of challenges to it."[18] Patrick Jones, author of *The Selma of the North: Civil Rights Insurgency in Milwaukee*, catalogs some of the ways a focus on northern Black freedom movements changes our understanding of the civil rights era: "Foregrounding northern struggles for racial justice complicates a number of debates that southern movement historians have been grappling with for the past couple of decades. It reinforces the 'long civil rights movement' concept, by further exploding the popular chronology that begins in 1954 and ends in 1968. It highlights the interactivity between formal politics, legal action, social movement activism and cultural politics."[19] Detailed studies of civil rights activism in the North by Martha Biondi (New York), Matthew Countryman and Lisa Levenstein (Philadelphia), Clarence Lang (St. Louis), Rhonda Williams (Baltimore), Brian Purnell (Brooklyn), Patrick Jones (Milwaukee), and others, including Jason Sokol's more regional study of the civil rights era in the Northeast, have further deepened our grasp of the significance of northern Black freedom movements. And yet remarkably, Boston has remained relatively absent from this growing scholarly literature.

Works on Boston's broader history are voluminous, including several important books on race relations and campaigns for civil rights during the nineteenth and early twentieth centuries.[20] Yet scholarship on the civil rights era is harder to come by. The strongest and most substantive work we have on Boston's Black freedom movement is Mel King's autobiography, *Chain of Change*, which demonstrates the ways in which the modern struggle for racial justice in Boston touched on every aspect of Black life and shaped the future of the city. Ruth Batson's *The Black Educational Movement in Boston* is more than just a personal memoir about her role in the school desegregation campaign; it offers the beginnings of a real conceptual approach to Boston's civil rights movement.

More recently, a new generation of historians has begun to point toward a fuller picture of not only the school desegregation movement in Boston but also the enduring struggle for racial justice in the city.[21] *Before Busing* builds on this work by expanding on the longer trajectory of school desegregation activism in Boston and placing it within an even deeper stream of racial struggle stretching back into the seventeenth century. In doing so, it knits together the previously disparate stories of people like Anthony Burns, William Lloyd Garrison, Phyllis Wheatley, Ed Brooke, Frederick Douglass, Booker T. Washington, William Monroe Trotter, W. E. B. Du Bois, Malcolm X, Ruth Batson, and Martin Luther King Jr., all of whom had significant ties to Boston during the century prior to the busing controversy.

In its six chapters, *Before Busing* outlines the history of struggles over race and racism in Boston spanning four centuries.[22] Chapter 1 focuses on the early origins of Boston's Black community, both enslaved and free, which grew up around Boston's waterfront and wharves, particularly in the North Slope of the Beacon Hill neighborhood. Like other port cities in this period, Boston's seafaring trade made great fortunes and brought a vast mix of peoples to the city. Given the centrality of the transatlantic slave trade, notions of liberty, democracy, and independence in Boston were intertwined with the tragic paradox of racialized slavery. It was not until a court decision in 1783 that slavery was outlawed in Massachusetts, the same year the Revolutionary War ended. By that point, racialized slavery had been a fact of Boston life for 150 years, making a deep and lasting impact on the "cradle of liberty."[23] It was in this context that Boston's Black community led a number of campaigns to achieve educational opportunity and equality, establishing education, broadly, and schools, specifically, as key sites of racial struggle. These efforts revolved around two related yet distinct strands of activism. The first was led by Black teachers and administrators who served segregated Black schools and who organized efforts to increase wages, improve classrooms, and receive more basic supplies. Rather than a struggle for "separate but equal," it might more aptly be termed a pragmatic fight for "equal within separate." On the other hand, Benjamin Roberts and other community leaders pushed for integration within the common school system, leading ultimately to a historic court case, *Roberts v. Boston*.

This case, which served as one of the first challenges to racial discrimination in public schools, occupies a central part of the latter part of chapter 1. The case involved Benjamin Roberts's five-year-old daughter, Sarah Roberts, who attended the underfunded Abiel Smith Common School for Black children, which was located at a great distance from the Robertses' home. In response, Roberts attempted to enroll his daughter in a whites-only school closer to their home and was denied, leading to the lawsuit that sought to end racial discrimination in Boston public schools. In 1850, the Massachusetts Supreme Judicial Court found in favor of the city, claiming no constitutional basis for the suit. The U.S. Supreme Court later cited this case in its infamous 1896 *Plessy v. Ferguson* decision, establishing the "separate but equal" doctrine. Nevertheless, back in Massachusetts, Roberts brought his claims to the state legislature, which in 1855 passed a law banning segregation in the state's public schools. It was the first such law in the United States. Both the court decision and legislative initiative would later play a role in the landmark 1954 *Brown v. Board of Education* decision.

As a result of the Great Depression and World War II, both of which brought economic issues to the fore, education as a central focus of the Black freedom struggle receded into the background. Following the war, some Black veterans used the GI Bill to augment their education, buy homes, and do a whole range of things they had not been able to do before. Although many were helped, just as many were denied these benefits due to segregation, restrictive covenants, whites-only schooling, and other impediments that were still in place. As such, those who did receive benefits helped to lay the foundations for the emergence of a true Black middle class and the civil rights movement.

As the nascent civil rights movement began to grow in the years after World War II, efforts to combat racial inequality were continually challenged by the precedent set by *Plessy v. Ferguson* (1896). In 1895, Black Louisianans decided to test the constitutionality of the new laws that were being passed that required separate railroad cars for Black passengers. Homer Plessy, a fair-skinned man with a fierce sense of social justice, who had been involved in civil rights gatherings and groups, sat down in a car reserved for whites and was arrested. Because he and his colleagues believed that they were protected by the Fourteenth Amendment and its equal protection clause, Plessy believed the Supreme Court would stand by him. It did not. The court upheld his conviction in a decision that would shape race relations for the next half century. In *Plessy v. Ferguson*, it ruled that "the 14th Amendment could not have been intended to abolish distinctions based upon color or a commingling of the races." In so doing, it created the bulwark and shadow against which the modern civil rights movement would mature and grow—and it would eventually be overturned.

In the decades that followed, the Jim Crow North took hold in Boston during the late nineteenth and early twentieth centuries. Chapter 2 discusses the vigorous debates that took place in the city over Black political leadership and the most effective response to the new system of white supremacy and racial discrimination setting in across the country. Initially, Booker T. Washington's accommodationist approach found a welcome audience in Boston among many middle-class Black leaders and the descendants of white abolitionists. Washington, who owned a summer home in a Boston suburb and sent his children to school in the city, founded the Negro Business League in Boston in 1900 to spur Black entrepreneurship. During the first two decades of the twentieth century, though, two other titans of Black politics with deep roots in Boston—W. E. B. Du Bois and William Monroe Trotter—rose to offer scathing critiques of Washingtonian accommodationism and put forth their own visions of racial uplift. Both men were leaders of the Niagara Movement and played a role in the foundation of the NAACP. Each rejected Washington's industrial education model and advocated a more direct attack on racial discrimination and segregation in Boston and beyond. Trotter left the NAACP to form his own organization, the National Equal Rights League. He used the pages of his newspaper, the *Guardian*, to level withering, often personal attacks on Washington and other Black leaders, including Du Bois. Trotter, often seen as a more militant leader, mounted several important public protests during this period, most notably against President Woodrow Wilson's decision to segregate federal offices and against the screening of D. W. Griffith's racist epic, *The Birth of a Nation*. Du Bois chose to work within the structure of the newly formed NAACP, preferring legal challenges to protest politics and leveling a more measured attack on Washington's leadership in the pages of the *Crisis* and in his classic book, *The Souls of Black Folk*.

It is notable that these hotly contested debates—between arguably the three most important Black political leaders of the early twentieth century—took place largely in Boston, underscoring the centrality of the city to national debates over racial uplift. The ideas, organizations, and strategic approaches of these three leaders would have enduring influence within the Black freedom movement throughout the twentieth century, and at the heart of each man's philosophy of racial change was an educational program. Finally, the tussling for influence in this early period highlights the fact that Black communities are not monolithic but complex and organic, made up of varieties of experiences, perspectives, and approaches to racial change. This, too, would be an enduring lesson (and challenge) for the Black freedom movement.

During the 1930s and 1940s, Black political activism centered on the fight for economic justice and the dire needs of the Black working class. Chapter 3 recounts how, as the city and nation slipped more deeply into the Great Depression, bread-and-butter issues dominated. Employment and economic opportunity, as well as housing, moved to the forefront of struggles for racial justice. New alliances between organized labor, radical movements, and the Black working class emerged. At the heart of these economic efforts was Boston's "Don't Buy Where You Can't Work" campaign, a local manifestation of a national movement during this period. The campaign in Boston was led by the League of Struggle for Negro Rights, a communist-organized successor to the American Negro Labor Congress. This chapter highlights the long-standing role that white radicals have played as allies in local Black freedom movements, as well as the possibilities, but also the significant challenges, associated with class-based interracial organizing. Finally, while the economic protest campaigns of the 1930s and 1940s did achieve modest success in opening up some new opportunities for Black clerks, delivery drivers, bank tellers, and even store managers, the scale and pace of change was nowhere near the level needed in the community, raising important questions about the effectiveness of this approach for racial change.

A new generation of Black political leaders emerged in the postwar period. Chapter 4 focuses on their efforts to challenge a range of issues within the context of a rising national movement for racial justice. One strand in this chapter is wound around Otto and Muriel Snowden's Freedom House, a nonprofit, community-based organization in Roxbury founded in 1949 and dedicated to civil rights and the empowerment of the Black community. Freedom House held not only social events but also a series of lectures, debates, and "coffee hours," which fueled intergenerational discussions regarding pressing political issues. It was out of this milieu that legendary Boston civil rights leader Ruth Batson emerged. The chapter charts her evolution as an activist at Freedom House to a leader in school desegregation. It also examines Operation Exodus, an innovative, self-funded, community-based effort led by Ellen Jackson and Elizabeth Johnson to bus Black students in Roxbury to open seats within the Boston school district. The program, which ran from 1964 to 1969, also provided tutoring, cultural enrichment programs, psychological services, and vocational training and was an important forerunner of the more well-known Metropolitan Council for Educational Opportunity, or METCO, a voluntary school desegregation busing program founded in 1966. METCO became a national model for voluntary desegregation programs across the United States and is still serving children in Massachusetts today.[24]

The second strand in this chapter explores a new cadre of young civil rights leaders and the linkages between Boston-area college campuses and local community organizing campaigns, including the Boston Action Group, a student-clergy alliance that pressured area businesses, like Wonder Bread, to hire Black workers; Stay Out for Freedom, a nonviolent direct-action boy-cott campaign against de facto segregation in the Boston public schools led by Noel Day and James Breeden in 1963–64; and the Northern Student Movement, formed in the wake of the southern student sit-in movement to provide moral, physical, and financial support to southern student activists and challenge northern racial discrimination. These organizations established tutoring programs for inner-city children, staged rent strikes against absentee landlords, protested housing discrimination, and fought urban renewal. Overall, this chapter underscores the many ways Black Bostonians drove local civil rights campaigns through the mid-1960s.

What followed was the tumultuous Black Power era. Chapter 5 looks to the racial polarization that gathered strength between 1967 and 1970, interrogating the idea of what I call "Boston Exceptionalism"—the claim that Boston did not suffer from the same racial problems as other northern cities during the late 1960s. The critically acclaimed 2008 documentary *The Night James Brown Saved Boston* offers a good example of this rosy narrative. The film juxtaposes images of widespread urban rebellion in the wake of Dr. King's assassination on April 4, 1968, with the riot-that-wasn't in Boston. On April 5, the night after King's death, James Brown was scheduled to perform at the old Boston Garden, a show the local authorities considered canceling out of concern that the large Black crowd might riot. Instead, city officials decided to televise the con-cert, with the goal of keeping Black Americans in their homes and off the streets. The televised concert furthermore gave the mayor a public platform from which to present a message of peace and unity. While the film presents an entertaining examination of an interesting moment in music history and, as such, provides an avenue to understanding the somewhat unique racial cli-mate in Boston, it also reifies the dangerous notion that Boston was excep-tional in an era of widespread urban rebellions. In fact, the previous year, three days of rioting, violence, and property destruction followed a sit-in demon-stration by the Mothers for Adequate Welfare at the Grove Hall welfare office in Roxbury, the culmination of growing urban tensions between local Black residents and Boston police. While Boston *was* one of the few American cities spared large-scale civil disorder in the immediate wake of Dr. King's murder, its Roxbury, North Dorchester, and South End communities all experienced modest bursts of racial violence, though not at the level as other major Ameri-can cities. In many ways, these simmering tensions set the stage for the racial crisis to come over busing during the early 1970s.

Finally, the book comes full circle in chapter 6 by examining and reposi-tioning the Boston busing crisis of the mid-1970s within the broader context of the long history of civil rights activism in the city. Instead of a narrative focused almost exclusively—and somewhat sympathetically—on white reaction, as has been the case in books like *Common Ground* or *Boston against Busing*, Black agency and activism take center stage, situating the busing program as the culmination of nearly three decades of consistent political organizing by Black Bostonians. In addition to community organizing and protest politics, this chapter also frames the busing crisis as part of a decades-long legal battle, pressed by community activists like Ruth Batson and championed by Black lawyers like Nathaniel Jones of the NAACP and their allies. The ultimate result was the historic *Morgan v. Hennigan* (1974) decision, which defined the busing controversy in the city for the next decade and a half. In this light, Black Bostonians were not merely pawns of Judge Garrity's "judicial activism," as is often suggested, but engaged participants in the unfolding drama, in which white resistance played a much deeper and more enduring role than commonly thought.

An epilogue provides a reflection on the impact of Boston's busing crisis on the city's educational and racial politics over the ensuing three decades, exploring the tangible gains that were achieved, as well as the intractable inequalities that persist. Forty years later, people still have strong feelings about desegregation and Boston's long civil rights movement. Modern-day projects like the Boston Busing/Desegregation Project, coordinated by the Union of Minority Neighborhoods, continue to work on dialogues around busing and have consistently found that social healing over busing and further action to redress racial segregation in education is still needed. Marking the fortieth anniversary of the busing crisis in 2014, the *Boston Globe* devoted a series of articles to a time that many Bostonians seemed unwilling to celebrate or remember, let alone learn from. The coverage reinforced the notion that Bostonians remain ambivalent about this crucial moment in their city's history and what it might reveal about ongoing urban challenges. As such, the true meaning of the busing crisis remains elusive, both for those who lived through it and for those looking back on it. Several of the stories retold here represent a narrative that has been "scattered"—told and retold not only in forums, symposia, and meetings but also in churches, barbershops, and quiet conversations between friends, neighbors, and families who lived through these years and participated in these campaigns, often without recognition, fanfare, and even acknowledgment.

As it was across the period explored in *Before Busing*, education continues to be a central touchstone of struggles over equality and opportunity, community and belonging, and democracy and social justice in Boston and throughout the United States. As this new telling of Boston's history reveals, the struggle over education intersected with other fundamental issues, such as economic inequality, housing, social segregation, transportation, political power, policing, nutrition, and mental health. Black Bostonians—from students, parents, and teachers to administrators and political leaders, as well as business and religious figures—have continued to fight for their own vision of educational equality, with and against forces that sometimes do, but often don't, have the best interest of their children at heart. In order to provide every child with a high-quality education, we must grapple with these complexities and develop a broad plan of action. This history provides one lens of analysis.

The Origins of Slavery, Freedom, and Jim Crow in the Cradle of Liberty, 1638–1896

God helping me, I would do my best to hasten the day when the
color of the skin would be no barrier to equal school rights.

—William Cooper Nell

In 1638, a Dutch ship bearing the designation *Desire* maneuvered its massive hull into Boston Harbor. Built in Marblehead, Massachusetts, this merchant vessel, sailed by Captain William Pierce (aka Peirce, Pearce) of Boston, did not make an especially remarkable sight as it sailed through the surging currents of the Atlantic. Its course from the Bahamas to Boston was perfectly ordinary, except that this ship carried in its keel a strange kind of cargo— namely slaves.

The origin of this long and difficult journey of racialized slavery in New England can be traced to an earlier historical moment, when the Old World of Europe and the New World of the Americas were violently thrown together with the arrival of Christopher Columbus in the Caribbean in 1492. On Friday, October 12, 1492, Columbus scrawled in his ship's log, "At dawn we saw naked people."[1] The naked people Columbus spoke of were the original inhabitants of the islands of the Bahamas, the site of Columbus's first landing. They would be all but wiped out through their struggle with the European invaders—first through the Europeans' attempt to enslave them; second through the Spanish encomienda system, which forced them to work in mines to satisfy a seemingly insatiable Spanish hunger for gold and silver; and third by the germs Europeans brought with them, against which the Indigenous populations were virtually defenseless.

Following in the tradition of their Spanish forebears, on November 9, 1620, one hundred two passengers of the Mayflower rounded the tip of Cape Cod and made landfall off the coast of Massachusetts. There they established Plymouth Plantation, which became a haven for sea-weary Pilgrims fleeing religious persecution and seeking a place where they could find rest.

The founder of the Massachusetts Bay Colony, John Winthrop—a Puritan lawyer, who would later serve as its first governor—led his band of newcomers from England to Massachusetts in 1630 to create the second major settlement in New England, after Plymouth, on the peninsula jutting out into the

Massachusetts Bay. The Native Americans called this place Shawmut.[2] The English would rename it Boston, after a small town in England. And Winthrop, quoting scripture, would call it a "city upon a hill."[3]

Boston—City of Myths

Mythmaking was an important aspect of Boston from the very beginning. A later moniker, the "cradle of liberty", would endure alongside "the city upon a hill" epithet to create an image of Boston as an idealized place—one that makes it all too easy to forget that slavery existed in the Massachusetts Bay Colony for some 150 years. As one of the oldest cities in America, Boston was a place of many firsts. Although enslaved Africans were first brought to Jamestown, Virginia, in 1607, Massachusetts became the first colony to officially sanction slavery when it passed the Body of Liberties in 1641.[4] Although not legally recognized until 1641, records dating as early as the 1630s reveal that slavery existed in the colony. The first record of a group of African people arriving in Massachusetts comes from Winthrop's journal.[5] Winthrop wrote in his diary on February 26, 1638: "Mr. Peirce, in the Salem ship, the Desire, returned from the West Indies after seven months. He had been at Providence, and brought some cotton, and tobacco, and negroes, &c. from thence, and salt from Tertugos. Dry fish and strong liquors are the only commodities for those parts. He met there two men-of-war, set forth by the lords, &c. of Providence with letters of mart, who had taken divers prizes from the Spaniard, and many negroes."[6] Initially, slavery was restricted to penal slavery, imposed as punishment for a crime. These crimes ranged anywhere from robbery to nonpayment of fines.[7] According to J. Anthony Lukas, whose depiction of northern slavery is rather benign: "Following the Hebraic tradition passed down through the Old Testament, the Puritans regarded slaves as persons divinely committed to their stewardship. Usually referred to as 'servants' rather than slaves, they were often treated as members of the family in which they lived."[8] As Jared Ross Hardesty writes in *Black Lives, Native Lands, White Worlds*:

> The New England colonies, home to around 1,700 slaves in the late
> seventeenth century, was not that different from other English
> settlements in North America. The region contained a small number of
> African slaves who supplemented the largely white workforce and settler
> population. . . . The first generations of New Englanders had a relatively
> ambivalent relationship with slavery. On the one hand, slavery was always

on the table and a tool of colonization. There was, however, a deep-seated
fear about the presence of so many enslaved "strangers" present in their
colonial experiment in the North American wilderness. Such attitudes
created a legal, albeit ill-defined form of slavery.[9]

With the Body of Liberties law, Massachusetts distinguished itself from
Virginia, which largely allowed slavery to develop incrementally in response to
societal custom. Instead, the Massachusetts Bay and Plymouth colonies sanctioned slavery by law and statute, passed a mere three years after the first Africans arrived on the shores of Massachusetts.[10] The next major date in the
history of race in Boston was 1644. Before that time, Massachusetts merchants
had occasionally brought in Black Africans from the West Indies; but in that
year, Boston traders imported slaves directly from Africa, when an association
of businessmen sent three ships there "for gold dust and Negroes."[11]

When we look at the documents from the earliest years of settlement, it is
clear that Massachusetts settlers were deeply involved in the kidnapping,
transporting, and selling of Africans.[12] New England colonists showed a marked
preference for Black slaves as opposed to white indentured servants. As early
as 1645, Edward Downing, the brother-in-law of Governor Winthrop, argued
that African slaves specifically were essential to the growth of the colony.
"The colony will never thrive," Downing wrote to Winthrop, "untill we gett . . .
a stock of slaves sufficient to doe all our business." He even went so far as to
express his interest in a "juste warre" with the Indians whereby he could ob-
tain Indian captives to exchange for Africans, possibly in the West Indies. As
late as 1723, a visitor to Boston, observing the preference for Black slaves over
indentured servants, noted that the New Englanders "will rather be burnt in
their beds by them [Africans] than suffer English servants to come hither to
work."[13]

Other factors contributed to the growth of racialized slavery in the Massachusetts colony. In 1696, the English Parliament revoked the monopoly
granted to the Royal African Company for slave trading, thereby enabling the
English to engage in the slave trade directly, already legal through the Royal
African Company. With the region's ample resources in shipbuilding, seamen, and enterprise in the maritime trades, New England became one of the
most active regions for the slave trade in America.[14]

Enslaved Africans were not passive victims in the institution of slavery, using whatever leverage they could find to maneuver. One tactic they employed
was the withdrawal of their labor.[15] A major strand of new scholarship on
slavery focuses on slaves' efforts to forge lives within slavery.[16] Laws were

eventually passed that allowed slaves to learn to read and write, so that they could read the Bible. By 1667, slaves could become Christians by baptism, but the conferring of baptism did not alter their slave status.[17]

In 1770, James, a slave of Richard Lechmere of Cambridge, brought an action against his master for detaining him in bondage. In doing so, James joined others protesting slavery in Massachusetts, including several slaves who petitioned the legislature to enact emancipation. The year 1773 saw increasing agitation among Blacks in Boston and Massachusetts for an end to slavery. Caesar Hendricks, a Black slave in Massachusetts, sued his owner for "detaining him in slavery." An all-white jury sided with Hendricks and awarded him damages.[18]

Noted Boston churchman and jurist Samuel Sewall wrote the first public antislavery tract, *The Selling of Joseph*, arguing that all men are the "sons of Adam." Liberty, he continued, is the real value of life; therefore, "none ought to part with it themselves or deprive others of it."[19] In doing so, Sewall joined an ongoing religious debate about the morality of slavery. These religious debates were informed by the Great Awakening, which helped to bring about the idea of the "covenant of works"—the notion that you could work your way into heaven—in the mid- to late eighteenth century.[20] This idea likewise inspired Edmund Burke to write an antislavery tract in 1756 on European slavery in America titled *A Vindication of Natural Society: or, A View of the Miseries and Evils arising to Mankind from every Species of Artificial Society*, denouncing the cruel treatment of Blacks as slaves and arguing for the need to either make conditions better or emancipate them.[21] Despite his criticism of slavery, Burke's arguments remained deeply influenced by the popular racist ideologies of the day that held that Black people by nature were stubborn and violent. As part of his diatribe, Burke argued that improved conditions would curb Black people's "natural" rebelliousness.[22]

As Massachusetts continued to grow as a colony, enslaved Africans played an important role in the context of the colony's economy, functioning as domestics, stevedores, and agricultural workers.[23] Lorenzo J. Greene argued for the importance of slaves to the development of New England in his own groundbreaking study, *The Negro in Colonial New England*.[24] The potential for a revolt began before African slaves even reached the shores of the New World. Because profit was made on each enslaved person who survived, traders loaded extra bodies onto ships like the *Desire*.[25] The practice became known as "tight packing." Insurance companies such as John Hancock wrote the policies to ensure these cargoes. It took between one to three months to get from Africa to parts of South and North America. Often, the most volatile and dangerous part of the journey was when the ships were waiting in port to receive more slaves, as those already on board would try to escape.[26] These attempts were risky because the bodies on the waiting ships were always heavily guarded—the people, shackled.[27] Employment on slave ships was not an attractive job or considered a prestigious assignment. Crew members were frequently outnumbered, and thus they were often reluctant to serve on these ships. Resistance among the enslaved continued even after the ships moved beyond sight of land. In one instance, one male and one female slave planned an attack on a ship. During the attack, two crew members were killed. In response, the ship's captain, Tomba, ordered the disobedient slaves to be whipped. The bodies of weak or dead slaves would be cast overboard without regard for their humanity, like waste.[28]

Slavery in New England was never based on the plantation economy, which had grown so strong in the South. New England slaveholders, few of whom had more than one or two slaves, often had them dwell in their homes.[29] In *Disowning Slavery*, Joanne Pope Melish argues that New England slaves, although small in number, were important members of the families and farms of New England slaveholders. The numbers of slaves and the types of farms on which they worked varied from state to state. Connecticut, for example, with its tobacco farms, mirrored something closer to a large southern, plantation-style economy. She suggests, "It is possible that by midcentury in Connecticut, Rhode Island, and Massachusetts (the three states with the largest populations of slaves), there were as many as one African for every four white families. Jackson Turner Main, surveying Connecticut estate inventories, found that in 1700 one in ten inventories included slaves, with the incidence rising to one in four by the eve of the Revolution."[30]

The American Revolution

The cemetery atop Boston's Copp's Hill Burial Ground is the final resting place of many notable figures from the revolutionary period.[31] One of those figures, Prince Hall, the son of an Englishman, Thomas Prince Hall, and a free Black woman of French extraction, was born in Bridgetown, Barbados, on September 12, 1748. Subsequently, Hall became an important leader in Boston's Black community, fighting in the American Revolution. In 1787, Hall founded Boston's African Lodge Number 459, the first African Masonic lodge, thus launching the beginning of Black Freemasonry in the United States. That same year, the newly drafted U.S. Constitution forbade Congress from interfering with the Atlantic slave trade before 1808. It also stated that for purposes of taxation and representation, slaves counted as three-fifths of a person.

The Revolutionary War and the Black figures who emerged from it form the cornerstone of the struggle for liberty in Boston. The first to die in the war was a fugitive mulatto slave from Framingham, just west of Boston, named Crispus Attucks. Born in 1723 to enslaved parents—an African father and a Native American mother who hailed from Nantucket—Attucks later escaped from slavery.[32] An advertisement placed twenty years earlier by William Brown in the *Boston Gazette* calling for his capture described him as "a mulatto fellow, about 27 years of age . . . well set, 6 foot 2 inches high, short curl'd hair, knees nearer together than common."[33] After his escape, Attucks became a sailor on a whaling ship that sailed out of Boston and, when he was in port, a rope maker—making his home in Boston. He worked ships out of the Bahamas and found himself on many voyages. As a part-time sailor for hire, he was worried about either becoming impressed into the Royal Navy himself or the competition that other British troops represented. Attucks may have remained an obscure figure in history were it not for the fact that in March 1770 he became the first casualty of the Revolutionary War after leading a group of fellow sailors in an attack on the British, later dubbed the Boston Massacre.

Attucks was not the only Black American to fight in the Revolutionary War. John Adams, who defended the British at trial and later became the second American president, famously dismissed the group as "a motley rabble of saucy boys, negroes and mullatoes, Irish teagues and outlandish Jack Tarrs."[34] Like their white counterparts in 1765, Black men demonstrated against the Stamp Act in Boston and rioted against British troops, an unwanted yet ever-present reminder of British tyranny and oppression.

William C. Nell, one of the first Black historians and the first of many protagonists in the struggle for equal rights in education, later wrote of Crispus Attucks and other Black Americans who fought in the Revolutionary War in his *Colored Patriots of the American Revolution*. In the introduction to this early achievement in Black historiography, Harriet Beecher Stowe wrote, "In considering the services of the Colored Patriots of the Revolution, we are to reflect upon them as far more magnanimous, because rendered to a nation which did not acknowledge them as citizens and equals, and in whose interests and prosperity they had less at stake. It was not for their own land they fought, not even for a land which had adopted them, but for a land which had enslaved them, and whose laws, even in freedom, oftener oppressed than protected. Bravery, under such circumstances, has a peculiar beauty and merit."[35]

In 1891, John Boyle O'Reilly immortalized Attucks in a poem, artfully recording his contribution as "first to defy, first to die."[36]

Attucks proved an exception with regard to the acknowledgment he received for his sacrifice, praised by Adams and eulogized in history books. Yet many Black Americans—both enslaved and free—fought in the war. While for whites, the Revolutionary War was primarily a struggle for or against independence from Britain, Black Americans, who fought on the side of both the revolutionaries and the British crown, the choice was often tied to the quest for freedom from slavery. Ultimately, however, the war resulted only in freedom from Britain—not slavery.

Since slavery was not abolished in the North until Vermont ended it in 1777, many Black slaves in the North risked life and limb to be emancipated for their service after the war's end, and some were. However, more flocked to the side of the British, particularly after the governor of Virginia, John Murray—more commonly known by his royal title, Lord Dunmore—proclaimed in 1775 that freedom would be granted to all slaves who enlisted in his "Ethiopian Regiment." However, this deal was offered only to those subjugated by slave masters fighting for the Patriot side. Runaway slaves belonging to Loyalists would be returned to their masters. Within a month of his proclamation, more than three hundred Black soldiers had joined Lord Dunmore's ranks, wearing uniforms emblazoned with the words "Liberty to Slaves."[37]

The American Revolution likewise gave support for an emerging Black maritime tradition, which would become an important and highly regarded position for Black men. Later, in the nineteenth century, the American shipping industry would come to employ more than 100,000 Black men per year. Frederick Douglass himself, in another generation, would rely on a retired Black sailor from the U.S. Navy, "Stanley," to lend him his Seaman's Protection Certificate—which proved American citizenship—so he could escape from bondage.[38]

Captain Paul Cuffe, who had made a reputation for himself and his family as a seafarer, navigated into southern harbors to conduct business as a trader. By 1780, Cuffe was quite successful and bought a small fleet staffed by his family and other Black sailors. Hailing from Massachusetts, he was a sea captain and the pioneer of an early version of Black nationalism. He owned his own shipbuilding company and built a wharf on the Westport River in Connecticut. As an extremely well-to-do free Black man, world traveler, and supervisor of many Black crews, Paul Cuffe was a memorable figure, providing a glimpse of what Black freedom could look like.

Black Americans participated in the Revolutionary War beyond the field of battle by engaging in the radical exchange of ideas. Indeed, the two—military or naval service and revolutionary rhetoric—often overlapped. In 1780, Cuffe and six other free men petitioned the General Court of Massachusetts for relief of taxation due to not being treated equally, including lacking the right to vote. In so doing, these men appropriated the revolutionary rhetoric of calling for "no taxation without representation" to demand racial equality. They were joined by men like Benjamin Banneker, who did not fight on the battlefield but likewise drew blood in the war for ideas, proving the mental facility of Black Americans and thus allowing it to become part of the revolutionary tradition.[39]

Banneker was born in Maryland to a mother of mixed-race background and a father who was African. Banneker's genius showed at an early age, and he had many teachers and kindly individuals who lent him books or took him into their kindness to help nurture his natural gifts and abilities. The layout of the nation's capital—what used to be known as Washington city but what is now Washington, DC—might look very different today had it not been for Banneker's photographic memory. In a letter to Thomas Jefferson, Banneker challenged the hypocritical and contradicting tenets established in the Declaration of Independence and the Bill of Rights. He directly positioned these utmost ideals of freedom and equality alongside the ongoing realities of slavery.[40]

Although many enslaved Black men, including those who joined the British side, were given their freedom at war's end, many were sold back into bondage in the West Indies. Others were brought to Nova Scotia and eventually settled in Sierra Leone. Many promises of land to these newly settled slaves were broken.[41]

For Africans in the colonies, the American Revolution represented both a paradox and an opportunity. Patriots and Loyalists alike recruited enslaved men, yet both continued to condone slavery. Some slave owners even sent enslaved men to fight in their place. But the war also gave Black soldiers a chance to escape and to earn their freedom. Enslaved Africans fought for their liberty and helped shape the Revolutionary era, inspiring uprisings across the Atlantic world.

By the time of the passage of the Declaration of Independence, adopted by the Continental Congress in Philadelphia on July 4, 1776, hopes were beginning to emerge that slavery could be abolished in Massachusetts and indeed throughout the thirteen colonies. On January 6, 1776, and again in

April and May, Black Bostonians sent petitions—first to Royal General Thomas Gage and next to the Massachusetts state legislature—denouncing slavery as "destructive of natural rights" and seeking the right to earn money to purchase their freedom. In doing so, they demonstrated the effect that the Revolutionary War had in terms of inspiring Black Americans to give meaning to the idea of "freedom and liberty for all" proclaimed by the new nation. Subsequent decades saw an increase in movements to bring about the manumission of slaves. In 1785, for example, the New York Society for Promoting the Manumission of Slaves was founded. By 1792, there were branches of the American Anti-Slavery Society set up in every state from Massachusetts to Virginia. These efforts paved the way for a wave of laws and proclamations that would soon transform the system of slavery in the North and the nation more broadly.

Quock Walker, a slave who sued for freedom based on his master's promise that he would be freed, was heard in court.[42] Walker sued based on Article I of the Constitution of the Commonwealth of Massachusetts, the Declaration of Rights, adopted in 1780, which declared that "all men are born free and equal, and have certain natural, essential, and unalienable rights; among which may be reckoned the right of enjoying and defending their lives and liberties."[43] Soon after the adoption of the declaration, Walker charged Nathaniel Jennison, his owner, with bodily assault. Jennison's defense was simple: Walker, he claimed, was his slave, so the law against assault did not apply.[44] In his ruling for the Massachusetts Supreme Judicial Court, Judge William Cushing rendered an opinion that slavery was inconsistent with the Massachusetts constitution in that it stated, "All men are created equal," and furthermore, that slavery was contrary not just to the Massachusetts constitution but to the "natural rights of mankind." The judge's ruling set a precedent that was understood by many around the country to be not only a reversal of but a complete rejection of the kind of exploitative society that Boston and the Massachusetts Bay Colony started out as. It was the beginning of an interpretation of Massachusetts as being a place where Black Americans had rights and where liberty perhaps breathed a little more freely. Before the Civil War, Black men petitioned their legislatures and the U.S. Congress to be recognized as voters. Eventually, rights for free persons in Massachusetts were expanded to include voting rights for free Black males who paid taxes.[45] Captain Paul Cuffe helped wage the struggle for the franchise for Black property owners in Massachusetts.[46]

This made the Bay State a place where Black males held the right to vote long before the passage of the Fifteenth Amendment—a right Black Americans would be fighting for some ninety-five years later in Selma, Alabama, during the civil rights movement—a right that one could argue is being fought for still.[47]

In the 1700s, the Black community moved to Beacon Hill, which became the center of a small, fiercely proud Black society that in 1806 manifested itself in the African Meeting House. The African Meeting House was a focal point of the relatively small band of souls that inhabited the hill from the eighteenth century through the early part of the twentieth century. Between 1800 and 1900, most of Boston's Black residents lived in the West End, between Pinckney and Cambridge Streets and between Joy and Charles Streets.

The first public school for Black children was founded there in 1807 through the efforts of George Middleton, who along with Black families petitioned support for a Black public school.[48] Although their numbers were small compared to other major seaport cities, Boston had a strong, vibrant Black community. There were Black businesses, fraternal orders, gathering places, and mutual aid societies. Centered on the north slope of Beacon Hill, barbershops were then—as they are now—an important forum for the discussion of political ideas, the exchange of community information, and the posting of job openings. The barbershops of Pete Howard and John J. Smith, both at the foot of Beacon Hill, were meeting places for antislavery forces and stations of the Underground Railroad.

In 1777, Vermont—not Massachusetts—became the first state to abolish slavery. Conversely, Rhode Island and Massachusetts granted slaves their freedom only in exchange for fighting. It was not until Massachusetts held its constitutional convention in 1780 that a Declaration of Rights was added to the state constitution. It is on that basis that Massachusetts abolished slavery three years later, in 1783. Although Black Massachusetts residents had high hopes that the commonwealth, and America, might come to realize the true greatness of its creed by ending slavery, those hopes soon proved to be just that, hopes. Independence and the birth of a new nation did not bring the end of slavery or discrimination.[49]

From the worldview of the enslaved, Boston's protestations must have seemed like a major contradiction. The Black community, both enslaved and free, which grew up around Boston's waterfront and wharves and produced notable leaders—David Walker, William C. Nell, Crispus Attucks, Maria Stewart, Paul Cuffe—articulated a vision that would help Boston come closer to living up to its lofty goals and those of the nascent nation, which proclaimed that "all men are created equal."

This situation began to change in the late eighteenth century as states in the North either abolished slavery outright or passed laws providing for gradual emancipation. With Vermont and Massachusetts leading the way, Connecticut also abolished slavery through its state constitution in 1784. States like Pennsylvania, New Jersey, and Rhode Island followed but did so only gradually. New York, which had the second-largest slave population in the North before the American Revolution, was the last northern state to abolish slavery. Indeed, the state had slaves as late as the 1820s. By 1790, slavery in the newly formed republic of the United States was primarily a southern institution.

Even though northerners were prohibited from owning slaves, they continued to participate in the slave trade. The international slave trade was abolished in 1808, but slaves were still traded internally from state to state. White northerners participated in and profited from this process of re-enslavement. Many newly freed northern Blacks, particularly from New Jersey, were sold back into slavery in the Deep South. With the invention of the cotton gin in 1794 and the purchase of the Louisiana Territory in 1803, slavery in the country as a whole expanded. Indeed, one of the things that enticed white settlers to newly acquired lands in the South and West was the continued allowance of slavery, fueling a growing cotton economy. By 1815, cotton was the single most important crop exported by the United States.

Building Boston's Free Black Community

In the decades after the American Revolution, Black Americans expressed many concerns, including securing housing and safe spaces. As slavery gained momentum in the South, the North became more associated with freedom. Free Black people built communities and established institutions that reflected their dual identities as Africans and Americans, leading to the emergence of an emerging African American identity. In 1796, the African Society for Mutual Aid and Charity, founded in Philadelphia, became one of the first organizations serving this purpose. The society provided social welfare services, financial relief, and job placement to its members and their families. According to Ruth Batson, "The original membership numbered forty-four. By July 14, 1808, the organization was supported publicly by two hundred Blacks. The society provided important welfare services for the needy of the community."[50]

Similar community development occurred in other cities with significant Black populations, including Boston. By 1800, some eleven hundred Black Bostonians made up one of the largest free Black communities in North America. Throughout the eighteenth century, free Blacks settled in the North End of Boston, where they worked on the docks and in the industry that grew up around the waterfront and the port. The long wharf, with its trade in molasses and rum, brought immense fortunes from the shores of the West Indies, Africa, and England. It was here, in the commercial heart of the city, that the first Black Americans in Boston worked as stevedores, longshoremen, crewmen, and at times captains of their own ships.[51]

The Abolitionists

The son of a slave father and a free Black mother, David Walker was originally from Wilmington, North Carolina, and inherited his free status from his mother, according to the law that stated that enslaved people followed the status of their mother. His freedom, however, did not prevent him from developing a real hatred toward the institution of slavery. Walker carried memories from childhood of things he witnessed. What his eyes saw and what his ears heard never left him, including a son being forced to whip his mother until she died. Walker moved around the country, eventually settling in Boston, where he was able to open a used-clothing store on Beacon Hill.

He soon became involved in the local antislavery and abolitionist movements, even contributing stories and articles to the abolitionist newspaper, *Freedom's Journal*. He came to know prominent Black leaders, who nurtured and encouraged his abolitionist activities, and by 1828, he had become one of Boston's leading Black abolitionists. Walker put pen to paper and made an argument against slavery and colonization, making separate appeals to four different audiences: free Blacks, enslaved Blacks, people involved in religion, and white Americans in general. He argued that it was neither natural nor divinely ordained for men to be in servitude. He wrote, "It does appear to me, as though some nations think God is asleep, or that he made the Africans for nothing else but to dig their mines and work their farms, or they cannot believe history, sacred or profane. I ask every man who has a heart, and is blessed with the privilege of believing—Is not God a God of justice to all his creatures? Do you say he is?"[52] His appeal made it clear that either slavery could be ended peacefully or it would end in a bloodbath.[53] In this sense, Walker invited the possibility of violence as a way to end slavery.

Not all of Boston's abolitionists were willing to go that far. William Lloyd Garrison was a pacifist. Still, he believed that one should not vote or participate in American politics and government in any way because to do so would perpetuate the institution of slavery.[54] He pointed out how places in the North like Massachusetts were complicit in slavery—for example, the textile industry in Massachusetts.[55]

With the help of people like Walker and Garrison, the abolition movement slowly gained traction. Across the Northeast, including in Philadelphia, Boston, and New York, the 1830s witnessed a rise in abolitionist organizations, composed of both white and Black people. In the period between 1833 and 1850, the abolitionist movement became increasingly more militant. This change in tone and outlook occurred for a number of reasons. In response to growing abolitionist power, race riots began to take place throughout America, mainly concentrated in the North. In addition, pro-slavery advocates seemed to be gaining power with the addition of new lands to the Union, stemming from the Louisiana Purchase and the Mexican-American War.[56] The American Anti-Slavery Society emerged to deal with these new threats, founded by Garrison, alongside Arthur and Lewis Tappan and others in Philadelphia in December 1833. The group laid out its goals in a manifesto, which was largely based on the Declaration of Independence and titled the Declaration of the Anti-Slavery Convention.[57] Garrison, who once burned a copy of the Constitution on the steps of Boston's Old State House, decried the original Declaration of Independence as a slavery document. Instead, believing in the principle of moral suasion, he and others hoped by exposing the sheer barbarity of the system, Americans would be morally bound to side with the slave.[58]

As the editor of an antislavery organization and a journalist, Garrison began printing the antislavery newspaper, the *Liberator*, as a challenge to the American Colonization Society.[59] The American Colonization Society (ACS) wanted Congress to set aside money to find either South American or African land for free Blacks to live in. In 1822, the ACS successfully acquired land and established a colony on the west coast of Africa that in 1847 became the independent nation of Liberia. In the 1830s, the society was harshly attacked by other abolitionists, who worked to discredit colonization as a slaveholder's scheme. Yet some Black Americans, including Martin Delany, supported this effort as part of a nascent Back to Africa movement, which would capture the imagination of various Black nationalist organizations in subsequent decades.[60] By 1867, the ACS had sent more than thirteen thousand emigrants to Liberia.[61] The ACS also started a newspaper and magazine called the *African Repository and Colonial Journal*.[62]

By contrast, Garrisonian abolitionists believed that slavery was a sin and that it was the moral obligation of every American to help eradicate it from the national landscape by freeing all slaves.[63] The first issue of the *Liberator* contained a statement against the ACS's plan for gradual abolition, which Garrison had previously supported, and for immediate granting of citizenship to the slave population.[64] The first known Black newspaper to be published was *Freedom's Journal*, published by editors Samuel E. Cornish and John B. Russwurm in 1827 in New York City. John B. Russwurm eventually left America with early Liberia settlers, never to return. Because the early Black newspapers were dependent on subscriptions for their survival, they didn't often last long.

As journalist Phyl Garland has written, "The year 1827 marked the beginning of an era in which African Americans would use the printed word as a means of political protest, when few other outlets for black public expression were available. Before the Civil War, newspapers in the North became a vital force in the antislavery movement; after the war, black newspapers in both the North and the South helped to forge cohesive communities of formerly enslaved African Americans. And when, following Reconstruction, racist violence targeted African Americans, the black press once again took up the mantle of political activism."[65] Though the abolitionists' arguments over methods and tactics raged on without a decisive conclusion, by the time the Civil War began, Boston was ready to enter the fray. Into that war marched the all-Black Massachusetts Fifty-Fourth Regiment, which distinguished itself in bravery under the leadership of its white commanding officer, Colonel Robert Gould Shaw, who had strong roots in Massachusetts and Boston.[66] The equestrian monument of Shaw and the Fifty-Fourth Regiment, designed by Augustus Saint-Gaudens, occupies pride of place on the Boston Common on Beacon Hill, directly across from the State House. Another important monument on the Boston Common honors those who were killed in the Boston Massacre, particularly Crispus Attucks, the Black man who was the first person to die for the freedom of the then American colonies from Britain. These two monuments commemorate not only the struggle for freedom from colonial or Confederate rule but the struggle for freedom from enslavement. In many ways, they symbolize the juxtaposition of both the ideals and the imperfections of the United States.[67]

The Beginning of the Black Education Movement in Boston

Throughout the post–Revolutionary War period, Black Bostonians fought tirelessly against the prejudice and discrimination that abounded in public schools. The Boston Latin School, the first public school in America, was founded in 1635. As such, it is the oldest existing school in the United States. The early history of American education unfolds in the New England colonies in the seventeenth century with some of the first schools being opened. Previously, public education was somewhat of a luxury, only for the more affluent classes who hired private tutors to educate their children. The first publicly founded elementary school, the Mather School in Dorchester, Massachusetts, was the first to be supported by taxpayer dollars when it opened in 1639. Named after Richard Mather, a Congregational minister who had emigrated and settled in Dorchester in 1635. In 1642, the Massachusetts Bay Colony made education compulsory for all school-aged children.

Beyond the basics of literacy, arithmetic, and writing, school was meant to acculturate young minds into the culture, communication, and way to think of adults and the world they are being prepared for. By the nineteenth century, the schools had assumed the role of parents themselves. American education theorists like John Dewey call this process socialization. He wrote in his classic 1916 treatise on the subject:

> The primary ineluctable facts of the birth and death of each one of the constituent members in a social group determine the necessity of education. On one hand, there is the contrast between the immaturity of the new-born members of the group—its future sole representatives—and the maturity of the adult members who possess the knowledge and customs of the group. On the other hand, there is the necessity that these immature members be not merely physically preserved in adequate numbers, but that they be initiated into the interests, purposes, information, skill, and practices of the mature members: otherwise the group will cease its characteristic life.[68]

The movement for Black education began when Prince Hall established a private school for Black students in Boston following the denial by the Boston School Committee to open a public school for Black children in 1798. The schoolhouse was the private home of Hall's son, Primus Hall.

While a small number of Black children did attend the city's white schools in the early 1800s, many others were denied admission. This led to protests to allow Black children to attend the city's public schools—an indication of the long history of school desegregation efforts. In 1787, Black parents carried their protests to the state legislature, where they decried "the severity of the prejudice and discrimination in the existing public schools."[69] In their petition, they argued that it was unfair for them to pay taxes to the city while their children's education was not being provided for. Ultimately, however, the Boston School Committee rejected their request to provide education for their children.

In 1800, Prince Hall petitioned the committee once again to include Black students in the Boston Public School system. George Middleton, a former commander of the Bucks of America—an all-Black company of soldiers during the Revolutionary War—initiated a petition, signed by sixty-seven Black parents, that the Boston School Committee establish a public school for their children. The petition was denied, the reason given being that "Blacks were not excluded by law from public schools."[70]

In 1806, the First African Baptist Church (later to be known as the African Meeting House) established a schoolroom for Black children. The classroom that Prince and Primus Hall had set up in their home was moved to the basement of the African Meeting House, making it the first "public" school for Boston's Black children. The "African School"—as it was widely known—was the only school in the city that admitted Black children. As part of this move, the church raised $180 to set up the classroom. Elisha Sylvester, who was white, was hired as the first teacher. Teachers at the African School were paid less than teachers at white schools. Black parents made financial contributions to keep the school afloat, paying a weekly sum of 12.5 cents per child for some forty students. Costs to maintain the classroom were covered by contributions from the community, including a $5,000 donation from Prince Saunders, the first Black teacher hired by the school.[71]

Another teacher at the school was John Russwurm, who, with Samuel Cornish, would later cofound the abolitionist newspaper *Freedom's Journal*, the first paper owned and operated by Black Americans. Russwurm taught for a short period before leaving the school to pursue higher education at Bowdoin College, becoming one of the earliest Black college graduates.[72]

After decades of petitions and protests, the Boston School Committee finally recognized the African School in 1812, still housed in a basement, as an official school. The committee also agreed to fund it partially, allocating $200 per year to the school. This move allowed the committee to assert its jurisdiction over the school; at the same time, by incorporating the African School, the committee restricted Black children from attending other public schools.[73] The basement of the African Meeting House became a hub for various activities when school was not in session, including community organizing. In 1832, the New England Anti-Slavery Society was founded there, and the charter meeting was held there as well.[74]

In 1815, a prominent white businessman, Abiel Smith, passed away and bequeathed $4,000 for the education of Black children in Boston, mostly due to the efforts of Prince Saunders, who made the original appeal to Smith for support. After Smith died, the African School was renamed the Abiel Smith

School in his honor. Further demonstrating their heavy-handed leadership, Boston school officials dismissed Elisha Sylvester, the school's first teacher. This action was taken without consideration of or in consultation with parents.

In criticisms that would be repeated by Black activists later in the century in support of school desegregation, Black parents and community leaders during this period levied charges that Black children received a subpar education in comparison to their white peers. With echoes of future history, the Boston School Committee established a subcommittee in 1833 to investigate charges that education in the Abiel Smith School was inferior. David Lee Child, a charter member of the New England Anti-Slavery Society and a member of the Boston School Committee, chaired the subcommittee, which found that "the problems of the classroom contribute to the poor attendance and low morale at the school."[75] The conditions of the school itself were also inferior to those of the white schools in Boston, and the Black community continued to fight for equal opportunities in education. A new building for the Abiel Smith School was opened on March 3, 1835, right next to the African Meeting House. Boston school officials thought that the new location of the school would quiet the objections of parents.

It soon became apparent that the inadequacies of the new school were too significant to overlook. The Smith School's curriculum offered only six of the eighteen subjects taught in the white schools. Although three of these subjects were necessary for admission to high school, there was not enough funding to support them.[76] In 1837, evening education classes began at the school. In 1841, a high school opened in the basement of the African Meeting House. Meanwhile, parents' complaints regarding the inferior education their children were receiving continued, amounting to what they perceived as abusive treatment of students by headmaster Abner Forkes. Subsequently, Black community members, supported by white antislavery supporters, led a nineteenth-century protest to end segregation in the Boston public schools, which they deemed as both unfair and a barrier to their goal of the best possible education for their children.[77]

One of the primary leaders in the protests targeting discrimination in education at the Smith School was historian, activist, abolitionist, and free Black Bostonian William Cooper Nell.[78] Nell was a frequent contributor to the *Liberator* and a loyal Garrisonian. Born into a Boston abolitionist family, Nell eventually went on to study law. He dedicated himself to antislavery work, lecturing, organizing meetings, and assisting fugitive slaves. He helped establish the Freedom Association in 1842, an organization of Black Americans who aided the Underground Railroad by providing escaped slaves with protection, food, clothing, and shelter. Nell began writing for the *Liberator* in the early 1840s, managing the paper's "Negro Employment Office."[79]

One of the most fearless advocates for school integration, Nell had once been a student at the Abiel Smith School himself. In 1829, he and two other Black students were awarded the prestigious Benjamin Franklin Medal, given to excellent students upon graduation. In lieu of the medal, they received biographies of Benjamin Franklin. Nell was incensed but found a creative way to protest this act of discrimination and racial prejudice. Although they were not invited to the award ceremony at Faneuil Hall, Nell convinced one of the waiters to allow him to help serve the white honorees and guests. As Stephen Kantrowitz writes, it was on this night that Nell dedicated himself to a life of activism in pursuit of racial justice. He is said to have vowed at that very ceremony, "God helping me, I would do my best to hasten the day when the color of the skin would be no barrier to equal school rights."[80]

In 1845, Nell led the way by encouraging Black parents to submit petitions to the school board to integrate the Boston Public Schools. He was also able to convince several white abolitionists to enter the fray, and together, along with the Black parents, they put a great deal of political pressure on the Boston School Committee.[81]

On February 6, 1846, eighty-six parents signed a petition to the Primary School Committee of the City of Boston in which they demanded that "the 'exclusive schools' (segregated) be abolished and that Black children be allowed to attend the schools in their respective districts in which they live."[82] On June 15, 1846, George Putnam and other Black citizens of Boston also petitioned the committee to abolish exclusive schools for Black children.[83]

On June 22, 1846, the committee gave its response: "Resolved, that in the opinion of this board, the continuance of the separate schools for colored children, and the regular attendance of all such children upon the schools, is not only legal and just, but is best adapted to promote the education of that class of our population."[84]

Over the next few years, more petitions were submitted. A group of influential white Bostonians opposed to slavery joined Nell and other Black leaders to put pressure on the Boston School Committee. Nell also encouraged Black parents to boycott the dilapidated Smith School until the Boston schools were integrated.[85] When Black Bostonians began to picket the Smith School, enrollment dropped from 263 in 1840 to 50 in 1849.[86] With their petitions denied and every option exhausted, parents had been left with no choice. Nell filed a lawsuit against the City of Boston in 1849, based on the

1845 law which stated "any child that is unlawfully excluded from the public schools can recover damages" and "students should attend the school closest to their home, unless special arrangements have been made."[87]

Every day, Sarah Roberts, the daughter of Benjamin Roberts, had to walk past five white public schools in order to attend the densely populated all-Black Smith School. This was, in his view, a clear violation of an 1845 Boston statute that held that "any child, unlawfully excluded from public school instruction, in this Commonwealth, shall recover damages therefor, [*sic*] . . . against the city or town by which such public school instruction is supported."[88] Roberts, like many of Nell's petitioners, appealed relentlessly to the school committee to allow his daughter to attend the school closest to her home, as mandated by the 1845 law. At one point, Roberts even went beyond appeals and enrolled Sarah in the school, but she was asked to leave—removed in fact. Roberts was so incensed that his daughter had been turned away that he decided to sue the City of Boston on her behalf. As one of the few Black men in the city who owned his own business, Roberts was well known and liked by the leaders of the city's Black political and social organizations, who supported his business, along with a number of white antislavery supporters. As a result, he had many friends to turn to.

Roberts turned to two Boston lawyers to represent his daughter. The first was prominent white attorney Charles Sumner, who would later become a lion of the Senate. The second was twenty-four-year-old Black attorney Robert Morris, the first Black attorney to ever win a jury case in America. Together, the legal team of Sumner and Morris forged powerful arguments against school segregationists in the North that reverberated down through American history and form a direct line to *Brown v. Board of Education*.

It was Boston abolitionist Ellis Gray Loring who found Morris in Salem. Unsatisfied with his legal assistant, Loring proposed the opportunity to Morris to study law. Morris was a very willing student, ultimately passing the bar in Massachusetts, making him only the second Black practicing lawyer in the country. Just before the Roberts case was to be presented in court, the Boston School Committee remodeled the Smith School, addressing Black parents' long-standing complaints about the school's condition. Sumner and Morris, however, opted to proceed with the case.

Segregation, though not formally legalized, had generally been customary in Massachusetts, as it was in other Northern states, through the mid-nineteenth century (and into the twentieth). Although no law dictated it, Boston's public schools were segregated. The school committee, which possessed the power to classify pupils, simply restricted the Smith School to

Black students. Sumner and Morris argued the case based on the distance that Sarah had to travel.

The fact that a first grader had to pass directly by five primary schools to get to the Smith School on Belknap Street, in the West End, was extreme. Roberts made no less than four separate attempts to enroll Sarah in one of the other public schools closer to her home, but her application was rejected every time. It was but one example of the travails many Black children had to undergo in the Boston system. That this case spoke for many Black parents and their children is what made it so important, but because it was not a class-action suit, Roberts faced the judge alone.

Sumner argued the case before a court headed by Chief Justice Lemuel Shaw, whose scholarship and legal decisions shaped American jurisprudence. Sumner threw open the proceedings with an appeal to the moral compass of the judge and jury:

> It would be difficult to imagine any case which could appeal more strongly to your best judgment, whether you regard the parties or the subject. On the one side is the city of Boston, strong in its wealth, in its influence, in its character; on the other side is a little child, of a degraded color, of humble parents, still within the period of natural infancy, but strong from her very weakness, and from the irrepressible sympathies of good men, which, by a divine compensation, come to succor the weak. This little child asks at your hands for personal rights. So doing, she calls upon you to decide a question which concerns the personal rights of other colored children which concerns the constitution and laws of the Commonwealth; which concerns that peculiar institution of New England, the common schools; which concerns the fundamental principles of human rights; which concerns the Christian character of this community. Such parties, and such interests, so grand and various, may justify challenge your most earnest attention.[89]

Sumner cited parts of the Massachusetts constitution that gave protections to an individual—which would one day be likened to the equal protection clause of the Fourteenth Amendment—and declared that every form of discrimination "in civil and political institutions" was therefore outlawed. Sumner argued that the intent to segregate Black children was tantamount to "brand[ing] a whole race with the stigma of inferiority and degradation." To do that, Sumner railed, would be "to place itself above the state constitution."[90] A very similarly worded decision would be handed down a little less than one hundred years later by the Warren court in *Brown v. Board of Education.*

Connecting distance and the question of unconstitutionality, Sumner pointed out that if the committee were going to impose discriminatory classifications, they must have a "reasonable relationship to the legitimate business of education." Children might be classified by age, by sex, or by moral and intellectual fitness when assigning them to schools and classrooms, but not by race or color. "A segregated school," said Sumner, "could not be considered as the equivalent of the white schools because of the inconvenience and the stigma of caste that mandatory attendance of it imposed on the Negro child."[91]

Sumner also referenced the psychological trauma Sarah suffered as a result of having to travel so far to attend a Black school and the stigma that this early "separate but equal" standard places on any Black school. Moreover, Sumner argued, segregation injured the white pupils as well: "Their hearts, while yet tender with childhood, are necessarily hardened by this conduct, and their subsequent lives, perhaps, bear enduring testimony to this legalized charitableness."[92]

The justices who would one day hand down the *Brown* decision would cite Sumner's argument in *Roberts*, but it did not have the same effect that day. Although few could doubt Sumner's brilliance and grandiloquence, Judge Shaw did not agree with the plaintiffs. In his written decision, he stated, "It is urged, that this maintenance of separate schools tends to deepen and perpetuate the odious distinction of caste, founded in a deep-rooted prejudice in public opinion. This prejudice, if it exists, is not created by law, and probably cannot be changed by law."[93] Judge Shaw's written decision was so influential that in 1896, when the *Plessy v. Ferguson* verdict was being handed down, it quoted Shaw extensively. In fact, it becomes apparent upon comparing the two decisions that *Roberts* was the legal cornerstone on which *Plessy* was built.[94] As J. Anthony Lukas writes, "Justice Shaw's ruling—the "separate-but-equal doctrine"—was to have a profound effect on the nation's history. The Roberts case was the chief precedent cited by the Supreme Court when it enshrined that doctrine in *Plessy v. Ferguson* (1896) and, thus, the genesis of the legal principle which was to govern the country's race relations until 1954."[95] Despite losing the lawsuit, Roberts and other Black leaders in Boston, including Nell, continued the fight for desegregation.

In April of 1855, Roberts and Nell brought their case to the state when they presented to the Massachusetts legislature a petition demanding an end to racial segregation in Boston public schools. The long boycott of Black-only schools led by Nell was the major reason for the successful petitioning of the state legislature. Cambridge, New Bedford, Worcester, Salem, Charlestown,

Roxbury, and Lowell had already integrated their schools. On April 28, 1855, the Massachusetts legislature passed a bill making segregated schools illegal in the commonwealth. This represented a victory in the struggle for equal school access waged by Boston's Black community in the nineteenth century. Where legal challenges in the courts had failed, boycotts and direct action had seemingly prevailed. With the April 1855 bill, Massachusetts became the first state in the United States to prohibit segregated schools. Following the victory, Robert Morris the attorney who had helped to represent the Robertses, declared, "Let us be bold, and they will have to yield to us!"[96]

Conclusion

Roberts v. City of Boston left a lasting impact on American history. The 1850 opinion of Chief Justice Lemuel Shaw for the Massachusetts Supreme Judicial Court made Boston the legal origin of the "separate but equal" doctrine. Southern jurists would soon come to cite the *Roberts* case to expand the legal justification for Jim Crow. Yet the case also serves as evidence that the Black community was active very early in the struggle for racial justice in Boston.[97]

Free Blacks in Boston fought valiantly not only for school desegregation but against segregation in theaters, segregation in railway cars, and laws against interracial marriage.[98] They formed the first Black army regiment and set an example of Boston as a place where Black organizing created powerful social change. Despite the actions of Black Bostonians and their white allies, racial segregation in the city of Boston would become more strident in the twentieth century, if not become even more entrenched. As Boston moved into the twentieth century, Bostonians found themselves at a racial crossroads. As Stephen Kantrowitz writes in *More Than Freedom*, "On some streets a black Bostonian could buy or rent whatever home he or she could afford, on others not at all; more than half of Boston's black population resided on a few streets on Beacon Hill and in the adjacent West End. The owners or operators of restaurants, hotels, and other accommodations excluded or segregated black men and women. Unlike the segregation imposed by some states in the later nineteenth century, these exclusions and insults were not official policies. Neither were they illegal."[99] On the one hand, they could pride themselves on living in a city with integrated schools—for the moment. However, as waves of European immigrants came, Boston became a city increasingly characterized by racial exclusion and segregation.

CHAPTER TWO

Boston Confronts a Jim Crow North, 1896–1934

We want laws enforced against the rich as well as the poor; against the capitalist as well as the laborer; against white as well as Black. . . . We want a decent education for our children. . . . They have a right to know, to think, to aspire.

—William Monroe Trotter

Education in itself is worthless. It is only as it is used that it is of value. Since most Negroes must stay and work in the South as farmers and artisans, their schooling should "meet the needs of conditions." In short, industrial education.

—Booker T. Washington

On May 31, 1897, a bright sunny day in Boston, Booker T. Washington rose to a platform in Boston Music Hall to address a distinguished interracial audience that included the governor of Massachusetts, the mayor, the sons and daughters of Black Civil War veterans, and an interracial group of abolitionists from the antebellum era. Washington was invited to christen a monument to the Massachusetts Fifty-Fourth Regiment, only a year after the *Plessy v. Ferguson* decision had been handed down. By welcoming Washington, Boston reaffirmed its commitment to "separate but equal," initiated during the *Roberts* trial several decades earlier.

Washington was held in high esteem by the governor of Massachusetts and the city fathers who now sat before him. As he rose to the podium to speak, the mood was a festive one; indeed, in many ways, the arena was overflowing with patriotism, as the *Boston Evening Transcript* described it: "When Mr. Washington rose in the flag-filled, enthusiasm-warmed, patriotic, and glowing atmosphere of Music Hall, people felt keenly that here was the civic justification of the old abolition spirit of Massachusetts; in his person the proof of her ancient and indomitable faith; in his strong thought and rich oratory, the crown and glory of the old war days of suffering and strife. The scene was full of historic beauty and deep significance."[1]

Washington proceeded to speak directly to Sergeant William H. Carney of New Bedford, a Black American who had carried the flag at the Battle of Fort Wagner for the Massachusetts Fifty-Fourth, saying, "To you, to the scarred and scattered remnants of the Fifty-fourth, who with empty sleeve and wanting leg, have honoured this occasion with your presence, to you, your commander is not dead."[2] His address at the unveiling of the statue resonated

Booker T. Washington, 1856–1915 (Frances Benjamin Johnston [photographer], Frances Benjamin Johnston Collection, Library of Congress Prints and Photographs Division, LC-J694-255).

with the old spirit of abolition and drew on the well-established sentiments and nostalgia for the Civil War that still burned in the hearts of those sitting in the audience. The crowd's warm reception affirmed the still mythical stature of Boston as the "cradle of liberty" and the birthplace of freedom while channeling its "separate but equal" traditions.[3]

At the same time, there was a deeper, more contested political meaning to Booker T. Washington's presence on that spring day. In a city like Boston, which had been at the vanguard of the abolitionist movement, the unveiling

of the great equestrian monument that honored Colonel Shaw and the Massachusetts Fifty-Fourth Regiment was a larger-than-life event. In many ways,
the juxtaposition of these unlikely constituencies symbolized the internal
contradictions that came to characterize racial politics in Boston in the progressive period, during which Washington would make many trips to Boston.
The question remains, however: Why did Booker T. Washington, who is best
associated with the Tuskegee Institute, associate so strongly with Boston?
Despite *Plessy v. Ferguson*, in 1896 it was still unclear what the fate of Black
residents in the North would be with regard to education. Would segregation
still be a uniquely Southern phenomenon, or would it reestablish itself in the
North as well? By inviting the premier Black leader of that era to christen a
monument to the Massachusetts Fifty-Fourth Regiment, the city fathers were
sending the message that they approved of Washington's formula of industrial education and implicitly Jim Crow education. Washington's presence
also marked in many ways the consummation of a dream he had harbored
since his entrance to Hampton Normal and Agricultural Institute. Washington had been profoundly shaped and influenced by the values of New England
Puritanism.[4] His philosophy of industrial education (had it been fully realized) would have potentially shaped the ways in which Black youths would
be educated across the country. Industrial education was slowly coming to
dominate schools in the North. While Washington was not the sole advocate
for industrial education, he argued strongly for its use for Black Americans.
This was part of his strategy to not threaten the social hierarchy of the races.

Washington had the support of one of the first national organizations
founded by Black people. Before the founding of the NAACP and the Niagara
Movement that gave rise to it, there was the National Afro-American League
(NAAL), which existed from 1887 to 1893.[5] Founded by T. Thomas Fortune,
editor of the vaunted Black newspaper the *New York Age*, and Bishop Alexander Walters of the African Methodist Episcopal Zion Church in Washington,
DC, the league "sought equal opportunities in voting, civil rights, education,
and public accommodations."[6] Another organization was the Afro-American
Council, first founded in 1898 and later reconstituted in Rochester, New York,
also by Fortune and Walters.[7] Among the Afro-American Council's many contributions was its role as the first organization to push for the use of terms like
"Afro-American" instead of "Negro." The council, largely displaced by the
Niagara Movement and the NAACP, lasted until 1907.

Both the Afro-American Council and the National Afro-American League
were heavily influenced by Washington, called by some "the Wizard of
Tuskegee" for the enormous influence he wielded. By 1900, Washington, who

William Monroe Trotter, Harvard College Class of 1895 Portrait (Harvard College Class of 1895 Class Album, Pach Brothers Firm/Harvard University Archives).

was already a prominent educator and political leader in the South, had received national acclaim following his speech at the Cotton States and International Exposition in 1895. With the death of Frederick Douglass in 1895, Washington was anointed the de facto leader of Black America, and Fortune would become one of his able lieutenants.

Washington, for his part, was very forthright concerning his views. Education in and of itself was worthless. Since most African Americans were agricultural workers, he reasoned, industrial education was the answer.[8] William Monroe Trotter, on the other hand, believed in the importance of education for all, although he did acknowledge that industrial schools such as Tuskegee Institute, where the curriculum was more agricultural in nature, did have some value. He even went so far as to occasionally carry advertisements for industrial schools in the *Guardian*, though never one for Tuskegee. Characteristically, his objection was more symbolic in nature. He opposed indus-

W. E. B. (William Edward Burghardt) Du Bois, 1868–1963 (C. M. Battey [photographer], Library of Congress Prints and Photographs Division, LC-DIG-ppmsca-38818).

trialism because, as he said, "The idea lying back of it is the relegating of a race to serfdom. That underlying idea, the innate mental inferiority of Negroes, must be admitted to be the reason why industrial education is more popular with the general white public than advanced or classical education. To prove their equality Negroes must seek and succeed at the highest forms of education."[9] Trotter had done it himself. Moreover, Washington, "this apostle of industrialism," according to Trotter, "was doing great harm by soliciting in the North for his 'practical' school."[10]

The Tuskegee program continued to garner wide acceptance across racial lines in Boston. As Stephen Fox writes, "Though a strong tradition of racial
militancy had come down from the abolitionist era, some of the most influential members of the city's Black community supported the Tuskegee program. Washington's best friend in Boston was probably his former protégé,
Dr. Samuel E. Courtney. The two men had known each other since the 1870s,
when Courtney had attended the first school taught by Washington back in
West Virginia."[11]

The debates between Washington, Du Bois, and Trotter in Boston marked
a turning point in the enunciation of the strategies that would shape the
Black freedom struggle in and beyond Boston in the years to come.[12] The Niagara Movement would help lay the foundations for the school desegregation
movement in Boston and the nation more broadly. There is a direct correla-
tion between the debates and struggles among these significant leaders and
the modern-day civil rights movement. Understanding these dynamics is
critical to tracing how we got to that point and, more specifically, how Black
Bostonians initiated their own struggle to rid their city of Jim Crow.[13]

Harvard University

In the mid-1890s, Harvard University was an important site of Black educational aspirations and political ambitions. Trotter graduated from Harvard in
June 1895, three months after Frederick Douglass's death and three months
shy of Booker T. Washington's Atlanta address. Booker T. Washington received an honorary degree there on June 24, 1896. In his letter of acceptance,
written on Tuskegee letterhead, Washington wrote, "Your favor May 28 in-
forming me of the desire of Harvard University to confer an honorary degree
upon me at the next commencement June 24, is received. In reply, I would say
that the information is a great surprise to me. I shall be present at the time
you name."[14] The university also nurtured the academic career of W. E. B. Du
Bois, who was the first Black student to earn a PhD (in history) from Harvard
University in 1895.[15] Du Bois was seated in the audience during Harvard's
1896 undergraduate commencement alongside William Monroe Trotter, who
received a master's degree from Harvard, when Washington received his honorary degree.[16] At that moment, these three men were absolute strangers to
one another. Yet larger historical forces were soon to bring them together.[17]

Du Bois, Trotter, and Washington each came to have very defined beliefs
regarding the best way to address disparities in Black communities. By the first
decade of the twentieth century, Washington was the more established of the

group.[18] By 1903, however, W. E. B. Du Bois was well on his way to becoming the preeminent Black intellect of the twentieth century. Du Bois advocated a struggle for political and social equality, calling early for a Black intellectual elite to "lead their race." As he wrote in *The Negro Problem*, "The Negro race, like all races, is going to be saved by its exceptional men. The problem of education, then, among Negroes must first of all deal with the Talented Tenth; it is the problem of developing the Best of this race that they may guide the Mass away from the contamination and death of the worst, in their own and other races."[19]

Booker T. Washington, by contrast, pushed for Black youths to be educated in the trades and other professions. He downplayed social activism, arguing instead for steady economic gain.[20] While Du Bois later butted heads with Washington, most famously in his 1903 screed in *The Souls of Black Folk*, "Of Mr. Booker T. Washington and Others," his conflict with Washington has sometimes been overstated. Indeed, Du Bois had once applied for a job at the Tuskegee Institute.[21]

In "Of Mr. Booker T. Washington and Others," Du Bois outlined the philosophical and ideological debate between the merits of the gospel of wealth and industry a strong political base devoted to the pursuit of higher education. In doing so, he exposed the contradictions in Washington's philosophy of social uplift. Diplomatic as it was, Du Bois sought to drive home the point that Washington had made a Faustian bargain with white people by carefully crafting a model of industrial education intended to please the labor needs of the South (and North) while not interfering with the hierarchical racial order sanctioned by *Plessy v. Ferguson* and its corresponding doctrine of separate but equal. While not without its merits, Du Bois's critique of Washington lacked the benefit of hindsight. In many ways, both Washington's Tuskegee model and Du Bois's "Talented Tenth" contained components of racial uplift philosophy and functioned to show how education played a central role within this broader movement.

Since the end of the Civil War, two prevailing schools of thought dominated the debate as to what strategy would best fit the aims of the Black community. One attitude held that the answer for Black people was to gain political and social equality by pursuing the avenues opened by a classical education. Proponents of this school argued that the greatest nations in the world were built on the foundations of culture and knowledge of a glorious and proud history. Furthermore, they argued that freedom for Black people lay in the ballot box and that franchise extended to at least the educated part of the race would secure the rights of all.

The prevailing school of thought had been that Black people needed to "put their hand to the plough" and gain industrial and agricultural training in the face of an oppressive and dominating South. This view was most closely associated with Washington, a former slave, mine worker, and Hampton Institute graduate. Washington spoke in glowing terms of pulling oneself up by the bootstraps and said that what the race needed were less politicians and more captains of industry. Ownership of property and education in the industrial and agricultural arts figured prominently into Washington's philosophy of economic empowerment.

Washington told Southern Blacks to "cast down your bucket where you are" in his infamous address at the Cotton States and International Exposition in Atlanta on September 18, 1895.[22] Washington asserted that although the two races must work together in economic matters, in social relations they "could be as separate as fingers on the hand."[23] Washington's ideas about industrial education continued to hold sway throughout much of the country.

While some Black Bostonians had severe concerns about Washington and his ideas, Washington was able to strike a chord with the wealthy white upper crust of Boston and with the neo-abolitionists, particularly the Garrison family. Washington's success in this area had as much to do with his unique talents and abilities as it did with the confluence of several historical forces from the period between 1895 and 1915. The descendants of the most famous abolitionist in American history and a legend in the abolitionist mythology of Boston, the Garrisons were by and large Washington supporters.[24] They wrote letters and editorials that supported Washington's position and helped finance his trips to Europe. They also participated in campaigns to secure his position among affluent whites, while boosting his legitimacy as a leader over that of other Black leaders.[25]

Booker T. Washington in Boston

While often associated with the South, Booker T. Washington created important ties to the Boston area.[26] His wife, Olivia A. Davidson, had attended the State Normal School in Framingham, a Western suburb of Boston, under the auspices of dowager and white socialite Mary Hemenway, graduating in 1881. Washington even established a summer home near Boston, in South Weymouth, Massachusetts. In 1900, Washington founded the Negro Business League in Boston, in the home of Dr. Samuel Courtney, his protégée from Tuskegee.[27] He sent his children to be educated nearby.[28] Although Washington reportedly spurned higher education in the liberal arts, he sent his daughter, Portia, to Wellesley College, located just outside Boston. She enrolled as a "special student," taking only a few courses in the fall of 1901.[29] His son, Booker T. Jr., took classes at the adjoining Wellesley School for Boys.[30] These ties only became stronger with Washington's decision to make Boston the next battleground in his decades-long war to promote industrial education.

In his speech at Harvard University's commencement, Washington attempted to bolster the support he already had among Bostonians. In his habitual way of catering to white audiences, he stated, "How shall we make the dwellers in the mansions on yon Beacon Street feel and see the need of the spirits in the lowliest cabin in Alabama cotton fields or Louisiana sugar bottoms? This problem, Harvard University is solving, not by bringing itself down, but by bringing the masses up." He continued:

> If through me, a humble representative, seven million of my people in the South might be permitted to send a message to Harvard—Harvard, that offered up on death's altar Shaw and Russell and Lowell and scores of others that we might have a free and united country—that message would be, "Tell them that the sacrifice was not in vain. Tell them, by the way of the shop, the field, the skilled hand, habits of thrift and economy, by the way of the industrial school and college, we are coming up. We are crawling up, working up, yea, bursting up,—often through oppression, unjust discrimination, and prejudice; but through them all we are coming up, and, with proper habits, intelligence, and property, there is no power on earth that can permanently stay our progress."[31]

Numerous influential white Bostonians were united in their support for Booker T. Washington and his educational philosophies, often out of direct opposition to William Monroe Trotter, whom they saw as a rabble-rouser. When Charles Eliot, president of Harvard, raised a glass at an event in Washington's honor to toast the man who had "done more than any other in the world to open the way of equal education to his race," he was probably speaking for most of the Boston Brahmin elite—many of them educated at Harvard University.[32]

The support Washington received from the Boston Brahmins caused him to see Boston as a key to his rise as a national leader. He made several attempts to preempt any actions by his enemies by convening meetings with the organic anti-Tuskegee element in Boston. Samuel Courtney, his longtime friend and protégée from Virginia, attended the Westfield Normal School and eventually settled in Boston.[33] Washington was continually stepping into

enemy territory either through his public appearances or under the clandes-
tine auspices of his personal spies, who tried to infiltrate the Boston radicals
in several instances. As Stephen Fox writes, "Washington saw Boston as a
threat to his role as national spokesman for the race." As a preemptive strike,
he arranged a reconciliation dinner with his Boston critics at Young's Hotel in
the spring of 1898.[34]

Washington had spies in Boston and loyal men who reported back to him
in exchange for high-level political appointments. Peter Jefferson Smith Jr.,
was one such individual employed by Tuskegee as a northern advance agent.
Clifford H. Plummer was another; born in Virginia, he was a Black Boston
lawyer and one of Washington's staunchest supporters.

As the budding leader of the opposition, a young Trotter, while still forming his unique brand of elitist militancy, was completely dedicated to the task
of organizing a group of men to stand in radical opposition to Washington's
leadership. In 1903, Trotter started to coordinate the efforts of Bostonians with
similar backgrounds and credentials to his own and those of militants elsewhere in order to do just that.[35] The Afro-American Council was particularly
strong in the Southern states because of Washington's influence there. Trotter,
a Northerner with ties to other radicals largely educated in the North, believed
he needed to gain influence among such constituencies if he was to garner
wider support for his ideas. In the spring of 1903, Trotter helped organize a
protest meeting for Black Americans in New England; and in June, he and an
associate, Clement G. Morgan, attended a similar affair in New York.[36] However, these efforts did not yield the kinds of results Trotter was looking for. The
radicals in Boston were strong; they were well heeled and highly educated, and
they had the necessary connections. But they were mainly communicating
among themselves and were distrusted by many Black Southerners due to their
perceived elitism. To become nationally known leaders, they needed to organize. To penetrate what were the leading civil rights organizations of their day,
they needed to meet said members of those organizations personally. Trotter
and his band of radicals would have to try to gain access in the South.

The sheer amount of power Washington brandished posed a threat,
but Trotter had a plan for stopping him.[37] He prepared for a confrontation
with the leadership of the Afro-American Council in April 1903, at a meeting scheduled to take place in Louisville. Some Black newspapers noted
that he had emerged as a dissenting voice at the meeting, but once again,
Washington rolled over the radicals. Trotter by this point had some legitimate objections to Washington's leadership style and his overall program.
The challenge that Trotter faced was clearly communicating his objections

about Washington's ideals and convincing the general population. Washington was a charismatic leader and thus able to avoid serious scrutiny except when it came to radicals like Trotter. Unfortunately, Trotter often derailed the impact of his concerns by turning his valid philosophical criticisms into personal attacks.[38]

The next opportunity that Trotter had was a meeting held by Washington associates at the Boston branch of the National Negro Business League on July 30. Trotter hoped the Boston radicals might have better luck in their own city. His group made arrangements to attend the public meeting at the African Methodist Episcopal Zion Church on Columbus Avenue in the South End.[39] In preparation for the meeting, Trotter and his associates drafted nine questions to pose to Washington and Fortune from the floor, questions specifically designed to embarrass and agitate. Although they covered all manner of things, they all had one common thread—questioning Washington's leadership.

What Trotter sought to do was to discredit Washington in front of Boston's Black leadership and the press, which were all in attendance. Trotter began, "In view of the fact that you are understood to be unwilling to insist upon the Negro having his every right (both civil and political), would it not be a calamity at this juncture to make you our leader? Don't you know you would help the race more by exposing the new form of slavery just outside the gates of Tuskegee than preaching submission? Are the rope and the torch all the race is to get under your leadership?"[40] At one point, Trotter climbed atop a chair and began shouting at Washington. Others soon joined in, creating a cacophony in the room. The situation escalated after someone threw cayenne pepper onto the stage, prompting everyone to begin sneezing, and a physical brawl broke out. This continued until the police arrived. In the end, Washington pressed charges, and Trotter spent thirty days in jail.[41]

Black newspapers, which carried stories of the meeting, characterized Trotter as angry, even hostile. The Washington *Colored American* captured the feelings of many, including Black leaders in Boston, when it wrote, "Last night at the A. M. E. Zion Church, on Columbus Avenue, at a public meeting of the Boston branch of the National Negro Business League, one of the most dis-graceful and riotous scenes in the history of Boston was precipitated by five men under the leadership of William Monroe Trotter, editor of the *Guardian*, who has become insane in his opposition to Dr. Booker T. Washington and his methods of leadership."[42] The event became known as the Boston Riot.

As these and other quotations make clear, Black newspapers were not so sympathetic to Trotter's protest. In discussing the event, the *Freeman*, an

Indianapolis-based paper, wrote, "When Mr. Washington was introduced the five men created so much disorder and confusion that the audience became panicky and riotous in temper. The managers of the meeting then decided to have Trotter and all of his fellow conspirators ejected from the church. A squad of policemen, commanded by a sergeant, was called in, and, in the confusion that ensued both inside and outside of the church, arrested Trotter and his sister, and two of his henchmen, and, with handcuffs on their wrists, marched them off to the station house."[43]

Although it must have been painfully embarrassing to be written about in this way by the majority of Black newspapers, it was a baptism by fire. This so-called Boston Riot proclaimed Trotter as the de facto leader of the Boston radicals. Indeed, this moment brought national attention to their cause.[44] Du Bois later outlined the events in his 1968 autobiography, published five years after his death:

> In the early summer of 1903, Mr. Washington went to Boston and arranged to speak in a colored church to colored people—a thing which he did not often do in the North. Trotter and [George] Forbes, editors of the *Guardian*, determined to heckle him and make him answer publicly certain questions with regard to his attitude toward voting and education. William H. Lewis, a colored lawyer whom I myself had introduced to Mr. Washington, had charge of the meeting, and the result was a disturbance magnified by the newspapers into a "riot," which resulted in the arrest of Mr. Trotter. Finally he served a term in jail.

Du Bois further recalled, "With this incident I had no direct connection whatsoever. I did not know beforehand of the meeting in Boston, nor of the projected plan to heckle Mr. Washington. But when Trotter went to jail, my indignation overflowed. I did not always agree with Trotter then or later. But he was an honest, brilliant, unselfish man, and to treat as a crime that which was at worst mistaken judgment was an outrage."[45]

Following the riot, Washington's presence was felt in Boston in all sorts of ways.[46] Despite the negative coverage, the controversy garnered Trotter growing support among those opposed to Washington's leadership. Trotter, it seemed, was the only person brave enough to take Washington head on, finally achieving his long-term aim of breaking the charm that Washington seemed to have over so many Americans—both Black and white. This transformation, however, did not come about overnight. There were those who remained critical of Trotter and continued to support Washington. In response to these skeptics, Trotter wrote in the pages of the *Guardian* in 1904: "The policy of compromise has failed. . . . The policy of resistance and aggression deserves a trial."[47]

In 1905, Trotter and Du Bois joined together, alongside a number of other people, including Ida B. Wells, to found a new organization to serve as a counter voice to the Afro-American League and the forces supporting Washington. This would result in the formation of the Niagara Movement.

William Monroe Trotter

During the late nineteenth and early twentieth centuries, William Monroe Trotter emerged as the most irreverent opponent of Washington and, too often, the lone voice in radical opposition to his ideas. At the time, industrial education was coming to dominate schools in the North. Had it not been for the leadership of Trotter, Washington's vision might have come to dominate the lives of Black Bostonians. Whether in his position as editor of the *Guardian* newspaper or as the founder of various political organizations that had several incarnations, Trotter as a so-called race man consistently delivered a scathing critique of the Tuskegee machine.[48] Although we often think of Du Bois as the chief architect of the movement against Washington's accommodationist strategy, Trotter attacked Washington most ardently, doing so three years before the more celebrated Du Bois joined in the fray with the publication of *The Souls of Black Folk* in 1903.

Trotter was a firebrand—a man who, for his own reasons and unique circumstances, had developed into a hard-nosed race man. Trotter and other Black leaders replaced the old guard whites from the abolitionist tradition. In that sense, Trotter and Du Bois replaced people like William Cooper Nell and Roberts in leading the Black struggle in Boston. During the 1920s, they helped reclaim Boston's legacy as an abolitionist stronghold and lay the groundwork for the political actors who fought for the race later in the twentieth century. In addition, they were friends.

Born in 1872 in Chillicothe, Ohio, William Monroe Trotter was the son of James Trotter, a Civil War veteran, author of a book on American music, and bona fide claimant to the mantle of what would later be called the "the Black Brahmin."[49] In the 1850s, Trotter's parents fled the South for Ohio, a free state and common destination for former slaves. With the outbreak of the Civil War, James Trotter moved to Boston—known to be a stronghold of abolitionism— to join the all-Black Massachusetts Fifty-Fifth Regiment, fighting for the North. According to historian Dolita Cathcart, "When the war [came] to an end, his service, the fact that he [became] an officer, that he [knew] many of the White abolitionists, help[ed] him move from having been a teacher in Ohio to essentially becoming a real estate magnate in Boston, and [he became] quite wealthy."[50] James Trotter taught his son to be a fighter—in every way imaginable. According to Carl Senna, a journalist and devoted biographer of Trotter's life in the pages of the *Bay State Banner*, Trotter's brother-in-law, Dr. Charles G. Steward, stated that James once told his son that "he could expect two beatings if he lost one to a white boy."[51]

Trotter could not have been more different from Booker T. Washington. The former was a Massachusetts man, raised in the well-to-do white neighborhood of Hyde Park. Washington was a Southerner, born into bondage in the last years of slavery. As a child, Trotter had all the advantages and went to all the right schools. In Hyde Park, Trotter was extremely popular and valedictorian of his school. He earned his undergraduate and graduate degrees at Harvard University. While at Harvard, Trotter was an avid participant in social clubs and athletics, helping to set up and run the Total Abstinence League. During his years at Harvard, Trotter established his lifelong reputation as a teetotaler.[52]

Trotter received his bachelor of arts degree magna cum laude in June 1895 and became the first Black member of Phi Beta Kappa. He also took extra courses during the 1895–96 academic year and received a master's degree in education in 1896.[53] Trotter's experience at Harvard served as "an inspiration," he wrote, "because it was the exemplar of true Americanism, freedom, equality, and real democracy. Harvard was a place where all races, proscribed in other sections, could find carried out in a practical way the policies and ideals that all beings want. Each individual was taken on individual worth, capability, and ambition in life."[54] Although Trotter's experience at Harvard was a positive one, it would not be without its pitfalls, a subject that would be addressed in Du Bois's later recollections. Their paths rarely crossed while Du Bois was enrolled at Harvard as a graduate student.[55]

As a boy, Trotter had expressed some interest in attending seminary. It was James Trotter's dream that his son might pursue this option. Instead, in 1897, a year after obtaining his master's degree, Trotter joined his father in the real estate and mortgage business.[56] Initially, Trotter was confident that his education and upbringing would all but guarantee his future success. At the time, the plight of Black men, women, and children across the country was nonexistent to him. That may have remained the case were it not for Trotter's experience with racism, including his exclusion from the white business world. This discrimination led him to ultimately pursue a life dedicated to the Black men and women of Boston instead.[57] It also led Trotter to identify with the working-class Black people in Boston.

Trotter's path to political leadership was not direct. He would later write of himself: "He did not seek a career of agitation and organization for equality of his race," speaking in the third person. "The burden was dropped upon him by the desertion of others and he would not desert the duty."[58] Over time, he increasingly became confident that he must do something meaningful for his people. He resolved to do race work. In later years, Trotter reflected on his chosen life of activism, "The conviction grew upon me that pursuit of business, money, civic or literary position was like building a house upon the sands, if race prejudice and public discrimination was to spread up from the South and result in a fixed cast of color."[59] At the same time, Trotter became increasingly aware of Washington's efforts to promote industrial education and determined to counter them.

Trotter's family fortune allowed him the freedom to start his newspaper, the *Guardian*.[60] On November 9, 1901, Trotter and friend George W. Forbes published the first issue of the *Guardian* newspaper with the motto "For Every Right with All Thy Might." The *Guardian* would be Trotter's central preoccupation for the rest of his life. Subsequently, Trotter used the paper to launch a full-scale diatribe against Washington. As early as 1901, Trotter was speaking out against Washington in the *Guardian* and stirring up quite a storm of protest among Black Bostonians and the white neo-abolitionist establishment. In editorial after editorial, Trotter hammered away at Washington and his network of support that spanned the country, especially in the form of other Black newspapers.[61] From the outset of his newspaper career, Trotter aligned himself with the strategy of agitation for equal rights for the race. Why would a wealthy, albeit middle class, Black person do that? As he wrote in the inaugural issue, "We have come to protest forever against being proscribed or shut off in any caste from equal rights with other citizens, and shall remain forever on the firing line at any and all times in defence of such rights."[62] In an early editorial, the *Guardian* accused Washington of fathering a system of "caste education" and for masquerading as an educator in order to bring into existence a political machine.[63] Second perhaps only to Du Bois, it was Trotter and his unflinching rhetoric and vitriol against Washington that kept the protest tradition alive. As the editor of his own newspaper, he was part of a grand tradition that was creating the opportunity for dissent and organizing against Washington. The *Guardian*, unlike many of the other Black newspapers of its time, contained no advertisements for hair straightening products or skin bleaching creams—an accomplishment that made Trotter very proud. Unbeholden to these kinds of businesses for ads, the independence of Trotter's newspaper afforded him a certain amount of freedom in his views and a more extensive degree of latitude within which to operate. And yet the question remained: How was Trotter able to keep advertisement revenue and remain independent—and thus not susceptible to white capital?

As the *Guardian*'s masthead stated, "Segregation for Colored Is the Most Damning Degradation in the United States—Fight It." Trotter became editor and publisher of the *Guardian* while idealizing the great and courageous abolitionist editor William Lloyd Garrison, publisher of the immortal *Liberator*. Trotter considered the launch of the *Guardian* in the same light as and purpose of the *Liberator*—the abolition of economic slavery, racial segregation, and injustice.

In 1908, seven years after starting the *Guardian* at his place of business, Trotter moved the *Guardian* office to 10 Pemberton Square, the same building site as the Garrison-edited *Liberator*. On his desk, Trotter kept a bust of Garrison. In many ways these two men were much alike, but one must also realize that Trotter had an uncompromising father—a former army officer and one of the first Black authors to come out of the Civil War. Trotter admired men like this, and his refusal to accept advertisements for skin creams or hair straighteners was a good example of how Trotter modeled an early notion of "Black is beautiful."

Nevertheless, like Garrison, Trotter was never a stay-behind-the-desk editor. Trotter was always out on the streets, as well as on rostrums at conferences and protest meetings throughout the country and even abroad. A dynamic moving force that attacked racial injustice wherever he found it, Trotter organized the first equal rights mass meetings in Boston, long before the rest of the nation even dreamed about such demonstrations. He organized the first National Equal Rights League and was first to bring the civil rights crusade into the churches, much as Garrison had similarly awakened the church's conscience against slavery. Trotter was the first to speak for Black freedom in Asia and Africa as well as the Americas when he later attended the Paris Peace Conference and foundation for the first League of Nations, an extraordinary story in and of itself.

While the *Guardian*'s editorials served as an effective consciousness-raising instrument for Trotter, they also gave readers a glimpse into a specific racial ideology that placed him at odds with many of his contemporaries. Trotter and Washington disagreed on many of the same points that Du Bois and Washington differed on; however, Trotter's exchanges were marked by a personal animosity that Du Bois and Washington's feud never had. There existed between Trotter and Washington a hostile bitterness that was to characterize relations between the two men until Washington's death. Trotter seemed, at times, a man possessed—always going to greater lengths not only to criticize Washington's ideas but to personally ridicule him as well. Part of that can be accounted for by Trotter's enigmatic personality and strong notions of masculinity—he often expressed his views in terms of manliness and claimed that others were not "real" men. This means of expression may have been overcompensation on Trotter's part as a response to his rather genteel upbringing. It seems that although Trotter lived—or was meant to live—the life of a gentleman, a Black Brahmin, as it were, he had the mentality, the doggedness, and the temperament of a working man. He was in many ways both very much a part of his class and a stranger to his class. He could have had a more comfortable life, but in many ways he rejected this to live a life dedicated to racial justice.[64] Some have argued that this sometimes petty personal criticism detracted from the arguments he made against Washington's accommodationist views.[65] As Fox writes:

> The *Guardian*'s vitriolic assault was a risk, because while it brought
> the paper fame and gave Trotter's case against Washington a wider
> circulation, in its freewheeling excesses it could alienate readers who were
> sympathetic to basic ideas of protest. Charles Chesnutt wrote to Trotter
> praising the *Guardian* as "interesting and instructive" and complimented
> "its uncompromising stand on all questions pertaining to the rights of the
> Negro." But, Chesnutt wondered, "are you not likely, with your strong
> feelings and impulsive disposition to make the matter too much a
> personal one and thereby injure your own influence?"[66]

Still, Trotter remained steadfast in his focus on racial justice. In that pursuit, he helped establish the Boston Literary and Historical Association, a forum where the most prominent Black intellectual leaders of Boston discussed various issues confronting Black people nationally, including the issue of industrial education versus liberal arts, and how that filtered down into the Boston schools.[67]

Subsequently, Du Bois, who penned the most famous attack on Washingtonian accommodationism, touted Trotter's role in fomenting anti-Washington sentiment within the Black political leadership class:

> All this naturally aroused increasing opposition among Negroes and
> especially among the younger class of educated Negroes, who were
> beginning to emerge here and there, particularly from Northern
> institutions. This opposition began to become vocal in 1901 when two

men, Monroe Trotter, Harvard 1895, and George Forbes, Amherst 1895, began the publication of the Boston *Guardian*. The *Guardian*, a weekly periodical, was bitter, satirical, and personal; but it was well edited, it was earnest, and it published facts. It attracted wide attention among colored people; it circulated among them all over the country; it was quoted and discussed. I did not wholly agree with the *Guardian*, and indeed only a few Negroes did, but nearly all read it or were influenced by it.[68]

Using the *Guardian*, Trotter continually skewered Washington. Editorials published by the *Guardian* had titles such as "Washington, the Politician" and "Always Playing Double."[69] Along with editorials, the *Guardian* featured cartoons about Washington in which he was hanged in effigy and subjected to all kinds of ridicule, including a "snapshot in Hades taken by the *Guardian* artist."[70]

Along with editing the *Guardian*, Trotter was the de facto leader of the Boston Radicals, a feisty group of Black people who had attended New England colleges and were opposed to Washington's philosophy. In Trotter's heaven or hell world, one either supported the Boston Radicals or was for Washington. A person was forced to choose. Fox writes that "the best known and most widely respected of the 'Boston radicals' at first was Archibald Grimké. But the principal impetus came from younger men of college training, Trotter, George Forbes, and two lawyers, Clement G. Morgan, and Butler Wilson. Beneath them in a loose orbit was a host of others—teachers, domestic servants, waiters, housewives. The *Guardian* was their mouthpiece, and the Boston Literary was their club."[71] Later, Trotter included Ida B. Wells in his gang of radicals.

Ida B. Wells, who became one of the most uncompromising voices in the promotion of Black rights of anyone—male or female—also began to use her voice to speak for the rights of Black men at a time when doing so threatened the lives of Black men themselves. She too was a journalist. When Wells learned that a "committee of leading citizens" had smashed her printing presses in Memphis after the publication of an incendiary editorial, she joined the *New York Age*, the leading Black newspaper of the time, edited by T. Thomas Fortune, known as the dean of Negro journalists.[72] Du Bois's major contribution was the notion of the Talented Tenth to lead Black folk to a better day. Both Trotter and Wells used journalism to organize and empower. Washington emphasized economic bootstrapping over the claim for rights.

By the early part of 1902, Trotter was eyeing Du Bois to join his camp, although the latter was cool to the idea. At this time, Du Bois still had amicable

relations with Washington and was reluctant to step outside his role as a social scientist to get caught up in the fray. What clinched it for Du Bois was the
Boston Riot, which crystallized the need for opposition to the machine,
which rolled over any sign of dissent. The late Elliott Rudwick wrote, "In July
of 1903, Du Bois took another step closer to Trotter when he made it clear
that the Tuskegeean was actually a political boss. He went further than he had
in his critique of the preceding spring and unfairly increased Washington's
responsibility for the attitudes of the whites in regard to Negroes."[73]

While Trotter and Washington clashed over many issues, at the heart of
this disagreement was an issue that Boston had been struggling with since the
Roberts trial. In 1903, Booker T. Washington published a piece in *Atlantic
Monthly* titled "The Fruits of Industrial Training," in which he mentions the
Boston opposition specifically. On April 24, 1899, a group of Boston Blacks
met at Young's Hotel to commemorate the forty-eighth anniversary of Charles
Sumner's election to the Senate. William H. Lewis gave the principal speech.
He said of the Tuskegee program: "The gospel of industrial education has
been declared to be the negro's only salvation. If it is meant by this that
through some mysterious process a trade will give to the negro all his rights
as a man and citizen, it is a sufficient refutation of the theory to say that the
South would not stand for it a single moment."[74]

Both men agreed that education was crucial for the Black man. However,
their emphases were quite different. For Washington, it would be practical
training leading to a good job. For Trotter, it was a necessary right that could
prove the quality of the Black man's brain. Stephen Fox calls it "the difference
between the Hampton man, and the Harvard man." At times Washington
showed traces of anti-intellectualism. His college-educated critics, he once
wrote, "know books but they do not know men"; they "understand theories,
but they do not understand things."[75]

It is an educational difference more than a question of different ideologies
that characterized the Washington-Trotter framework, and the question of
education should, therefore, be integral to any understanding of their differ-
ing positions.[76] The critical debate as to whether Black people should learn
industrial rather than liberal arts, accept social segregation rather than strive
for racial integration, be resigned to political impotence rather than to exercise the franchise, is a debate mainly about education and the civic good. As
such, it is interesting to see how that debate played out in Massachusetts—
home to both Du Bois and Trotter.

Trotter could also be very inconsistent in his beliefs. For example,
when Trotter left the Niagara Movement, he refused to join the newly formed

NAACP, although Du Bois invited him. He claimed to be unable to support the fledgling organization because of its white leadership. Yet Trotter had dedicated most of his life to doing just that—and would continue to do so. His emphasis was on integration, legal rights, and the importance of persistent agitation for the right to political power. He saw that power as emanating from the federal government and made many attempts to bring that power to bear through his protest activities, which ran the gamut.

Boston has pride of place as the site of the first branch of the NAACP in 1911. A significant force in the race for power in Boston, the esteemed civil rights organization was the oldest in the nation. Bostonian involvement in the organization was significant from the beginning, including among those who participated in the earlier Niagara Movement. In 1910, the Boston Committee to Advance the Cause of the Negro, which grew significantly in terms of membership and activity that year, chose Boston as the site for the first annual conference of the NAACP. The ad hoc committee became the first branch of the NAACP when the second annual conference was held at the Park Street Church in Boston in 1911.[77]

The organization's initial membership included leading Bostonians, such as Moorfield Storey, William Monroe Trotter, Archibald Grimké, and members of the Garrison family, providing a link back to the abolition movement. When the NAACP held its 1911 national convention in Boston, it seemed, in the words of Albert Pillsbury, "like an old-fashioned anti-slavery meeting."[78] The abolitionist impulse was likewise palpable on the evening of February 8, 1911, when 506 Bostonians, many of whom were descendants of abolitionists themselves, gathered at the Park Street Church to receive the official branch charter. As the many sons and daughters of nineteenth-century New England abolitionist leaders looked on, the charter inscribed with the following statement of purpose was read aloud: "To uplift the colored men and women of this country by securing for them the full enjoyment of their rights as citizens, justice in all courts and equality of opportunity everywhere."[79]

By the end of 1912, less than a year since its founding, the Boston branch of the NAACP claimed over 250 members.[80] Moorfield Storey, a Bostonian and a founding NAACP member, served as the first national president of the organization.[81] He also served as the first president of the Boston branch until 1916, when his successor, Butler Wilson, a Black lawyer and a founder of the branch, was elected branch president. It was a position Wilson would hold until 1936, earning him distinction as an early Black leader of the NAACP. It would not be until 1919 that the national organization itself had its first Black president, James Weldon Johnson.

During the early twentieth century, the NAACP led a number of campaigns on behalf of Black Bostonians. In 1914, the branch won a victory when it persuaded the Boston School Committee to withdraw from the schools a book titled *Forty Best Songs*, which included which included a number of racist epithets for Black people. Black children had been returning home from school upset over the fact that these songs were being taught to them and that white children were taunting and jeering them as a result. The vote of the committee to discard the songbooks was unanimous.[82]

The next major fight that the NAACP undertook occurred in response to the 1915 anti-Black film *Birth of a Nation*, the movie version of the best-selling novel *The Clansman* by Thomas Dixon Jr. The branch published a leaflet explaining its opposition and spent thousands of dollars in a campaign fighting for the removal of the film from a Boston theater. A mass meeting was sponsored by the branch at Tremont Temple to protest not only the release of the film but also pending legislation in Congress that was discriminatory against Black Americans. Despite the protests of the majority of Boston's Black institutions, agencies, and leadership, the city ultimately allowed the film to complete its scheduled run at the Tremont Theatre through the summer of 1915. Six years later, however, when the film was scheduled for a rerun at the Shubert Theatre in Boston, William Monroe Trotter and the Boston NAACP managed to have the film banned after about six hundred citizens attended a demonstration protesting the film.[83]

In 1918, only two years after Wilson took over, the chapter faced its greatest battle yet when a Black girl was threatened with suspension from a Boston elementary school over a misunderstanding about the young girl's attendance record. The misunderstanding proved to be the result of errors in the roll, an observation that was revealed during the case brought about by the NAACP. The branch came to her defense with legal aid and won her case, allowing her to stay in school. The case proved typical of the organization. While occasionally engaging in direct action, such as the protest of *Birth of a Nation*, the NAACP relied more on legal strategy than on protests and pickets.

By 1919, the Boston branch of the NAACP reported a membership of approximately 2,700, including over 447 new members in the previous year alone.[84] That same year the *Crisis*, the official newspaper of the NAACP, reported that the Boston chapter had maintained the lead among branches in the diversity of its membership, which represented a variety of races.[85] The Boston chapter continued to play an important role in the national organization. At the insistence of the Boston branch, led by Wilson, the national board called for a congressional investigation over the treatment of Black soldiers at home and abroad who were fighting for democracy overseas in World War I and facing discrimination upon their return home. Even so, some in the city had begun to question the organization's dominance.

Following his refusal to join the NAACP, Trotter cast out on his own, founding a radical political organization called the National Independent Political League as an alternative to the newly formed NAACP. This organization subsequently went through several incarnations before eventually becoming the National Equal Rights League.[86] From his position leading the all-Black league, Trotter quickly became a vocal critic of the NAACP for its lack of Black leadership. While cooperating minimally with the Boston chapter, Trotter could be just as caustic in his critique of the NAACP as he was about Washington's Tuskegee machine.[87]

By the 1900s, Boston, like much of the South, was being infected by the deadly scourge of Jim Crow, which had seeped into the bedrock of the nation. After the 1896 *Plessy v. Ferguson* decision was handed down, making "separate but equal" the law of the land, segregation began to creep into all corners of the country. Trotter disagreed with Washington so vehemently on the question of so-called industrial education that he called it "caste education." Trotter was, if anything, an apostle of the good that could come of a well-rounded liberal arts education, which he viewed as being bound up with the franchise. Washington saw the vote as something of a luxury for Black people, while Trotter saw it as a right that must not be conceded under any circumstance. Interpolating the language of the Dred Scott decision, the *Guardian* charged that "the northern Negro has no rights which Booker Washington is bound to respect. He must be stopped."[88]

In Boston, Trotter was beginning to witness a slow deterioration of the rights that Black Bostonians had formerly taken for granted. Giving voice to the change that was slowly happening in the city of Garrison, Ray Stannard Baker wrote that while "no hotel or restaurant in Boston refused Negro guests" in 1900, just a few years later "several hotels, restaurants, and especially confectionery stores, will not serve Negroes."[89] From Trotter's point of view, as long as Washington, the foremost leader of the race at that time, refused to condemn such a deterioration, he was complicit.

W. E. B. Du Bois

At the turn of the century, Boston, like other Black communities, was divided over the best path for racial uplift. Some supported Booker T. Washington's philosophy of industrial education, while others looked toward the emerging progressive approach touted by people like Du Bois and Trotter. The debate was a vigorous one, taking place amid the shadow of widespread discrimination, lynchings, and racial violence, all of which reached new heights amid Jim Crow—not just in the South but in the North as well.[90] In the end, the story must be told that Du Bois and Trotter were friends. In many ways, the pairing of Du Bois and Trotter was unlikely.[91] Trotter did not command the eloquence, the charisma, or the influence that the Atlanta professor could bring to their struggle. Conversely, Du Bois "was not an organization man," but he thought perhaps the two could work together. Du Bois was more willing to get involved in the fight after Trotter's arrest because he saw how it could help his project of forming what would become the Niagara Movement. Alone, they were ineffective, but together they built one of the most influential movements to rival even the National Afro-American League and the Afro-American Council. The Niagara Movement, rooted deeply in Boston, began in earnest following the Boston Riot.

Du Bois writes, "I sent out from Atlanta in June 1905 a call to a few selected persons for organized determination and aggressive action on the part of men who believe in Negro freedom and growth. I proposed a conference during the summer to oppose firmly present methods of strangling honest criticism; to organize intelligent and honest Negroes; and to support organs of news and public opinion."[92] The meeting was held on the Canadian side of Niagara Falls because Du Bois could not find a hotel willing to host the Black group in the United States.

About that fateful day, Du Bois recalled, "Fifty-nine colored men from 17 different states eventually signed a call for a meeting near Buffalo, New York, during the week of July 9, 1905. I went to Buffalo and hired a little hotel on the Canadian side of the river at Fort Erie and waited for the men to attend the meeting. If sufficient men had not come to pay for the hotel, I should certainly have been in bankruptcy and perhaps in jail; but as a matter of fact, 29 men, representing 14 states, came. The 'Niagara Movement' was incorporated January 31, 1906, in the District of Columbia."[93]

Twenty-nine Black men in all, from all over the country, gathered at Fort Erie. Of the men gathered, seven were from New England, six hailed from the South, eight were from the Midwest, four were from the mid-Atlantic, and four were from Washington, DC. Du Bois served as general secretary, alongside a general treasurer. Together, they acted in conjunction with an executive committee made up of the chairmen from each state's local chapter.[94]

The executive committee endorsed a Declaration of Principles drafted by Du Bois and Trotter. The declaration made a plea to white America in plain, unambiguous language. It read, "The Negro race in America, stolen, rav-ished, and degraded, struggling up through difficulties and oppression, needs sympathy and receives criticism; needs help and is given hindrance, needs protection and is given mob-violence, needs justice and is given char-ity, needs leadership and is given cowardice and apology, needs bread and is given a stone. This nation will never stand justified before God until these things are changed."[95] This was bold, courageous language that bespoke of the eloquence and collective years of education of the leadership of this new initiative. The declaration went on to state:

> Persistent manly agitation is the way to liberty, and toward this goal, the Niagara Movement has started and asks the cooperation of all men of all races. . . . Any discrimination based simply on race or color is barbarous, we care not how hallowed it be by custom, expediency or prejudice. . . . And while we are demanding, and ought to demand, and will continue to demand the[se] rights . . . , God forbid that we should ever forget to urge corresponding duties upon our people: The duty to vote . . . to respect the rights of others . . . to work . . . to obey the laws . . . to be clean and orderly . . . to send our children to school . . . to respect ourselves, even as we respect others. . . . We refuse to allow the impression to remain that the Negro-American assents to inferiority, is submissive under oppression and apologetic before insults.[96]

Opposed to the kind of direct action proposed by the Niagara Move-ment, Washington and his allies portrayed Trotter, Du Bois, and others as troublemakers and worked to undercut them. Yet the radicals persisted. A number of leaders of the Niagara Movement, including Trotter, Du Bois, and Wells, were invited to join the newly formed NAACP. Trotter and Wells however, were ultimately maneuvered out of power within the fledgling organization.[97]

One of the biggest reasons for the eventual dissolution of the Niagara Movement was the fact that the Tuskegee machine had infiltrated it, tried to isolate it within the race, and opposed it in a variety of ways, all the while minimizing its importance in public. Shortly after the founding of the Niag-ara Movement, Washington and Fortune held a strategy meeting and agreed to keep news of the radical group out of the press.

The Niagara Movement likewise suffered from internal fissures related to Trotter. As Du Bois wrote, the Niagara Movement "began to suffer internal strain from the dynamic personality of Trotter and my own inexperience with organizations. Finally, it practically became merged with a new and enveloping organization of which I became a leading official—the National Association for the Advancement of Colored People."[98]

Conclusion

In many ways, the Boston of the early twentieth century was a city at odds with itself over its past, its future, and the question of educating Black Bostonians. It was a city that created a myth of having been a crucible of liberty, freedom, and education for all, a myth that started with the words of John Winthrop when he called Boston "a city upon a hill." Winthrop quoted that piece of scripture in a sermon written aboard the brig *Arabella* during its passage from Southampton, England, to New England in 1630. Aboard the ship, the company's leader, Winthrop, laid out the towering expectations they would be measured by:

> Now the only way to avoid this shipwreck and to provide for our posterity is to follow the counsel of Micah: to do justly, to love mercy, to walk humbly with God. For this end, we must be knit together in this work as one man; we must hold each other in brotherly affection; we must be willing to rid ourself of our excesses to supply others' necessities; we must uphold a familiar commerce together in all meekness, gentleness, patience, and liberality. We must delight in each other, make others' conditions our own and rejoice together, mourn together, labor and suffer together, always having before our eyes our commission and common work, our community as members of the same body.[99]

John Winthrop is actually proclaiming that the Puritans had made a covenant with God to establish a truly Christian community "in which the wealthy were to show charity and avoid exploiting their neighbors while the poor were to work diligently. If they abided by this covenant, God would make them an example with the world—a 'city upon a hill.' But if they broke the covenant, the entire community would feel God's wrath."[100] Roger Williams led his religious converts to Rhode Island, naming the city Providence. The Bible defines "faith" as "the substance of things hoped for, the evidence of things unseen."[101] Who is to say that faith did not lead these religious dissidents to Boston or Providence? What if Boston really was designated to be like the shining city upon a hill, as mentioned in the book of Matthew in the Bible. It reads, "You are the salt of the earth. But if the salt loses its savor, how can it be made salty again? It is no longer good for anything, except to be thrown out and trampled by men. You are the light of the world. A city on a hill cannot be hidden."[102] Many white Bostonians saw the city as "the hub of the universe," a beacon of the light of education, learning, and religion that was shown to the rest of the nation.[103]

Some Bostonians would remain true to that creed and very ambitious charge given by this piece of scripture and Winthrop's vision: "So shall we keep the unity of the spirit in the bond of peace. . . . We shall find that the God of Israel is among us, and ten of us shall be able to resist a thousand of our enemies."[104] The problem, however, is one of conquest, and what Gerald Horne calls the "apocalypse of Settler Colonialism."[105] The myths that emanate from this sermon predict the future history of this small settlement on the slender peninsula nestled between the Mystic and Charles Rivers, which the Native Americans called Shawmut and the English would call Boston. The story of Thanksgiving itself came out of this unlikely confluence of different peoples and the imperial gaze. The Native Americans who received blankets festooned with smallpox from Lord Jeffery Amherst, the man for whom the beloved Western Massachusetts college town is named, would probably have found it confusing that the English subscribed to this ideal. Winthrop's last line, "He shall make us a praise and glory that men shall say of succeeding plantations, 'The Lord make it like that of New England.' For we must consider that we shall be as a city upon a hill. The eyes of all people are upon us."[106]

In many ways, Winthrop's words become prophetic. Boston as a city would not be hidden; much to the contrary, it would be there for all to see. This is Boston's "Magna Carta"—the closest thing to a founding document. The contortions with race and equality of the new colonial outpost of what would become the Massachusetts Bay Company city and eventually the city and Commonwealth of Massachusetts, as well as the struggle to live up to the stated ideals upon which it was founded, are America's same problems. Boston would miss achieving its vaunted ideal many times. But in wrestling with the ideals set out by its founder in both words and deed, myth and reality, it kept Boston and America on a path of mythmaking and using said myths to control the body politic in ways beneficial to the ruling class.

This myth sharply contrasted to the reality of the Jim Crow North, which emerged in Boston during the late nineteenth and early twentieth century. This expansion of racial discrimination inspired vigorous debates among the city's, and indeed the nation's, Black leaders regarding the most effective response to the new system of white supremacy and racial discrimination, debates that became even more relevant as Jim Crow set in across the country. Initially, Booker T. Washington's accommodationist approach found a welcome audience in Boston among many middle-class Black leaders and the descendants of white abolitionists. In time, two other titans of Black political leadership with deep roots in Boston—W. E. B. Du Bois and William Monroe Trotter—rose to offer scathing critiques of Washingtonian accommodationism and put forth their own visions of racial uplift. Both men were founders of the Niagara Movement. Each rejected Washington's industrial education model and advocated a more direct attack on racial discrimination and segregation in Boston and beyond. As stated earlier, Trotter ultimately left the NAACP to form his own organization, the National Equal Rights League, and used the pages of his newspaper, the *Guardian*, to level withering, often personal attacks on Washington and other Black leaders, including Du Bois.

Subsequently, Trotter went on to mount several important public protest campaigns, most notably against the screening of D. W. Griffith's racist epic, *The Birth of a Nation*, and against President Woodrow Wilson's decision to segregate federal offices. Meanwhile, Du Bois chose to work within the structure of the newly formed NAACP, preferring legal challenge to protest politics, and leveled a more measured attack on Washington's leadership in the pages of the *Crisis*.

These hotly contested debates between arguably the three most important Black political leaders of the early twentieth century took place largely in Boston, underscoring the centrality of the city to national debates over racial uplift. In addition, at the heart of each man's philosophy of racial change was an educational program. The ideas, organizations, and strategic approaches of these three leaders would have enduring influence within the Black freedom movement throughout the twentieth century.

CHAPTER THREE

Small Victories on the Way to Freedom, 1934–1945

There is no enemy too big for the L.S.N.R. to fight; there is no Negro worker too "insignificant" for the L.S.N.R. to fight for. In the sight of the League of Struggle for Negro Rights, there is no Negro worker who is an insignificant person. Stand up and fight for Negro rights in Boston!

—Eugene Gordon, introduction to *The Borden Case:*
The Struggle for Negro Rights in Boston

How did Boston go from being the home of abolitionism to being considered one of the most racist cities in America? To understand this critical change-over requires an investigation of the changes to Boston's demographics in the Gilded Age. The first Irish mayor of Boston, Hugh O'Brien, was elected in 1885. His election represented a shift of power in many ways from the so-called Boston Brahmin—an English descended Anglo-Saxon Boston that literally "went back to the Mayflower"—to the Irish American. In capturing city hall, the Irish took the municipal jobs, appointments, and patronage that went with it, including control over police, fire, and the Boston Public Schools. Boston's political structure during the twentieth century was one in which the mayor was the most influential figure in the city. This structure led to a system of politics and patronage along severe ethnic lines. By 1920, four Irishmen had served as mayor for a total of sixteen years.

Thomas O'Connor writes in his book *The Boston Irish*:

In the South End, a group of local Black political leaders traded power for patronage much as the Irish ward bosses had done some years earlier. Dr. Silas F. ("Shag") Taylor, a pharmacist, became boss of Ward 9 with the help of his organization, the Massachusetts Colored League. During the prewar years, Shag and his brother Balcom ("Bal") worked with the Curley machine: They set up meetings, organized rallies, ran ads in the local newspapers, and pressured their constituents to support white candidates. The Taylors were among the many Black politicians who switched to the Democratic Party in the 1930s when Roosevelt's New Deal offered them a chance for social and economic security. Beyond this, however, they accepted the segregated system as a political fact of life, assuming, like everyone else, that in Boston you had to "go along to get along."[1]

This issue is crucial because it has been a sticking point in the busing narrative and, at the same time, a missing element to many discussions around busing. Tom Sugrue wrote, "Boston's Irish-Americans, the largest ethnic group in the city and the most visible of its anti-busing activists, cast themselves as the victims of history, Blacks as feckless and undeserving, and advocates of school desegregation as oppressors. In a peculiarly American version of victimology and self-reinvention, they invoked their ancestors' tales of workplace signs that read 'No Irish Need Apply,' and claimed that through hard work and gumption they had risen above oppression while Blacks continued to wallow in self-pity."[2] This was a false narrative that belied their experience in Boston. At the same time, David Roediger wrote in his classic *Wages of Whiteness*:

> Low-browed and savage, groveling and bestial, lazy and wild, simian and sensual—such were the adjectives used by many native-born Americans to describe the Catholic Irish "race" in the years before the Civil War. The striking similarity of this litany of insults to the list of traits ascribed to antebellum Blacks hardly requires comment. Sometimes Black/Irish connections were made explicitly. In antebellum Philadelphia, according to one account, "to be called an 'Irishman' had come to be nearly as great an insult as to be called a 'nigger.'"[3]

Between these two extreme opposing points of view lies the truth about the complicated historical relationship between the Irish Catholics of Boston and Black Americans—intertwined in certain ways in their shared oppression—misinterpreted by many scholars, who went too far in either direction in their interpretation. What is not in dispute is that these two groups were often pitted against each other economically—with Black Americans often used as strikebreakers, and the Irish placed socially below them in Boston—and the long list of ways these two groups have been playing against each other to the benefit of the ruling class.[4]

For all their efforts during these years, Black Americans could not change the entrenched nature of racial animosity in Boston. Doing so would have required much more of an acknowledgment of said racism by *all* parties in Boston and a profound transformation in the city's political economy, educational structures, and job market. Efforts to shift the very nature of race in Boston would rely on the evolution of Black politics from the early twentieth century through the Great Depression, which would set the stage for later activism in the postwar period.

For most white Bostonians, whether natives or transplants, the issue of race loomed larger than the issue of class. One notable exception can be found in the life of John Boyle O'Reilly, a political exile and poet of the Irish national struggle for independence, who arrived in Boston in 1870. Writing for the Irish American newspaper the *Pilot*, he began to find points of commonality between the Irish American and the Black struggle. He had empathy and understanding for the struggle of Black Americans perhaps because of his own background as the member of an embattled race. In essence, O'Reilly saw the fate of Black Americans and the Irish as one. Referring to O'Reilly's dream of brotherhood for all, Mark R. Schneider laments that "by 1920, that dream had vanished."[5] Although the city always had a small Black population, it was perceived as a place where Black residents could make a living and have a real chance for upward mobility. That had changed by the 1930s, however, and Boston moved toward residential segregation, along with educational and economic inequity.

In the decades leading up to the Second World War, new political possibilities and challenges emerged in Boston as labor activism, political radicalism, and struggles for economic justice worked in tandem with Black civil rights campaigns. As in other cities, Black Bostonians attempted to leverage wartime military service to open up new possibilities in the city's manufacturing base, port-related industries, and service economy. Yet as was often the case, class-based solidarity regularly broke on the rocky shoals of persistent racism.

During the 1930s and 1940s, the struggle for and over education moved to the periphery as economic security and economic justice came to the fore. As the city and nation slipped more deeply into the Great Depression, abstract ideological debates like the ones between Washington and Du Bois gave way to make room for bread-and-butter issues, including employment and housing, which were important to the Black working class. Of course, the two phenomena were linked, but one had been more ignored than the other for so long that they may have appeared to Bostonians at that time as mutually exclusive. At the same time, new alliances between organized labor, radical movements, and the Black working class emerged. This new emphasis on the economy was on full display during Boston's "Don't Buy Where You Can't Work" campaign, led by the League of Struggle for Negro Rights, a communist-organized successor to the American Negro Labor Congress.

Boston's "Don't Buy Where You Can't Work" campaign was a local manifestation of a national movement. This chapter highlights the role that white radicals played as allies in local Black freedom movements, as well as the possibilities, but also the significant challenges, associated with class-based interracial organizing. The economic protest campaigns of the 1930s and 1940s achieved modest success in opening up some new opportunities for Black workers—including as clerks, delivery drivers, bank tellers, and even store managers—through broader direct-action methods targeting jobs. This was important for the shape of the struggle to come and pushed the long tradition of Black organizing in Boston in a new direction.

Eugene Gordon and the League of Struggle for Negro Rights

George Borden had done nothing wrong. He was a janitor, a father, and a hard worker who stayed out of trouble. Except for a minor traffic infraction, he had no criminal record.[6] Even so, his previous experience with the Boston Police Department, like so many Black men in Boston before him, had taught him to be afraid.[7] On the balmy afternoon of July 8, 1934, while having a meal with his wife and three young children and a family friend, two swaggering white men in civilian clothes knocked at the door of his Copeland Street cellar apartment.[8] They were both armed, and they gave the impression that they might be street thugs. One said he was a motor vehicles inspector named Everett Gardner, and that the man with him, William Harmon, was a police officer. They had come to serve a warrant for Borden's arrest for "driving without a license."[9]

Borden was frightened by the appearance and the actions of the men. He asked for permission to telephone a friend from a neighbor's apartment upstairs. Granting the request, Gardner and Harmon accompanied him upstairs. Gardner kept his hand on his firearm while he waited for Borden to telephone his supervisor. No one answered. Terrified for his life, that these men had come to possibly kill him, he made a sudden dash for the stairs, hoping to escape through the basement.[10] As the janitor for this housing block, Borden was familiar with the building and its environs. While being brought down the rear staircase, Borden ran up to the third-floor apartment. Harmon gave chase. Borden opened the back door to the third-floor apartment, slamming the door behind him. Harmon, however, was able to prevent the door from slamming shut—smashing his hand in the process—and continued the chase through the apartment and down the front staircase. On reaching the inner door at the main entrance, Borden threw the door violently back at him. Harmon threw himself forward in an effort to pin Borden, resulting in Borden's head smashing against the pane of glass. Harmon fired one shot in the air and another into the ground. Inspector Gardner, who had been guarding the rear entrance of the apartment block on Waverly Street, ran around to Copeland Street. Borden ran to the back of the house and made his way into the cellar of number 12 Copeland. Perhaps having realized things had gone awry, Harmon remained at the top of the stairs. Inspector Gardner, however, walked through the alley.

Inspector Gardner stationed himself in front of the house at number 12 to await Borden's next move. He heard the sound of breaking glass. Gardner moved in to see that a pane of glass in the cellar bay window had been smashed. A moment later, Borden emerged from an adjoining window in what the inspector interpreted to be a threatening attitude. As Borden stood in a semi-crouch, defenseless, terrified, and unarmed, Inspector Gardner opened fire.

Inspector Gardner later claimed that Borden had his right hand in the rear pocket of his trousers as if in the act of drawing a weapon. Gardner was a full forty feet away from Borden when he fired. At that distance, it would be hard to determine if someone had a weapon in their hands or not. Wounded and bleeding, Borden ran along the alleyway seeking refuge in back of number 14 Copeland. He managed to make his way to the rear of the house and then collapsed. Having witnessed most of the episode, a neighbor said he at first thought it was a holdup and that he saw Borden, whom he knew, attempting to escape. Borden had bullet wounds in his left side, right ankle, and right wrist. He was taken to Boston City Hospital in critical condition, and a blood transfusion was necessary. Borden ultimately succumbed to his wounds.

The deputy superintendent of police, William W. Livingston; Captain Thomas S. J. Kavanagh of the Dudley Street station; and Lieutenant Louis DiSessa of the Homicide Division at police headquarters investigated the affair, stating that Inspector Gardner was justified in shooting Borden, as his own life and that of patrolman William R. Harmon of the Dudley Street station, who had accompanied the inspector, were in danger. The police claimed that Borden had a black object, which was believed to be a revolver. After failing to locate any weapon, they later claimed an object had been thrown aside in the rear of 14 Copeland Street and later picked up by a friend of Borden's. Police searched for the revolver, but none was ever found.[11]

Borden's death at the hands of a motor vehicles inspector was believed to be the first time that an inspector of motor vehicles had fired his weapon to bring about the arrest of a suspect, in this case an unarmed twenty-nine-year-old Black man—married and a father of three. And yet the shooting of an unarmed Black man was an all-too-common experience in Jim Crow

America. Borden's experience undercut Boston's self-proclaimed status as the birthplace of freedom. Despite being a father, a worker, and a generally law-abiding citizen, Borden's skin color and class status made him vulnerable to the capricious whims of a discriminatory vigilante in a dubious position of authority, another Black man who may or may not have had a weapon being targeted, even though he was in his own home, in the middle of a meal with his family. It was murder plain and simple.

Borden's murder may have gone unnoticed were it not for Eugene Gordon. Arriving in Boston as part of the post–World War I migration, Gordon joined the white-owned daily *Boston Post* as a staff writer, where he garnered the respect of Boston intellectuals, organizers, and leftists for his outspokenness on behalf of Boston's forgotten. In 1925, Gordon became the paper's editor and chief columnist. Using the power of the pen, Gordon marshaled his considerable intellectual weight to spread the word about injustice for Borden and other Black Bostonians.[12]

As perhaps one of the most respected Black communist writers, he refused to let the police get away with another killing of an unknown Black man—a worker, a comrade, a father. In his steadfast commitment to fighting for justice for Borden, Gordon came to represent not just Black or White Boston but what he called "Red Boston"—a loose affiliation of left-leaning progressive organizations that, in the 1930s and 1940s, pushed some of the more traditional civil rights organizations to ever greater heights of community engagement and mobilization.[13] Gordon used his post to shed light on a number of less explored causes and campaigns. Where he really shined, however, was as an essayist. In various pieces, Gordon used the longer form to continue to hammer away at bourgeois and middle-class life in Boston, pointing out how race worked in more sophisticated ways than most people were used to thinking about.[14]

Gordon joined the American Communist Party in 1931. He was the cofounder of the Boston John Reed Club and was the first editor of its magazine, *Leftward*. The John Reed Clubs were an American federation of local organizations targeted toward Marxist writers, artists, and intellectuals, named after the American journalist and activist John Reed. Gordon also covered the historic 1955 Afro-Asian Bandung Conference in Indonesia for the *National Guardian* newspaper.[15]

The crash of the stock market in 1929 was a dramatic event, but the complex set of economic problems that led up to it had been growing steadily for years. The American economy had been involved in overproduction and overly optimistic speculation. Conditions quickly worsened for urban

Blacks as competition for jobs intensified. With jobs in scarce supply, preference was given to white workers. Since Black workers predominated in service occupations, their jobs were easily eliminated by cost-conscious employers. Many Black men found work as porters and waiters on the railroad. Their work in construction and mining was hard hit by the Great Depression. Generally speaking, the unemployment rates of Black workers were 30 to 60 percent higher than those of white workers during the Great Depression.

The Great Depression and the 1930s in America brought about great economic difficulties for Black workers, many of whom made a living from the programs of the New Deal. As such, they were especially hard hit during the depression. The federal programs of the New Deal often gave way to local Jim Crow practices in implementation. Black workers were paid less, while many Black service jobs fell under the minimum wage codes. Black women competed for domestic jobs with white women, who had been thrown out of factory jobs. In northern cities like New York, "slave marts" existed for domestic servants, who worked for radically depressed wages of ten cents an hour for families in Long Island and Westchester. Employers were deceitful with their poorly paid "help." In some cases, they adjusted clocks to gain an additional hour of work, promised return carfare, and included lunch in the wages, without delivering on the promises agreed upon. In New York City alone, over two hundred slave marts existed by 1935.

The Great Depression had a tremendous effect on the generation growing up under these circumstances and forever shaped their vision of race, equality, and the American dream. The administration's half-hearted support for unionization added to the surge in labor organizing. Between 1933 and 1935, over 1,470,000 workers participated in 1,856 work stoppages—but these were mainly white-only union shops. The American Federation of Labor's business unionism was losing ground to militant class struggle. But with a scarcity of jobs combined with a preference for white workers, Black workers suffered more and longer than others in the Depression.

The established civil rights organizations encountered a great deal of competition from the Communist Party of the United States (CPUSA) in the 1930s, attracting some Black members because of its strong stance on racism, economic issues, legal equity, and social justice. The CPUSA garnered significant support through its dedicated commitment to the Scottsboro Boys case. The well-documented struggle during these years between the CPUSA and the NAACP played out in countless legal cases that gained national and international attention, including the Borden case.[16]

In the aftermath of Borden's murder, the League of Struggle for Negro Rights (LSNR) jumped into action, sending representatives to visit Borden's wife and attempting to get a warrant for the arrest of the police assailants from the city. As part of their efforts to secure justice for Borden, LSNR members also interviewed witnesses. Meanwhile, the NAACP followed a pattern of "wait and see." This strategy was typical of the NAACP at the time, as it only took on legal cases when it thought it stood a chance at winning.[17] This strategy did not mesh well with the sense of urgency that increasingly permeated Black communities in Boston and other cities. Far from an isolated incident, Black Bostonians rightly saw the Borden shooting as one in a series of incidents involving police brutality and demanded a response.

Borden did not die immediately from his gunshot wounds. On the Friday following Borden's shooting, the LSNR and the International Labor Defense jointly called a mass meeting in Roxbury. Police attempted to intimidate the gathering by amassing at the entrance and turning off the lights. At the exact moment that a speaker was denouncing these characteristic police tactics to the mass meeting of Black and white Bostonians, word came that Borden had died.[18] In this moment of great despair, Gordon took his place at the rostrum. He gave an emotional plea that resonated deeply with the distraught attendees. In his booming voice, he told the audience that they must "Stand up and fight for Negro rights in Boston!"[19]

In 1934, Gordon noted that there was one organization in Boston that was supposed to look after the interests of people like Borden—that is, friendless people who find themselves overwhelmed by the brutal forces of society. That organization was the National Association for the Advancement of Colored People, headed by Black lawyer Butler R. Wilson.[20]

The NAACP, according to Gordon, had fallen behind the times with regard to working-class Black Bostonians. The LSNR was speaking directly about the issue of police brutality, which was the focus of the Borden case, in a way that was not being done by any of the other more middle-class, bourgeois organizations. In addition to police brutality, the LSNR focused its efforts on jobs and the overall material conditions affecting Black Bostonians, issues it perceived as of importance to working-class Black Bostonians.[21] The LSNR, which was backed by the Communist Party, was joined by groups affiliated with the Socialist Party. Although the Socialist Party did not adopt a racial position until after the Communist Party did, it was visible in scattered local campaigns on issues affecting Black Americans. However, it was the Communist Party that became the most active in the 1930s.[22] The established civil rights organizations encountered a great deal of competition from the Communist Party in the 1930s, which not only took a strong stance on racism and economic issues but pursued legal equity and social justice for Black people.

While the LSNR helped popularize economic issues in its fight with the NAACP, it was not the first organization in Boston to do so. Several decades earlier, at the turn of the century, some of the first Black labor organizing in the city occurred in response to an increase in European immigration. As European immigration increased, Black men, who had historically held positions as stevedores and longshoremen in the city's bustling port, found themselves ousted out of those jobs. Similar circumstances permeated the service sector, where premier jobs once held by Black men and women in many of the city's best hotels and restaurants, like the Hotel Vendome, were given to European immigrants. In response to this situation, some Black waiters decided to unionize. In 1890, they organized the Boston Colored Waiters' Alliance and affiliated with Local 183 of the International Union of Hotel and Restaurant Employees.[23] These were men of the highest order, whose organizing example made it possible for a Black man to rise in the world.

The Boston NAACP

The success of the "Don't Buy Where You Can't Work" campaign had lasting effects on the city's long-standing civil rights organizations, including the NAACP, which was perceived to have fallen out of step with the times. In particular, Black Bostonians increasingly criticized the NAACP's fleeting and largely unsuccessful attempts to address the economic conditions that faced poor and working-class people.[24] Amid the difficulties of the Great Depression, which permeated every aspect of American society, Black Bostonians found themselves in a bad situation grown considerably worse. By 1934, almost 34 percent of Boston's Black workforce was unemployed. The situation increasingly found coverage in the *Boston Chronicle*, which decried the circumstances in which Black citizens experienced the highest unemployment and were otherwise confined to menial, low-paying jobs. Throughout the 1930s, there was barely any Black representation at the management level of big business establishments.[25]

Despite these conditions, the NAACP remained largely quiet with regard to the "Don't Buy Where You Can't Work" campaign in Boston, choosing instead to lead its own campaign to assist Black Bostonians suffering during the Great Depression. In 1932, the Massachusetts legislature heard testimony from a longtime member of the NAACP on a proposed bill calling for state and unemployment insurance programs to pay those who were out of work $2 a day. Alfred Baker Lewis, an avowed socialist who served as a member of the Boston NAACP from 1924 until his death in 1980, drew up the first bill for unemployment insurance ever presented to the Massachusetts legislature.[26] The bill was of vital importance to the Black unemployed because of the pervasive racial discrimination and unemployment that existed in the city.[27] Lewis also served as a member of the NAACP's board of directors, its treasurer, and secretary of the Massachusetts Socialist Party from 1924 to 1940. He also ran twice as a socialist candidate for the United States Senate, in 1926 and 1928, and as the socialist candidate for governor of Massachusetts several times in the 1930s.[28]

In 1935, Butler Wilson, the longtime Black president of the Boston NAACP, was replaced by Irwin Dorch, a Black lawyer. Dorch received a favorable assessment in the *Boston Chronicle*.[29] During Dorch's tenure, the NAACP increasingly took on the issue of employment discrimination in the city's various industries, starting with insurance companies and public utilities. At the organization's annual meeting that year, Dorch stated that he "would . . . lead the branch in dealing with economic and labor concerns."[30]

Subsequently, in 1937, the newly formed NAACP Youth Council began a drive to pressure the manager of a movie house in the Dudley Square section of Roxbury to hire Black ushers. Their claim was based on the fact that 40 to 50 percent of the theater's patronage came from Black customers. "The delegation appealed to Mr. Levin first on the basis of fair play; that since the theatre enjoyed a large Negro patronage, he should have some Negroes on his operating staff."[31] Dissatisfied with the manager's response, the Youth Council staged demonstrations against the theater and other Lower Roxbury businesses that tended to hire teenagers.[32]

As the *Boston Chronicle* reported, the Youth Council "began a drive against those business enterprises operating in Negro neighborhoods which refuse to employ negro help. The campaign is the result of a survey recently undertaken by a committee of the youth council." On Monday morning, June 21, a delegation of three Youth Council members called upon the manager of the Dudley Theater to present their concerns. The council members had contacted other theaters in the chain in Italian and Jewish neighborhoods and were told that they hired Jews and Italians in those theaters. They contacted other theatres in the M & P. Theatre chain. Including ones located in Jewish and Italian neighborhoods. They asked the other managers if they hired Jewish and Italian help. *The Boston Chronicle* tells of their ingenious organizing tactic, explaining "that the manager of one of these theatres said that although his theatre is one of a city-wide chain, he as well as other managers had the sole right of hiring and firing." The obvious conclusion was that there was nothing preventing the Dudley theatre from hiring African Americans except a definite policy of exclusion. As the young representatives stated, "In Jewish neighborhoods they hire Jewish help; in Italian neighborhoods they hire Italian help; but in a Negro community they balk at hiring Negro help."[33] The Youth Council helped to spur further negotiations with the management to bring about a change in their policies. The delegation, stated "should these negotiations fail, the Council will have a definite plan and program to meet the situation." And so it was that the M & P Theatre in the Dudley Square section of Roxbury hired its first Black usher.

Even so, frustration at the failure of existing civil rights organizations, including the NAACP, to address the increasingly dire situation faced by poor and working-class Black Bostonians continued to mount. This frustration, combined with the death of William Monroe Trotter in 1934, helped pave the way for a wave of new organizations to take the stage in Boston. Quite a few of these organizations proved to be quite progressive in their nature and scope, dedicated to dealing with the pernicious effects of unemployment.

In Freedom's Birthplace

In 1914, John Daniels, a white settlement house worker, authored one of the first studies of Black workers in Boston, "Industrial Conditions among Negro Men in Boston," in which he divided the jobs that Black men in Boston held into four categories: (1) certain inferior occupations in which most Black Americans were to be found; (2) waged, salaried, or commissioned occupations of higher grade; (3) business proprietorships; and (4) professions.[34]

Comparatively speaking, race relations in New England were often better than they were in other regions of the United States. In terms of gaining access to jobs other than the most menial, however, most Black men and women in Boston found economic opportunities in New England quite difficult to come by.[35] Cross-race alliances, however, were difficult to forge, due in part to the fact that employers often used race to drive a wedge between white and Black workers. As in many major American cities, Black laborers in Boston were used as strikebreakers, including during the longshoremen's strike in August 1929. During the strike, one hundred Black men were employed to take the place of white longshoremen protesting a doubling of their loads. Despite their initial role as strikebreakers, Black longshoremen later used the strike as motivation to organize for better working conditions.[36]

This labor organizing, which continued in the years between the long-shoremen's strike and the Borden case, took on a new meaning in the context of the Great Depression with the help of the LSNR and other left-leaning organizations. The LSNR was able to re-center the Black working-class narrative in the struggle for racial justice in Boston. In addition to re-centering economic issues, the LSNR also helped frame Boston's Black freedom struggle in internationalist terms. As its founding document stated, "The League of Struggle for Negro Rights comes forward with a program for the liberation of the Negro people based upon the experiences and traditions of three centuries of struggle against slavery and oppression. We proclaim before the whole world that the American Negroes are a nation—a nation striving to manhood but whose growth is violently retarded, and which is viciously oppressed by American imperialism."[37]

The LSNR and the "Don't Buy Where You Can't Work" Campaign

With the exception of some labor organizing, including the 1931 longshore-men's strike, and prior to the emergence of the LSNR and other left-leaning organizations, the job of addressing the unemployment crisis among Black Bostonians fell largely to the Boston Urban League and other social welfare organizations. Incorporated in 1919, the Boston Urban League immediately became an affiliate of the National Urban League. At its beginning, the Boston Urban League offered the same services as settlement houses; however, its focus quickly shifted to education and employment opportunities.[38] Years later, Melvin King—who would become a stalwart champion of Boston's working people and would one day helm the New Urban League of Boston—remarked somewhat disparagingly that the initial Urban League affiliates basically served as job referral agencies, an assignment decidedly less productive in the face of mounting unemployment rates.[39] Even so, the Urban League played an important role by helping Black workers, especially southern and West Indian migrants, find employment.

In addition to the Urban League, the Women's Service Club and the League of Women for Community Service were both founded in the 1920s by Black women to aid other Black women, especially newcomers to the city. In her trailblazing study of Boston's Black upper class, the late Adelaide Cromwell describes these various "charitable, social, local, non-clique limited clubs" as "extremely important institutions in Boston."[40] Located at 558 Massachusetts Avenue for over a decade, the League of Women for Community

Service operated a settlement house and performed relief work, all while suffering from a diminishing budget. The league provided lunches to schoolchildren from families in need, and its prenatal assistance programs offered fresh fruits, vegetables, and milk to expecting mothers, and provided furnishings and clothing for newborns. It also provided clothing to destitute households and distributed baskets of food to families in the South End and Lower Roxbury.[41]

Topper Carew, who became a well-known television and film director (including creating the TV show *Martin*), was aware of the work of these organizations and recalls with fondness the role of Black women organizing in Boston: "The most organizing that I am aware of as a young person was being done by women. . . . [They] had these women's clubs and they would put on teas, man, to raise money for scholarships, you know, from the churches, . . . to try to pay for kids to go to college."[42]

Growing up nearby, Veronica A. Deare attended the settlement house as a child and recalled the love and fondness she felt for the work of the league. But even with these women's auxiliary organizations, more social welfare was needed to aid the Black community. Here, the role of the Black church cannot be overstated, as it is a critical yet often underreported factor in understanding the architecture of the Black movement in Boston. To be clear, the church played a very prominent role in Black Bostonian history—from the day that the African Meeting House first opened its doors on the north slope of Beacon Hill in the nineteenth century. The oldest extant Black church in America, the African Meeting House still stands triumphantly in the tony Beacon Hill neighborhood. Beginning in the 1900s, Black Americans began migrating toward the current-day heart of the Black community, first to the South End and later to the neighborhoods southwest of Beacon Hill, a mere six miles away. Their houses of worship soon followed. Churches with names like St. Augustine St. Martin, Twelfth Baptist Church, and Charles Street AME Church closed the doors to the buildings they once occupied in Beacon Hill and moved to the current heart of the Black communities where they are now located.

Together these organizations worked to aid Black Bostonians amid the Great Depression. As conditions worsened, a number of organizations resorted to more overt political expressions of protest, including working to strike down barriers to employment. In doing so, they sometimes used tactics that went against the NAACP's more traditional approach.[43] Many of these were Communist Party–affiliated organizations, including unemployment councils and tenant advocacy organizations, which won significant concessions from white-owned businesses.

This was the political climate in which the "Don't Buy Where You Can't Work" campaign emerged. This campaign (also known as "Buy Where You Can Work") first emerged in Chicago and grew out of the "double-duty dollar" ethos that American ministers preached from the pulpit. Many churches promoted the strategy in mass meetings and through their congregations. The primary aim was to help Black businesses financially and to advance the race economically and socially. The "Don't Buy Where You Can't Work" campaign spread to at least thirty-five cities during the Great Depression, where it helped draw attention to Black unemployment rates, which were often double or triple the national average.

Although initiated locally by the Boston Urban League, where it experienced measured results, the "Don't Buy Where You Can't Work" campaign eventually became a major organizing framework for the LSNR.[44] In 1932, the LSNR began a campaign to have supermarkets on Tremont Street hire Black males for positions as clerks and managers. As in other cities, the Boston campaign brought together multiple organizations, some of which had previously taken stands against one another. For this, they were unified.

On January 23, 1932, the *Boston Chronicle*, which played a vital role in the campaign, declared that it "would pursue vigorously a policy of exposing those establishments most culpable of excluding Blacks while acknowledging those making strides toward more fair hiring practices."[45]

By late 1933, after continued inquiries of store owners and managers in the South End and Roxbury as to why businesses in those neighborhoods refused to hire Black employees created no changes, Black activists started using more serious and sustained efforts. The LSNR established a committee to visit branches of the First National and A&P (the Great Atlantic & Pacific Tea Company) food stores to demand that the stores, which were heavily dependent on Black trade, hire Black workers.

Throughout the "Don't Buy Where You Can't Work" campaign, organizers and sympathizers relied on the sustained support particularly of Black women, since women generally made household grocery purchases, so that "we can show those in power that we mean business."[46] In addition to putting pressure on white-owned businesses that failed to hire Blacks, the campaign contributed to renewed calls for self-help through its work promoting Black businesses. In 1934, the *Boston Chronicle* printed a series of ads calling on "thinking Negroes" to "help the race, help the community, [and] help yourself." These ads praised Black consumers for shopping in stores that were owned and operated by Black people or in stores that employed Black workers.

The same article likewise provided an update on the campaign, reporting: "On Saturday night, January 27th, 1934, a large number of citizens picketed the First National Stores on Tremont Street. A few policemen were in evidence, but there was no violence attempted."[47] Promising to continue picketing until their demands were met or until they had forced the stores to close due to lack of business, demonstrators carried signs and placards reading "We demand jobs . . . jobs for Negroes in First National Stores as managers and clerks," and "Negroes, the chain stores can use your money but they won't use you."[48]

After three months of picketing during the spring of 1934, First National offered a partial concession by agreeing to take on two Black males as trainees to "test the viability of Negro clerks and managers."[49] Edward Cooper was hired and trained for the manager's position at the store on Columbus Avenue and later at the Shawmut Avenue location. Cooper's success and popularity brought hope that First National would continue to hire and promote other Black men to managerial positions. Cooper's position at First National also put him on a trajectory to community leadership. He went on to become a stalwart and venerated champion for Black rights in Boston for more than four decades.[50]

In the immediate aftermath of Cooper's appointment to First National, Black Bostonians rallied to keep the movement going. Responding to Cooper's appointment, as well as that of Leon G. Lomax, who was appointed branch manager of the South End Electric Company, the *Chronicle* encouraged its readers: "Let us get behind Lomax and Cooper and let the white world know with dollars and cents they can get a break when they give us one."[51] As previously noted, the newspaper played an important role, alongside Black women consumers, in sustaining the "Don't Buy Where You Can't Work" campaign. In December 19, 1936, the *Chronicle* similarly celebrated the hiring of "five colored girls" as part-time clerks at the Woolworth's five-and-ten in Roxbury. Although they were hired only for the 1936 Christmas season, and it was done with little fanfare, it represented a victory nonetheless.[52] It certainly helped that Ruth Worthy, one of the five clerks hired, was the daughter of socially prominent and politically conscious parents. As the efforts in Boston continued, they also increased in Cambridge, where the Kresge department store hired a Black male clerk, and a local drugstore was pressured to hire Black sales help.[53]

The Black Press and Boston Garveyites

In addition to the church and political organizations like the NAACP, the importance of the Black press cannot be overstated in this period. One of the reasons Boston's local Black press was so vibrant is due in part to the new Black migration to Boston, which took place during and following the 1920s and included large numbers of Caribbean migrants.[54] In 1915, when the West Indian population in Boston was still only a few hundred strong, a group of Jamaicans formed the Square Deal Publishing Company, which was head-quartered on Tremont Street in the heart of the business district of the Black neighborhood of the South End. Published every Saturday, the *Boston Chronicle* catered to a "West Indian" sensibility—that is, to the tastes, interests, and needs of the city's Black community, whether they were of Caribbean origin, had a New England background, or had roots in the Black south. The *Boston Chronicle*'s motto was "Fearless and Uncompromising Advocate of Justice, Rights, and Opportunities."[55] The *Chronicle* often competed with the Boston *Guardian*, published by William Monroe Trotter.[56] Although far less celebrated than Trotter, William Harrison—the longest-serving editor of the *Chronicle*, who served during its most important years of reporting—was a prominent architect of Black political protests and thought in Boston. Harrison had immigrated to Boston with his parents from Jamaica around the period of World War I, and he lived in the Humboldt Avenue middle-class area of Roxbury.[57] Like Trotter, Harrison was a graduate of Harvard University.

During the 1930s and 1940s, the *Chronicle* served as a venue for two of the period's most influential ideologies, namely communism and Pan-Africanism. These two ideologies existed alongside, and often in tension with, each other. The official Communist Party line discouraged Black nationalism in favor of working-class interracialism. Indeed, the Communist Party's 1921 program considered Black nationalism "a weapon of reaction for the defeat and further enslavement of both [Blacks] and their white brother workers."[58] It was only later that party leaders came to believe a truly Black working class existed as part of the international class struggle against the dual forces of global capitalism and imperialism. This Black working class was formed as the result of decades-old discrimination and racial exclusion.

Following Harrison's own ideological moorings, a number of *Chronicle* reporters flirted with communism. Like other Black newspapers at the time, including the *Pittsburgh Courier* and the *Baltimore Afro-American*, the *Chronicle* also served as a major venue for the expression of Pan-African sentiment. The paper regularly advertised meetings of the Universal Negro Improvement Association (UNIA), a Black nationalist organization founded by Marcus Garvey, which had established a Boston chapter.[59] Although the agenda of the Boston chapter seemed radical on the surface, Garveyism in Boston was often more rhetorical than practical in its orientation and accomplishments. The *Boston Chronicle* gave more attention to the Black diaspora than did the *Guardian*, such that migrants could see their lives reflected more in this paper.[60] As Mel King, whose family had migrated from Barbados, recalled in *Chain of Change*, "I grew up on the one hand feeling positive about being a West Indian and Black; but on the other hand, I had to grapple with the negative imagery of being a Black child in the United States, not wanting to identify with people who were slaves and who behaved in a Steppin Fetchit, Rochester model. Every time one of those movies was shown, we had to fight the next day in school because someone would come up and mock you."[61] He continued, "The coming together of Black folks happened around people who joined the Marcus Garvey Movement. In those days there was a column in the *Afro-American* newspaper (published in Baltimore) about Boston and two Black newspapers, the *Chronicle* and the *Guardian* which documented activities in the Boston-Cambridge community."[62]

Conclusion

Historian Gerald Gill has written, "Although many blacks living outside of New England in the mid-to-late 1940s viewed the city as one of 'America's 10 Best Cities for Negroes,' then-NAACP president Julian Steele described his hometown as 'something of a paradox,' a city where African Americans could enjoy most civil rights socially and politically, but were still restricted to the most menial jobs."[63]

In 1941, the Boston affiliate of the National Negro Congress set up picket lines in front of the supermarket in Roxbury. This campaign led to the hiring of two Black workers. In 1943, a coalition of Black activists, also led by the LSNR, called for the recruitment of more Black people as police officers, public utility workers, salesclerks in downtown department stores, and telephone operators, and for positions other than janitors on city buses and trolleys. Moreover, in 1945, a Boston Urban League earned a victory when New England Telephone hired Black women as telephone operators. This victory came after months of negotiations between J. Caswell Smith—head of the Boston Urban League—and New England Telephone, which resulted in the company modifying its previous "no Negroes" hiring policy.[64]

Although these movements were indeed triumphs, they did not have a dramatic impact on the overall picture of Black unemployment. For much of the period, most of the victories in employment were qualified successes.[65] The diversity of the campaigns of the Black community were mounting during the 1940s, raising concerns about employment, racial segregation, and police brutality.

A specific imperative emphasized the collective good. Socialist nationalism sought to develop wealth to benefit the group as opposed to the individual. A kind of socialist nationalism found expression in A. Philip Randolph's socialist newspaper, the *Messenger,* and in his organization of the Brotherhood of Sleeping Car Porters, a predominantly Black union. Nearly twelve thousand porters worked for the Pullman Company and lived in northern cities, having been recruited in the South. At the same time, a porter's base pay was only $810, while their tips averaged $600 a year. These porters had to prepare the cars during unpaid hours and had to purchase their own supplies and uniforms.

Although job opportunities for Black Americans were limited, the role of the Pullman porters carried with it a certain amount of pride, and those men were seen as leaders of the community. Robert Hayden, who interviewed men who had been sleeping car porters in Boston for a massive oral history project, argues, "Many Black men were attracted to railroad work because they were excluded from other occupations and because the Pullman Company and others recruited them." Andrew Buni and Alan Rogers likewise point out, "Job discrimination, for example, systematically deprived Black artisans of their trades. This meant that many men were forced to seek low-paying, unskilled jobs in the rail yards and station of the South End."[66]

In 1941, A. Philip Randolph became the nation's most famous Black political figure. According to Hayden, "As a pioneer of the modern civil rights movement, Randolph developed a philosophy of protest based on the principles of non-violent disobedience. He influenced a whole generation of civil rights activists, including Roy Wilkins of the NAACP and Martin Luther King, Jr."[67] Black Bostonians were also very involved in the March on Washington movement and had a Boston chapter by 1941.[68]

While local activists had devoted much of their attention in the 1930s to securing new employment opportunities for Black residents, competition around jobs was only one source of racial tension in the city; the contestation over de facto residential segregation and urban renewal had more far-reaching consequences. The historically racially restrictive housing market, propelled by redlining and discriminatory lending practices, prevented Blacks from moving into areas such as Hyde Park and West Roxbury, where many white working-class people owned their own homes. Redlining likewise kept Blacks out of poorer white working-class neighborhoods, such as South Boston, Charlestown, and East Boston.[69]

Boston was a place with many divisions, not only between Black and white but between rich and poor, Protestant and Catholic, Irish and English, African American and West Indian, southern and northern. By the 1920s, local politicians began to align themselves with Jim Crow and southern sympathies. This retrenchment of progressive politics in Boston created space for the resurfacing of redemption sympathies in Boston. In this ethnically and racially polarized municipality, dominated by Irish Catholic politics, the small population of Black Americans possessed little political sway, nor did they have much of a political voice at even the lower levels of Boston politics. As Gerald Gill has written:

> From 1945 to 1955, African American men and women—whether leaders, organizers, or rank-and-file activists and members within secular, political or religious groups—devoted themselves to the causes of true and complete racial equality and economic justice in Boston. Seeking to build upon the belated gains made by black workers in the city during the war years, many of these individuals hoped that ongoing struggle and protest would lead to further victories—big and small, symbolic and more real. Bolstered by optimism and tempered by realism, they were poised to continue their efforts towards making racial democracy real "in freedom's birthplace."[70]

During the 1950s, which are discussed in chapter 4, the NAACP and the Boston Urban League became more comfortable in terms of negotiating with economic and political elites; however, the primary campaign in Boston at this particular time would revolve around efforts to increase housing and decrease employment discrimination.[71] In the context of the growing red-baiting of the 1950s and the Cold War, organizations like the LSNR would fade, while the NAACP survived. However, it did so with a greater sense of attention to the material concerns of Black Bostonians.

CHAPTER FOUR

Mobilizing for Freedom

Community-Based Activism in the Post–World War II Era,
1949–1965

Discrimination in education is symbolic of all the more drastic discriminations which Negroes suffer in American life. The equal protection clause of the 14th Amendment furnishes the key to ending separate schools.

—Charles Hamilton Houston, 1934

Boston stands alone in the state and the nation as a city that refuses to recognize the de facto segregation problem.

—James Farmer

One voice crying in the wilderness of a busy insensitive city may well be the salvation of thousands of children and youth who are deprived of quality integrated education. Your vigil in behalf of truth shines forth from Beacon Street into the dark ghettos of American life encouraging thousands of your brethren. One man determined to bear witness to the truth can save a city. Your sacrifice may well be the wedge which crumbles the wall of de facto segregation in Boston Schools. You have our total admiration and support in your effort. God bless you.

—Martin Luther King Jr., June 1966

The late Adelaide Cromwell, who joined Boston University's faculty in 1951, once tried to explain the connections between Boston and race. "Boston was a funny place, a paradoxical place. . . . The image that this was freedom's birthplace . . . first of all, people were not particularly well-off. . . . And what's more there were places you could not go and did not go. Restaurants did not welcome you. . . . The local people conspired to keep the silence. They wouldn't tell you not to go to this or that place. Everybody maintained this fiction that this place was a free place. It wasn't a free place."[1]

In a short film about Dr. Martin Luther King's somewhat brief but very impactful time in Boston, the late Dr. Cromwell's son, Anthony Cromwell, explored these ideas further. Upon his arrival in Boston in the fall of 1951, having driven from Pennsylvania to Massachusetts in the shiny green Chevrolet his father gave him as a reward for graduating from Crozer Theological Seminary that spring, Martin Luther King Jr. encountered a very different Boston from the one that exists today. As voices from the film explain, "The Mass Turnpike was not there. The skyscrapers were not there. The tallest building in Boston was still the Custom House Tower, in McKinley Square, originally constructed in 1847."[2] As the son of a segregated South, reared in Atlanta in a state that was mostly rural and somewhat provincial, Boston must have seemed like another world. Its legacy as freedom's birthplace and the home of abolitionism, combined with the progressive reputation of Boston University and its School of Theology, were a powerful draw. But as the Cromwells make very clear—one in print and the other on film—when it came to issues of race and social justice, Boston presented a paradox.

After skipping two grades at Booker T. Washington High School, King matriculated at Morehouse College as a fifteen-year-old freshman in 1944. Under the influence of Morehouse mentors, including college president Benjamin Mays, he decided to focus his studies on the social sciences.[3] In 1948, just a month after turning nineteen, King was ordained as a Baptist minister and joined the staff of Ebenezer Baptist Church. After receiving his bachelor's degree in sociology from Morehouse, King enrolled at Crozer Theological Seminary in Chester, Pennsylvania.[4] In 1951, after earning his bachelor of divinity at the top of his class at Crozer, King enrolled at Boston University, with the ambition of studying systematic theology under the tutelage of Professor Howard DeWolf, who would become his thesis adviser, and Rev. Howard Thurman, who was perhaps one of his most important mentors. His dissertation was titled "A Comparison of the Conceptions of God in the Thinking of Paul Tillich and Henry Nelson Wieman."

Studying theology in Boston made a great impression on King's personality, ideas, and thinking.[5] While in Boston, King also served as a guest minister at the Concord Baptist Church. Formerly the United Presbyterian Church, it was established in 1946 and located at 190 Warren Avenue. Later, King served as a student minister and preached at the Twelfth Baptist Church under the tutelage of Rev. Michael E. Haynes. In King's studies and ongoing understanding of America, including his keen insights about American history and how it all worked, he seemed to be saying that the North represented the "true" America, and the South was an exception due to its (longer) history with slavery. Being a Southerner himself meant that he of course would have to begin in the South, but the North was always the eventual trajectory. Jeanne Theoharis makes the point that "while most scholars have tended to argue that King's attention turns North after the Watts uprising [in 1965], King was talking about Northern racism, standing with Northern movements, and calling out the limits of Northern liberalism from the very beginnings of SCLC [Southern Christian Leadership Conference]."[6]

The story begins with King's experiences as a student first at Crozer Theological Seminary and then at Boston University. King's years at Crozer show that some of his experiences there (in both Pennsylvania and New Jersey) likely shaped his view of the North and the segregation replete in the North—and the unwillingness of northern liberals to address it. In June 1950, King was a young seminary student at Crozer, residing at 753 Walnut Street in Camden, New Jersey.[7] King lived at the Walnut Street house from the end of 1948 to 1951 while attending Crozer, which was in Chester, Pennsylvania. The discovery of a legal complaint signed by King following a June 12, 1950, incident in nearby Maple Shade sheds an interesting light on his first experiences in the North, or what some might call "Up South." In what is believed to be the first time King took legal action in the name of civil rights—at least in the North—the legal complaint reads: "King and his Camden roommate, fellow Crozer student Walter McCall, and two other individuals were unceremoniously tossed out of Mary's Café, a Maple Shade bar. . . . King and his companions went to the local police station and filed a civil complaint against the owner of the bar."[8] According to the article, the president of the local NAACP chapter and an NAACP lawyer represented King and his companions in the case, which was dismissed after the white witnesses who had agreed to testify failed to show up in court."[9]

Similar things happened in Boston, given the kind of segregation and racism in the city. King told the *Boston Globe* in 1965 that when he first moved to Boston in 1951, he encountered a lot of housing discrimination when trying to find a place to live. During his Boston years, King lived in four different apartments, including one in Dorchester.[10] As Jeanne Theoharis notes, "I think this context in Boston is important for how King always talks about how segregation was national and that Northern liberals needed to be actually liberal at home (from the beginnings of SCLC onward, King is saying this over and over and getting more strident about . . . the 'vanity' and 'veneer' of Northern liberalism)."[11]

It's evident when looking at certain interviews and lesser-known talks and speeches that King was trying to make a deeper point about the North. Of course, Boston figures into this but, as Theoharis point out, earlier experiences do as well. It seems evident that the North was always on his radar. Theoharis states, "There's an investment in making it seem like Boston was a place of freedom for King, which I'm sure in some ways it was, but also not to have thought or investigated how it would be more mixed and that King would have left these six years in the North with a keen sense of Northern racism and the limits of Northern liberalism."[12] During his time in Boston, King became very involved in the Black Bostonian world, mainly through his sermons at Twelfth Baptist Church. King gave a sermon at Twelfth Baptist titled "The Negro Past and Its Challenge for the Future" for Negro History week in 1954.[13]

"King . . . was looking for more than just another degree" recalled Haynes. "He wanted to get a different perspective on world issues and race issues then he would be getting if we were directly in the south. I got the impression earlier at that time in the 50s . . . he was struggling really between his father's tug and pull for him to come back to Atlanta. At that time Daddy King was concerned about him theologically coming up to Boston University a shift too far to the left."[14] The seminary at Boston University at that time was actively looking for students who were potentially "prophetic" voices—those whose work and scholarship would be "transformative" to the social justice landscape. This alone—in addition to the fact that Martin would be on his own in a northern city—may have given the senior King reason enough to be concerned about him. As a result, Martin Luther King Sr. sought the help of the Hesters, friends of his, to keep an eye on young Martin.

Once in Boston, King Jr. first found an apartment in a rooming house at 170 St. Botolph Street, where he lived briefly before moving to apartment no. 6 on the top floor of 397 Massachusetts Avenue, which was a little closer to the action of the bustling Black community of Lower Roxbury and the South End. He remained there between 1952 and 1953. Nearby, various establishments, including Slade's Barbeque Chicken, Estelle's, the Hi-Hat at the corner of Mass and Columbus, the Savoy, Eddie Levine's, Wally's could be counted on to play first rate jazz music, as well as serve up delicious food and drinks. Regarding King's years in Boston, Haynes further recalled:

> He knew the story of South Boston, he knew about Charlestown, he knew about the strong Irish control in the political world of Boston . . . and he encouraged me to talk when I considering running for the House of Representatives . . . because the only way we would win our "struggle," the word he often used, was "movement," struggle and movement. . . . The only way to win our struggle is by having friends and allies inside. And he felt that God was revealing to him that he had a task to address the issues from the outside of government, but he realized that he needed to have allies inside the government.[15]

King himself echoed Haynes's recollections when describing why he chose to donate his records and papers to Boston University:

> I have chosen Boston University for several reasons. I guess first is the fact that Boston University is my alma mater. I had the privilege of studying here for three years, and it was this university that did so much in terms of formulation of my thinking and the ideas that I've gotten in my life. And Dr. Harold Dewolf, my major advisor, my major professor here, certainly has been a great inspiration in my life. And we had the privilege of talking about this collection a great deal before the decision was made, so that I was very happy to make the decision to turn the papers over to Boston University as my alma mater. And secondly because I think this is a great university. And thirdly, I made the decision because of the fact that I felt that this university was desirous enough of having these papers to give them the kind of attention that I think they will need and give the kind of staff to them in dealing with it in the kind of detail and responsible way that can make it the kind of collection that will add to and give research persons needed information that they will want as the years unfold.[16]

At the time, Coretta Scott was enrolled as an opera student at the New England Conservatory of Music. Like many Black women, Scott worked her way through the conservatory as a domestic. She lived at number 558 Massachusetts Avenue, home of the aforementioned League of Women for Community Service, a pioneer institution in the national Black women's club movement. Like her work, Scott's choice of living was a result of her being a Black woman, unwelcome in the dormitories. Amid these conditions, the league provided a place to stay for respectable young Black women going to school in Boston. The young women were not allowed to entertain in their rooms, but they could receive guests in the ballroom. There was a house mother, and there were curfews. There were hours they had to adhere to, and if they went out, they had to be back by a certain time.[17]

Martin Luther King Jr. and Coretta Scott had their first (blind) date on February 29, 1952, at Sharaf's Cafeteria at 187 Massachusetts Avenue. The date was arranged by Mary Power, a friend of King's from Atlanta who was a student at the New England Conservatory of Music with Scott and who worked as a secretary to Rev. Hester, King Sr.'s friend, at the Twelfth Baptist Church. King quickly fell in love with Coretta. According to oral histories conducted by Anthony Cromwell Hill, friends recalled that when King met Coretta, it clicked because she was somebody who was on the same wavelength as him in terms of interests.[18] Coretta, however, was less enthused about dating a southern minister. King proposed marriage to her that very night. She declined, as King had failed to impress her. He would persist, though, and the two continued dating.

Scott had grown up in rural Alabama, where she worked on her family's farm before earning a scholarship to Antioch College. It turns out she was not the only one with misgivings; King's parents were initially unsure about the match themselves. Despite his parents' reservations, Martin and Coretta were married on June 18, 1953, on the lawn of Coretta's parents' house in Marion, Alabama. After their wedding, Martin and Coretta returned to Boston and took an apartment in a now-demolished building at 396 Northampton Street, in the South End.[19] In 1954, after passing his oral examinations for his doctorate, King was appointed pastor of the Dexter Avenue Baptist Church in Montgomery, Alabama.[20] He and Coretta moved to Montgomery straightaway.

Despite his short time in Boston, King's experiences in the city made a lasting impression and gave him a lifelong affection for the city—one that remained with him through the early days of the northern school desegregation movement. As Haynes later recalled, "King . . . never forget what he had learned in and about Boston where Blacks had held the franchise long before the brutality of Selma spread passage of [the] Voting Rights Act."[21] Even after leaving Boston, King continued to make a mark on the city, encouraging old friends, such as Haynes and his fraternity brother Ed Brooke, to run for public office in Boston. King subsequently returned to the city multiple times, including on October 28, 1956, when he spoke on "A Realistic Look at Race Relations" at Jordan Hall, and on December 11, 1960, when he gave a speech titled "The Future of Integration" as part of the Ford Hall Forum.

On April 22, 1965, King addressed a joint session of the Massachusetts legislature on the topic of education. In his speech, he declared, "Let me hasten to say that I come to Massachusetts not to condemn but to encourage! It was from these shores that the vision of a new nation conceived in liberty was born, and it must be from these shores that liberty must be preserved; and the hearts and lives of every citizen preserved through the maintenance of opportunity and through the constant creation of those conditions that will make justice and brotherhood a reality for all of God's children." Speaking not as an outsider but as an honorary Bostonian, King continued:

> We can point to that momentous moment in 1954 when the Supreme Court of our nation rendered a great decision which said in substance that the old Plessy Doctrine of 1896 must go; that separate facilities are inherently unequal; that to segregate a child on the basis of his race is to

deny that child equal protection of the law. And so, we can all be proud of the fact that the Brown Decision brought our nation a long, long way toward the realization of a great and noble dream.[22]

The next day, a March on Boston was held, and Martin Luther King Jr. led an estimated five thousand marchers from William E. Carter playground to the Boston Common, where twenty-five thousand people gathered for the speaking program. Rev. Gil Caldwell served as master of ceremonies. King, the last speaker, declared, "I would be dishonest to say Boston is Birmingham or that Massachusetts is Mississippi. But it would be irresponsible for me to deny the crippling poverty and the injustices that exist in some sections of this community. The vision of the New Boston must extend into the heart of Roxbury. Boston must become a testing ground for the ideals of freedom."[23] After the march, King and a twelve-member delegation of local civil rights leaders met with Mayor John F. Collins, presenting him with a "bill of particulars" that called for ending racial discrimination and injustices in housing, welfare, and employment in Boston.

King was not the only prominent civil rights figure who spent time in Boston. By a twist of fate, when King was a student at the Boston University School of Theology, he and Malcolm X were in Boston at the same time— getting very different kinds of educations. Their twin destinies were still being forged—one at the finest institutions of higher learning and one in the streets of Boston—and would come to define the divergent intellectual and political trajectories of Black America in the 1950s and 1960s.

When a young Malcolm Little moved to Boston in 1941, zoot suits, hair conking, and the lindy hop were all the rage. Little immersed himself in the fast life of reefer smoking, woman chasing, and hustling, quickly transforming from an A student into a self-described con artist, a hustler of gambling and women. By day he worked a variety of odd jobs—shoeshine boy, busboy, soda jerk, factory and shipyard worker—but by night he plied his true craft at places like the Roseland Ballroom.

In New York they called him "Detroit Red"; in Boston they called him "New York Red." In 1945, he organized a gang to burglarize the homes of prominent families in Beacon Hill and other affluent parts of Boston. The other gang members included his friend Malcolm "Shorty" Jarvis; his white girlfriend, Bea; and two other white women. Little and his gang were arrested for larceny, carrying firearms, and breaking and entering. On February 27, 1946, Little began serving an eight-to-ten-year prison term in Charlestown, Massachusetts.

Malcolm Little's time in prison proved transformative. While there, he engaged in a period of intense study of Islam and became a follower of Elijah Muhammad.[24] When he was released from prison in 1952, he was taken in by Muhammad's family in Detroit, where he lived and worked for a short time, changing his name to Malcolm X to stand in for his lost African surname and replace his "slave name." In Malcolm's case, his X replaced the name Little. By September 1953, Malcolm X had become a minister in the Nation of Islam and returned to Boston to help found the Nation of Islam's Temple No. 11.[25] The minister of that temple, Louis Walcott, once a promising calypso singer, had joined the Nation of Islam, taking on the name Louis X. One day he would be known by another name—Louis Farrakhan.

The Road to *Brown*

In the decades since *Plessy*, various activists and organizations had challenged the ruling by contesting the decision's notion that segregation was legal as long as the segregated facilities were equal in quality. In particular, opponents argued that Black institutions were unequal to that of whites. The hope was that by requiring qualitatively equal conditions for Black Americans, segregation would become a burden and therefore dropped.[26] Others legitimately wanted separate but equal educational institutions and were less concerned about integration.[27]

Perhaps none of it would have happened had it not been for the visionary leadership of a man named Charles Hamilton Houston. Houston came from a privileged background. His mother had been a teacher, and his father was a lawyer. Houston attended Amherst College in Massachusetts, graduating at the top of his class in 1915. He was accepted to Harvard Law School, becoming the first Black editor of the *Harvard Law Review*.[28] During World War II, Houston volunteered to serve in a segregated army "to make the world safe for democracy," as the saying went. When he returned, Houston made it his mission to develop a legal challenge to Jim Crow. Such a challenge, Houston surmised, would require a cadre of brilliant Black lawyers armed with a passion for righting the wrongs of segregation and bringing about a world of social justice. As dean of the Howard University Law School, Houston was able to build such a team. He used the resources available to him to attract and recruit young law students who shared his vision of fighting Jim Crow tooth and nail. Among those whom Houston trained was Oliver Hill from Virginia, who would go on to become the first Black person to be elected to the Richmond City Council. Houston's own cousin, William Hastie, also joined the

Thurgood Marshall, attorney for the NAACP, 1908–1993 (Thomas J. O'Halloran [photographer], Library of Congress Prints and Photographs Division, LC-DIG-ppmsc-01271).

faculty at Howard before going on to become the first Black federal judge. Perhaps the most famous person to emerge from Howard University Law School at this time was Thurgood Marshall, a young man from Maryland who would become the first Black justice on the Supreme Court.

Together, Houston and Marshall took on the legal battle against Jim Crow. To do so, they needed an organization with the ability to reach Black communities across the country. The National Association for the Advancement of Colored People had been founded in 1909 in response to a rising tide of racial violence. As such, it became the ideal organization to work with, and Houston was appointed special counsel in 1934. He had the people and the organization; now he needed a strategy. Houston saw a key weakness in the "separate but equal" doctrine, and he believed that attacking this principle in education specifically was the key to destroying it from within.

Working together in the NAACP's Legal Defense Fund (LDF), Houston and Marshall took up the painstaking and time-consuming work of identifying campaigns, helping local groups seek legal redress, and guiding appeals that would eventually lead to challenging *Plessy v. Ferguson*.[29] Rather than challenge the "separate but equal" principle directly, they first filed precedent cases demanding that Black schools be made absolutely equal to white schools. And they stayed away from the elementary grades, going instead after graduate schools. This strategy was very effective due to the small number of Black applicants. There was no practical way of building a new Black law school or a new Black dental school or medical school for the application of just one or two Black students. But the law simply said "separate but equal"; it said nothing about the demand. Armed with this brilliant strategy, Houston and his team went to work. During this time, Houston did nothing but work. Friends, colleagues, and associates don't remember him doing anything besides work, even after his doctor told him to slow down. Houston would not live to see the fruits of his labors, dying from a heart condition in 1950. But this only pushed Marshall and other members of the team harder.

Following Houston's death, Marshall continued the work of the LDF, challenging *Plessy*. Each victory served to provide precedents to the larger challenge of eliminating segregation in education—first in higher education and later in K–12 public school education. Marshall was not alone in this legal quest. Constance Baker Motley, who worked for the LDF while earning her law degree from Columbia University, worked with Marshall, preparing legal briefs for *Sipuel v. Board of Regents of the University of Oklahoma* (1950) and *Sweatt v. Painter* (1950). The former revolved around a young woman from Oklahoma named Ada Sipuel, who in 1946 applied for admission to the University of Oklahoma College of Law. The state denied her application and told Sipuel to reapply to a separate law school for Black students that would soon be established.

Subsequently, the LDF took on Sipuel's case, taking it all the way to the Supreme Court, where Marshall argued that the facilities had to be immediately available to meet the "separate but equal" standard. In the Sweatt case, the applicant to the University of Texas School of Law was offered attendance at a temporary law school in the basement of a building near the Texas capitol. He declined and sued, citing denial of equal protection of the law under the Fourteenth Amendment of the Constitution. In a final case, *McLaurin v. Oklahoma State Regents* (1950), the student was admitted to the graduate school as a candidate for the doctor of education degree "with certain restrictions." These restrictions included sitting in a room adjacent to the classroom, sitting in a separate study area of the library, and eating at a specific table and at a different time than the other students in the cafeteria. The most galling was that McLaurin would have to sit in the hallway, where he could merely hear the lecture but not participate. These restrictions prevented him from receiving equal protection of the laws.[30]

Having had some early successes, Marshall began to see the dawn of the removal of segregation in higher education. Therefore, he felt his team was now ready to challenge K–12 education. Many of the institutions they had challenged were public, meaning the only distinction of this new challenge would be K–12 versus higher education. As a critical member of the team, Constance Baker Motley, who graduated from law school in June 1946, again played a major role in the preparation for the 1954 *Brown v. Board of Education* case. The case took its name from one of the plaintiffs, Oliver Brown, whose daughter Linda Brown had to travel over one mile to her segregated school, while a white school existed just seven blocks from her house. Although the case being brought was filed under the name of Oliver Brown by the courts, it represented five separate cases of unequal treatment in K–12 public schools. In *Brown v. Board*, Thurgood Marshall and his team argued that Black schools were allocated fewer funds and resources than were white schools, as opposed to the notion that Black schools were inferior simply because they were Black schools.[31] These cases together challenged not only the degree to which education was unequal but also the principle of separate but equal, proving that separate was *inherently* unequal. In order to do this, the NAACP relied on a combination of lawyers, historians, and social scientists. This included the husband-and-wife team of Columbia University–trained psychologists Drs. Kenneth and Mamie Clark, who provided social scientific evidence that Black children enrolled in separate schools presumed their own inferiority, which in turn limited their self-concept and sense of self-worth.

The Clarks' testimony was based on experiments they had previously conducted with schoolchildren in the South. Dr. Kenneth Clark and his wife had tested twenty-six children in Clarendon County, South Carolina, using white and brown dolls. J. Anthony Lukas writes:

Not until black demands for integration found an ally in the burgeoning social sciences did a systematic critique of educational performance begin to develop. As NAACP lawyers framed the attack on school segregation in the fifties, they turned for support to a young social psychologist at New York's City College. Kenneth Clark and his wife, Mamie, had been playing some interesting games with dolls. Their four baby dolls were identical in every way, except that two were brown and two were white. After showing them to Negro children aged three to seven, the Clarks said, "Give me the doll that looks bad," "Give me the doll you like best." The majority of Negro children tested—many of them in Boston and neighboring Worcester—showed "an unmistakable preference for the white doll and a rejection of the brown doll."[32]

As a result of these experiments, the Clarks concluded that the children had been irreparably harmed, made to feel inferior. Based on the psychological, social, and scientific effects of segregation, Dr. Clark had published on this subject and described a similar experiment with Black students in the integrated schools of a northern city. In summary, Dr. Clark concluded that 52 percent of schoolchildren in the South thought that the white doll was nicer than the Black doll; in the North (including results taken from Boston and Worcester), 68 percent thought so. In the South, 49 percent of the children thought that the Black doll was bad; in the North, 71 percent thought so.[33]

Although *Brown v. Board of Education* went to court in 1952, the case was not decided until 1954. This delay in judgment was indicative of the fact that the court was reluctant to get rid of segregation in schools. The court wanted to be unanimous and couldn't get total agreement. Supreme Court justice Fred Vincent died in the middle of the case, which required the appointment of a new justice. Eisenhower appointed former California governor Earl Warren in 1953. Ironically, Eisenhower appointed Warren because he believed that he wouldn't take any radical actions on the court. Although he had every reason to assume Warren was a safe choice based on his tenure as governor, Warren became a changed man politically and philosophically. During the case, Felix Frankfurter was the holdout. A Vienna-descended Jew, some might have thought Frankfurter's background would have made him sympathetic to the NAACP's case. However, his shrewdness and thoroughness with regard to every aspect of such a broad social proposal led him to resist siding with the plaintiffs. Upon joining the court, Warren made overtures to Frankfurter, whom he was eventually able to convince.

There were likewise concerns having to do with the balance of power. According to the Constitution, the Supreme Court had the power to interpret—and even enforce—the laws, but it relied on another branch to write them. Some feared that if the court ruled in favor of *Brown*, the court would be advancing a social custom that was beyond the scope of the Supreme Court. Frankfurter in particular thought that if they were at least unanimous in their decision, then it could be more easily accepted. In what seemed like just another frustrating delay at the time to Marshall, the Supreme Court asked the NAACP and Marshall to consider four questions.[34] Marshall provided measured but satisfactory answers to all the questions.

On May 17, 1954, the Supreme Court handed down the *Brown* decision. In a unanimous decision, the Supreme Court ruled that separating children solely because of their race "generates a feeling of inferiority . . . that may affect their hearts and minds in a way unlikely ever to be undone. . . . Any language in *Plessy v. Ferguson* contrary to this finding is rejected. We conclude that in the field of public education the doctrine of 'separate but equal' has no place. Separate educational facilities are inherently unequal. . . . It is so ordered."[35] Even with the court's decision, segregation in U.S. public schools persisted. Indeed, a full ten years after *Brown v. Board*, only 2 percent of schools were desegregated. An important point to understand is that the court was calling for desegregation, not integration. When the court talked about desegregation, what it meant was the removal of legal barriers to integration.[36]

But housing and residential segregation in the North had created de facto segregation—something which *Brown* did not cover—a major contributing factor to why schools remained segregated even after *Brown*. As J. Anthony Lukas writes in *Common Ground*, "Ironically, Boston was the only city to which the Court in *Brown* had given a clean bill of health. To gain maximum support for that landmark decision, Chief Justice Earl Warren had not wanted to point an accusing finger solely at the South; after all, *Brown* itself was a Kansas case."[37]

In January 1961, almost seven years after the *Brown v. Board* decision, James Howard Meredith, then a student at the all-Black Jackson State College, applied for admission to the University of Mississippi. He was denied and subsequently took his case to the NAACP Legal Defense Fund. The LDF filed suit on his behalf in U.S. district court, charging that Meredith was refused admission "solely because of his race." After more than a year of legal battles and appeals, on September 10, 1962, the U.S. Supreme Court upheld Meredith's right to be admitted to Ole Miss. Mississippi governor Ross Barnett famously refused to let Meredith be admitted.[38] Meredith eventually enrolled, but not until the federal government intervened, making him the first Black student admitted to the University of Mississippi.

Desegregation likewise faced direct opposition from many whites—not only in the South but indeed throughout the country. Middle- and upper-class whites in the South formed citizens' councils with the intention of maintaining the racial status quo in the South. While perhaps less obviously racist, staunch opposition also existed in the North. Many whites accused the Supreme Court of trying to make the laws, which they argued was not the function of that branch of government. This later became a constant refrain, galvanizing opponents to desegregation across the South and later in northern cities like Boston. Throughout the 1950s and 1960s, the defenders of segregated schools denounced the Supreme Court's ruling outright. They challenged the *Brown* decision on constitutional grounds and called for the impeachment of the Supreme Court's chief justice. In Boston, that sentiment was expressed as the preferences of a liberal suburban judge. Southerners were more likely to directly challenge the constitutionality of *Brown*, while Bostonians and other northerners couched their opposition in the rhetoric of calls for "neighborhood schools."

Muriel Snowden and Freedom House

While all of this was happening, a parallel struggle was playing out in Boston, as the Black elite worked to improve living conditions on a neighborhood-by-neighborhood basis. Inspired by social possibilities made by *Brown*, Freedom House was founded by Black social workers Otto P. and Muriel S. Snowden, emissaries of Boston's Black elite who had an acute sense of social justice and activism. Boston was very much transformed during the years of their leadership, between 1949 and 1986. With Freedom House, the Snowdens' expanded the movement for racial equality beyond the traditional boundaries of civil rights organizations and established what would become a critical meeting place for civil rights activities throughout the 1950s and up to the present day. Freedom House was founded in Upper Roxbury in 1948 as a "non-sectarian meeting place for all groups in the community; a reference point for all matters pertaining to civic improvement; and a focal point for the development of interests and projects which will help to make the community a unified one."[39]

The original goal of the organization, created "without respect to race, religion or national origin," was "to make Roxbury a better place to live."[40] Although the Snowdens were often called on to serve as spokespeople for the

Black community in Boston, Freedom House served multiple purposes. It was used as a cornerstone for the Black middle class in Boston, with its cotillions, debutante balls, and social events, as well as a meeting place for speakers with divergent points of view. It also hosted lectures at its popular coffee hours, where various speakers would discuss current political and social topics of the day. Later, Freedom House became an incubator for would-be social activists and future organizers, such as a young Sarah-Ann Shaw, who recalls attending those events.[41]

Freedom House grew out of the Snowdens' initial community organizing with the Council on Community Affairs of Upper Roxbury between 1947 and 1949. The initial goal of Freedom House was to "centralize community activism in the fight for neighborhood improvement, good schools, and harmony among racial, ethnic, and religious groups in Roxbury, Massachusetts."[42] Otto Snowden had been the director of St. Mark's Social Center when he married Muriel Sutherland Snowden. They were determined to remain in Roxbury and work to ensure its stability as a middle-class, racially mixed neighborhood. As directors of Freedom House, the Snowdens hoped to achieve their goals by linking the community to existing services and creating services where they were lacking. Freedom House would become an important base of operations in the Black community through successive movements, including civil rights, urban renewal in Roxbury, and even Black Power.

As the city moved from the Great Depression into the postwar era, Boston's relatively small Black population continued to grow as more and more migrants from the South and the Caribbean arrived in the city in search of jobs and improved political and economic opportunities. Although increased opportunity led to some occupational gains, income levels for Black workers, when compared to whites, remained low. At the same time, Boston was undergoing many structural changes, most notably urban renewal. Often framed as a means of modernizing cities, urban renewal proved devastating for Black Americans, demolishing entire neighborhoods to make way for the city's expansion. Ghettos began to emerge in the areas surrounding the Grove Hall section of Roxbury and North Dorchester.

As historian Gerald Gill writes, "The Great Depression and the subsequent New Deal spurred African-American activism in the city and led to the beginnings of newer, more militant campaign efforts that sought both economic relief and the broadening of employment opportunities. Although blacks composed less than three percent of the city's population in the 1930s, black male and female workers were disproportionately unemployed during the decade."[43]

Unlike other cities that had sustained periods of Black migration, Boston's Black community had difficulty achieving political parity with the longer established white ethnic population because of their relatively small numbers. Thomas Atkins, a Black American, was elected as a district-wide city councilor in the 1960s, but without a large constituency, Black candidates were unable to win many seats in local and state government. Black Americans also held few municipal jobs, which were often reserved for the relatives of white elected officials.

In lieu of electoral power, Black Americans in Boston fought racism through traditional civil rights organizations. During the late 1940s and early 1950s, the Boston Urban League focused its efforts on campaigns against race-based discrimination and segregation in the allocation of housing. The Boston Urban League participated in creating legislation against discrimination in housing, held housing clinics, and advocated for fair employment policies in local companies. They were joined by the Civil Rights Congress (CRC), an American civil rights organization dedicated to protecting the civil rights and liberties of Black Americans and suspected communists. The CRC was established in 1946 after three organizations closely associated with the Communist Party of America—the National Negro Congress, the International Labor Defense, and the National Federation for Constitutional Liberties—decided to merge. At its peak, the CRC had ten thousand members. During its relatively brief existence, the CRC fought for the protection of civil rights and liberties of Black Americans and suspected communists primarily through litigation, political agitation, and the mobilization of public sentiment. Communist leader and lawyer William Patterson served as executive secretary of the organization for the duration of its existence. In 1949, representatives of the CRC staged ongoing demonstrations against the Timothy Smith Company, as the store had not hired any Black employees.

Meanwhile, Boston's local NAACP chapter continued to play an important role in the city. In 1946, Reverend Kenneth P. Hughes was elected NAACP branch president. That same year, members of the NAACP Youth Council staged demonstrations in downtown Boston against those insurance companies that still refused to hire Black men and women for white-collar positions. Hughes's term was short. In 1947, John Lane was elected president of the Boston branch of the NAACP; later that same year, Black activists protested the small and in some instances nonexistent number of Black municipal employees in Boston.[44]

This turnover in such a short period of time is reflective of turmoil within the NAACP. Between 1948 and 1951, Mrs. Florence Lesueur was elected the first woman president of the Boston NAACP. During her administration, Boston's Black working class initially swelled the branch's membership. However, branch membership declined in 1950 as a result of the Loyalty Act; the NAACP had to purge its ranks of individuals who had been or who were members of the Communist Party. As Gerald Gill has written:

> The overall political climate in the United States led the national NAACP to enact resolutions barring local branches from working with or allowing Communists to join the organization. Following national edict, Lesueur helped to deter or to dissuade the involvement of publicly known black and white leftists in branch activities. The purges had a debilitating impact upon the Youth Council as the young adult wing of the organization would be weakened throughout the 1950s of the further loss of an energetic, able and creative cadre of men and women. Similarly, the branch would experience a noticeable drop in paid memberships.[45]

From *Brown* to Boston

When Lyda Peters moved from New York to Roxbury in her teens, she graduated from a predominantly white Catholic high school and then from a predominantly white Catholic college in Massachusetts. As a young Black teacher, she began her teaching career in the Boston Public Schools in September 1965, choosing to teach in a section of North Dorchester that was predominantly Black. She found the Quincy E. Dickerman Elementary School, where she could have a supervised practicum experience. As she writes in her doctoral dissertation, "I learned to teach under the supervision of a wonderful, caring third grade teacher, Mrs. Bethel, who was one of too few Black teachers in the city. She graduated from Boston Teacher's College. Only graduates from this college could find employment in the Boston schools and those few Black teachers who were employed by the Boston schools knew that this was the primary route to a teaching position in the city."[46]

All of twenty-one years old, Peters was assigned to the Dickerman school. A newly minted first-grade teacher, she entered her classroom that September. It had an enrollment of nearly forty-five six-year-olds. She loved teaching but would soon come to understand, on a personal level as a Black educator, the institutional challenges that the Black community and its children faced. The Quincy E. Dickerman Elementary School was in the Phillips Brooks district and was an eight-minute walk from her home. Built in 1915 and named after a schoolteacher who taught in Boston for half a century, Dickerman was the feeder school for children living on Magnolia Street and the surrounding area in Roxbury. It was located in a densely populated, residentially segregated, low-income Black neighborhood.[47]

As Peters later recalled, on Friday, May 17, 1968, on the fourteenth anniversary of the *Brown* decision, Jacqueline, a seven-year-old first grader, was left in a cloakroom on a Friday afternoon after school was dismissed. "Her teacher confined her to the cloakroom shortly after lunch, with tape placed across her mouth, as punishment for talking. All students in the school were dismissed for the weekend, leaving, as the only adults on the premises, three teachers and the school janitor. I was one of the three teachers." This incident became known as the "Cloakroom Case."[48] As a result of her being there, Peters was asked by the legendary Ruth Batson, who would become perhaps one of the most well-known figures in the drama around school desegregation and the eventual fight for busing, to provide testimony before the Massachusetts Commission against Discrimination, which Batson co-chaired with Fr. Robert Drinan.[49] Batson asked for an account of the events at Dickerman, which Peters provided.

Following her testimony, Mrs. Batson called Peters once again, to offer her employment in a newly funded program of "urban-suburban exchange," which Batson directed. The exchange was called the Metropolitan Council for Educational Opportunity (METCO) and was a voluntarily program in which Black Boston school students could attend one of seven suburban school systems. At the time, METCO was in its second year. Peters's responsibility would be to interview elementary students, select the schools to which they would be assigned, and develop programs for them, as needed. The staff was small, and they worked in concert. In addition to Ruth Batson as director, there was Elizabeth "Betty" Johnson, assistant director and one of the founders of Operation Exodus, a parent-led community organization that used Boston's open-enrollment policy to transport Black children to white schools where there were empty seats.

Batson had organizing in her blood at a very young age. A young Lenny Alkins, who would head up the Boston NAACP through the 1980s and 1990s, lived upstairs from Batson in the segregated Orchard Park housing project in Roxbury. Batson drafted the young man into a picket of a local store that would not sell to Black customers. At the time, the civil rights movement was just beginning to blossom in the North. As Alkins pointed out, they did not know they were being discriminated against until the movement came by way of the boycott. They went to school with white children; they played with white children; they went to their homes. Black children at that time went to Carson Beach, City Point, and did not have problems. As he says, "We had turf battles that were based on economic development more so than race."[50]

Batson subsequently went on to play a central role in Boston's Black freedom movement as an educator, civil rights activist, philanthropist, and historical preservationist. Following the boycott involving Alkins, Batson fought for the proper reading of history, while making plenty herself. As Batson wrote in a 1963 letter to the editor of the *Boston Globe*, she responded to critics of school desegregation by saying, "Raising educational standards without eliminating the basic problems of segregation in fact is no more than separate but equal."[51]

Batson was a lifetime resident of Boston, living the majority of her life in Roxbury. She and her three daughters graduated from Boston schools. In 1949, Batson made a fateful decision that would influence the future course of history in the city when she joined the Parents' Federation, a predominantly white women's organization organizing around school inequities. Subsequently, Batson was appointed the organization's executive secretary. In 1951, as executive secretary of the Parents' Federation of Greater Boston, Batson ran unsuccessfully for the Boston School Committee.[52] As a parent, Batson had been quite critical of the overcrowded and antiquated schools in her neighborhood. Batson's involvement with the Parents' Federation proved short-lived, however, as the organization soon disbanded following a slew of red-baiting. Following her involvement with the Parents' Federation, Batson continued to document disparities between white classmates and her daughter in home assignments. In 1950, Ruth Batson contacted the NAACP with a discrimination complaint about her children's education. It was in this same year that the Boston branch of the NAACP purged its ranks of individuals who had been or who were members of the Communist Party.

In 1953, Batson approached Lionel Lindsay, who had been elected president of the Boston branch of the NAACP in 1951, to inquire as to whether the organization had knowledge of the conditions and administration of the schools, and to make a complaint about them. Although the NAACP did have an Education Committee, it only dealt with "scholarships and guidance." After that meeting, Batson received a call in which she was asked if she would be willing to chair a newly formed subcommittee on schools.[53] The newly created Public School Subcommittee was charged with the responsibility of advocating for students attending Boston public schools.

Of course, Boston activists rejoiced over the Supreme Court's 1954 decision in *Brown v. Board of Education*, but with the national NAACP focusing on the South, Boston activists pressed their case in the schools with little results. Long-standing patterns of discrimination were now joined with the fact that the Black community was suffering from institutional and other kinds of racism in the form of residential segregation. Although some protests were taking place, there was no real sustained action on behalf of the Black community in challenging the status quo. "No one can take your education away from you" her mother would always say. Batson inherited this determination to seek and to hand down this resolve to her children. "When my concerns for the educational growth of my children developed into an organized community effort, I began a new collection of reports, letters, and newspaper and magazine articles." During her time with the Parents' Federation, Batson received the best kind of education—one in organizing and learning how to combat the disparities taking place in the Boston schools, which had been documented in "The Strayer Report," a study and general survey of the Boston Public Schools, commissioned by the Boston Finance Commission and released on January 25, 1944. Batson writes:

> I learned so much from the discussions at Parents' Federation meetings, and soon became a faithful and avid member. With the exception of my friend Kate and me, the Federation's membership was white and mostly women. . . . Our affiliation with this group opened Kate and me up to series of seminars that expanded our minds beyond my expectation. The group was divided geographically—members lived in West Roxbury, Dorchester, Roxbury, and the South End. Because Kate and I were the only black parents, we were in charge of Roxbury and the South End. At that time, there were very few black residents of Dorchester. "The Strayer Report" was our primer and we studied the findings.[54]

Thomas Atkins was not originally from Boston. He grew up in Elkhart, Indiana, and was the first Black student body president of his high school. It seemed wherever Tom Atkins went, he achieved. He was also the first Black student president at Indiana University Bloomington, where he attended college, as well as the first in the Big Ten. Like so many Black Americans who came to Boston from elsewhere and made a major impact on the city—Byron Rushing, Chuck Turner, Hubie Jones—Atkins would be drawn to the Black historical significance of Boston. And, like others, he found himself shocked that the great abolitionist citadel of Boston was not a place always hospitable to Black Americans, even those native-born or long-residing Black citizens. Atkins graduated from Indiana University in 1961 having earned a bachelor's degree in political science. In 1963, he earned a master's degree in Middle Eastern studies from Harvard University, and in 1969 he graduated from

Harvard Law School. It was while he was a student at Harvard—during the time of increased activism and protests that accompanied the 1960s—that Atkins served as executive secretary of the Boston branch of the NAACP.

Interviewed for the landmark documentary film *To Secure These Rights*, produced by WGBH-FM, he said about the climate at that time:

> The segregation is segregation that is based . . . that is the result, primarily, of housing patterns. And this we recognize. We have said, to the School Committee, "segregation exists." The fact it is the result of housing patterns is another problem. The fact that it exists, is the School Committee's problem . . . and our problem. Now, we are living up to the responsibility of recognizing the situation as it exists—de facto. This is what we have said. Now we are asking the School Committee to look to their part of the responsibility and that is to work with this problem toward a solution.[55]

When Hubie Jones first came to Boston from his native New York to attend the School of Social Work at Boston University, he could not have known how much Black people were suffering in "the birthplace of liberty" or the indelible impact he would have on his new adopted city. According to Kenneth Cooper and Don West, Jones was inspired by a course he took as an undergraduate at the City College of New York with Kenneth Clark, the psychologist who had provided the core evidence that proved the *Brown v. Board of Education* case. They write, "Clark was in the throes of proving that segregation does psychological damage to black children. He shared with his class the draft legal brief for *Brown v. Board of Education* before it was filed with the U.S."[56] They further explain that it was both the influence of Clark and a chance to hear Martin Luther King Jr. speak as a graduate student in social work a few years later at Boston University—"two titans of the civil rights movement"—that really touched the life of Hubie Jones as a young man. According to West and Cooper, "they inspired him to spend 50 years working to solve social problems in Boston, in order to create what he calls 'a wholesome society.' They appealed to his emerging sense of social justice."[57]

On June 11, 1963, 300 Black and white Bostonians marched on city hall to protest school segregation and on June 14, Black community leaders planned school boycotts in protest of school conditions. Students were warned to attend school on June 18, or face fines of up to $50 or six months in prison for persons "causing or encouraging the delinquency of a child."[58] On June 15, the Boston School Committee met with Black leaders to avert the school boycott. It would be at this meeting in which Black leaders would present their demands to the committee. On June 16, the Catholic Interracial Council of the Archdiocese of Boston released a statement expressing confidence in the sincerity of the planned school boycotts.[59] The next day, Gov. Peabody and his staff met with the Boston NAACP concerning the boycotts. The Superintendent of Schools Dr. Frederick Gillis argued that Boston was not segregated and that the city's schools were integrated. On June 18, the first "Stay Out for Freedom" school boycott was held, protesting school segregation, in which half of the five thousand African American students at Boston's junior and senior high schools stayed out of school. Instead, boycotters attended "Freedom Workshops" held at St. Mark's Social Center. Speakers included the Episcopal Bishop of Massachusetts, the Rt. Rev. Anson Phelps Stokes, Jr.; the Northeast Methodist Bishop, Rt. Rev. James K. Mathews and Celtics legend, Bill Russell."[60] On June 19, the Boston School Committee approved the establishment of a group of Black community leaders to help carry out the proposals of the NAACP. On July 9, 1963, the Boston School Committee took its first steps toward forming a committee of community members to address problems at Roxbury and South End schools, appointing Irene Robinson, Paul Parks, Archie Williams, Theodore Peters, Rev. Nathan Wright, Ruth Batson, Ernest Headley, Ms. George Keeley, Ms. Harry Elam, and Alice Yancey for committee membership.[61]

Jones's wife, Katherine Butler Jones was very involved in coordinating busing for schoolchildren. In 1966, she organized the Newton community to join the effort to desegregate seven suburban schools.[62] Today there are over thirty-three hundred children going to thirty-five suburban schools in Boston, and METCO is the most enduring educational infrastructure in the country. In February 1964, in the second Stay Out for Freedom, Jones was asked to mobilize suburban students. Lots of those kids came into Boston, many of whom participated in the Freedom Schools held in churches and community centers.

At a 2006 conference on the civil rights movement in Boston in the 1960s, Hubie Jones stated, "It was a time of overdue turbulence, enormous energy, great creativity and optimism. When I arrived here in 1955 from New York City, I described Boston as being up south because of practices of racial deep north discrimination and segregation in public bodies, such as the Boston Public Schools, the Boston Housing Authority, and the Boston Police and Fire Departments."[63]

Like many who have made this observation, it often takes the perspective of coming from outside to see things clearly. "I got here in '55," Jones said, "coming out of New York. There were no retail workers in the downtown department stores who were Black except in upfront positions serving the public. Those who were being hired were folks who were working in the stock room or on the loading decks bringing merchandise in. A neighbor of mine in Cambridge . . . had an upfront job, a retail job at Gilchrist's. He was like one of two people of color working in the downtown retail store."[64] As Jones observed, in the mid-1950s, "there were five bus drivers who were Black—maybe. There were no Black motormen driving the subway cars here in the mid-fifties. And so, there were these patterns of discrimination and basically the Black community was suffering from this kind of institutional and other kind of racism. And although there were some protests around, there was no real forceful sustained action on behalf of the Black community in challenging the status quo."[65]

Jones would go on to provide that kind of sustained action on behalf of the Black community when he got involved in the school desegregation movement in the 1960s. Subsequently, Jones was a professor of social work at Boston University from 1977 to 1993 and dean of the School of Social Work for many years. He also served as acting president at Roxbury Community College, which he guided through a time of crisis, before joining the University of Massachusetts Boston as special assistant to the chancellor for urban affairs. An indispensable champion of people, Jones served as a social worker, as a builder of literally dozens of community organizations, as either board president or chair of innumerable agencies, and as the executive director of the Roxbury Multi-Service Center for nearly four decades.[66]

"In the early 1960s," recalled Jones, "the pressure cooker was being stoked by the Civil Rights demonstration in the south, its horrific images flashing across television screens in Boston. Although there was some activism by Black leaders concerning our grievances, they were not vigorously challenging political and corporate power. That posture was about to change."[67]

By the 1960s, the NAACP Public Schools Subcommittee had collected enough information to show that there was at least the effect of segregation, if not segregation in fact. Black students were primarily in Black overcrowded schools in Black neighborhoods, and white students were primarily in white schools in mostly white neighborhoods. In 1963, the Boston branch of the NAACP took its findings to the Public Schools Subcommittee.[68] On June 11, 1963, members came before the all-white school committee and its newly elected chair, Louise Day Hicks. They not only explained how Black kids were primarily in Black schools but laid out how those schools were worse off in terms of their physical facilities and lack of supplies, and how the schools had been educationally segregated. The room that night was already packed when Hubie Jones arrived at the school committee's chambers at 15 Beacon Street in downtown Boston. It was "a hot night in a crazy, crazy room," Jones later recalled.[69]

Seated behind a long brown table on a raised platform sat Thomas Eisenstadt, Joseph Lee, Louise Day Hicks, William O'Connor, and Arthur Gartland, school committee members who had been elected at-large to represent the interest of all the children in the city. It was Boston's version of "a jury of your peers"—all white. On the floor directly in front of the committee at a "witness stand" sat Ruth Batson and Paul Parks, chair and member of the NAACP's Education Committee, respectively. Together, Batson and Parks presented the NAACP's case as the school committee stoically listened.

Batson began: "We are here because the clamor from the community is too anxious to be ignored, the dissatisfaction and complaints too genuine and deep seated to be passed over lightly, and," she continued, "the injustices present in our school system hurt our pride, rob us of our dignity and produce results which are injurious not only to our future, but to that of our city, our commonwealth and our nation."[70]

In their report, Batson and Parks asserted that de facto segregation existed in the Boston Public Schools and that Black children assigned to predominantly Black schools were being shortchanged as a result of inferior conditions. They cited overcrowded schools for facility repair and maintenance, and an inadequate supply of books and instructional materials as evidence. Subsequently, they presented the NAACP's program for corrective action, the first point calling for public acknowledgment by the school committee that de facto segregation existed in the Boston school system.

Saying that it was "too late for pleading," it was this first point that the Boston School Committee rejected, thus triggering the Stay Out for Freedom boycott. The remaining points read as follows:

1. An immediate review of the open enrollment plan to allow transfers without present limitations. This plan to be put into operation by school opening in September.
2. In service training program for principals and teachers in the area of human relations.
3. The establishing of a liaison between the school administration and colleges so that training programs may be set up for prospective teachers in urban communities.
4. The assignment of permanent teachers to grades one to three and the reduction of these classes to twenty-five.

"Picket parade" with signs at the Boston School Committee, August 7, 1963 (*Boston Globe* staff photographer, Boston School Desegregation Archival Resources, Archives and Special Collections, Snell Library, Northeastern University).

5. The use of books and other visual aids that include illustrations of people of all races.

6. The establishment of a concentrated developmental reading program in each school in grades one through eight.

7. The expansion of the school adjustment counselor program in the congested Negro school districts.

8. The expansion of the vocational guidance program to include grade seven and the selection of qualified un-biased counselors.

9. The elimination of discrimination in the hiring and the assigning of teachers.

10. An investigation into reasons as to why Boston has no Negro principal.

11. A review of the system of intelligence testing.

12. The adoption in toto of the Sargeant report that refers to Roxbury and North Dorchester.

13. Our most important proposal is as follows: We seek the right to discuss the selection of a new superintendent in detail with Dr. Hunt.[71]

At one point, Hicks, the new chair from South Boston, spoke; this was the first time many had seen her in action: "Mrs. Batson, surely you do not believe that this committee has any responsibility for housing veterans in this city," Mrs. Hicks intoned. "That is beyond our control. We assigned children to schools nearest to their homes. We reject the charge that this committee has deliberately segregated students in our school system based on race." School committee members joined the rebuttal to fully and enthusiastically support Mrs. Hicks's position with the exception of Arthur Gartland. Moderate to progressive by persuasion, Gartland agreed that it was proper to admit that de facto segregation existed, but through no fault of school committee action. His other colleagues, however, would have none of this accommodation. Amid the committee's objections, Parks repeatedly rose to recast the NAACP's position but was quickly joined by Hicks.[72] Hicks and other members of the committee would not abide the accusation of the Boston schools being segregated, so organizers were forced to find other ways of explaining the problem. "The NAACP is not blaming the school committee for segregating the schools. The courses of segregation are irrelevant here. De facto, Black students are in mostly segregated schools and experiencing hardships not present for white students. Regardless of the cause, the school committee has a responsibility to take positive corrective action."[73]

Their protestations, however, were to no avail. By the time the other four committee members had finished their orations, mainly designed for media consumption, it was clear that the "jury" had arrived at a verdict before the NAACP had even finished presenting its case. Subsequently, the school committee retired to its private chambers on the upper level of the building. As they deliberated, the sound of people singing civil rights songs downstairs carried through the open windows, a sign that the civil rights movement was alive in Boston that night.

Batson later recalled the standoff with the school committee:

We were naive. And when we got to the school committee room, I was surprised to see all of the press around. We thought this is just an ordinary school committee meeting, and we made our presentation and everything broke loose. We were insulted. We were told our kids were stupid and this was why they didn't learn. We were completely rejected that night. We were there until all hours of the evening. And we left battle-scarred, because we found out that this was an issue that was going to give their political careers stability for a long time to come.[74]

According to Hubie Jones, the school committee's response was: "We don't segregate the schools. We send students to the schools closest to where they live and we're not going to stand for you suggesting that we had deliberately segregated the schools. And we will do nothing, nothing to change what's going on here." Jones adds half-jokingly, "The Boston schools [were] a giant employment agency for white Irish Catholic folks."[75]

As Jeanne Theoharis writes, "To continue the pressure on the Boston School Committee, Black community leaders turned to direct action. A week after the hearing, they organized a school boycott and nearly half of the city's Black high school students stayed out of school, participating in Freedom Schools instead. The school committee then agreed to a second hearing with the NAACP, but shut the meeting down when civil rights leaders used the phrase 'de facto segregation.'"[76]

In trying to make the case, Batson recalls, "We said to them that this condition that we were talking about was called de facto segregation, and that by that we didn't mean at all that anybody on the school committee or any official was deliberately segregating students, but this was caused by residential settings and so forth, but that we felt that this had to be acknowledged and that something had to be done to alleviate the situation."[77]

Formed in 1789 after Massachusetts passed the nation's first comprehensive school law, the Boston School Committee had historically been a revolving door for white, mainly Irish American patronage—a way to repay favors, procure jobs, and pay off political debts. In other words, the school committee was a gateway to higher office. By the 1960s, fights over desegregation dominated.[78] Louise Day Hicks chaired the Boston School Committee into the mid-1960s. In 1965, there was not one single Black principal in the Boston Public Schools. Although one in four students was Black, only one in two hundred teachers was Black.

Batson recollects, "At one point [Hicks] said, 'The word that I'm objecting to is *segregation*. As long as you talk about segregation, I won't discuss this.'"[79] With the school committee's intransigence, the Black community resorted to large-scale protest in the form of a lockout. Following the June 11 meeting, members of Boston's Black community, led by the NAACP, created a lockout at the school committee building by joining hands and preventing people from coming into work. So high were passions and emotions, says Jones, that one of the school committee members "did a football thing where he crashed through the line to get to his office."[80]

Tom Atkins and others stayed overnight in the building and refused to leave. Meanwhile, makeshift dumbwaiters were made out of ropes so that people could send food to the people who were staying overnight. It was finally what organizers and parent-activists had worked to bring about—a real confrontation. Unable to get the protesters to leave the premises, authorities resorted to floating a rumor that a bomb had been set and that there was going to be a tragedy. Whether it was true or not, those protesters who had remained in the building knew enough about the history of white terrorism to know that it might be true and made the decision to leave, ending the protest. As Atkins recalls:

> The Boston School Committee has to accept responsibility for implementing and introducing programs to eliminate racial imbalance or "de facto Segregation" in the Boston School system. This is the very same reason it brought us originally to the School Committee on June the 11th. This is the very same reason that tied us up in the negotiation with the School Committee on the 14th of June. This is the very same reason that brought us to a meeting on the 13th of August that ended after 15 minutes. It is the reason that brought us here today and it's why I'm here now and I'll be staying here—all night.[81]

The end of the lockout, however, did not mean the end of protests against segregated schooling. Throughout the remainder of the summer of 1963, the Black community continued to put pressure on the Boston School Committee with marches, rallies, lock-ins, and other overnight sit-ins. On June 15, a meeting was held in an attempt to avert the walkout. On June 18, seven days after the infamous school committee meeting, James Breeden led a Stay Out for Freedom walkout—what amounted to a school boycott. During the boycott, organizers asked Black students in junior and senior high (not elementary school) to stay out of school to protest the fact that the school committee would not admit to the fact of segregation or do anything to correct it. As a result, more than three thousand students stayed out of school that day. During the protest, students attended ad hoc Freedom Schools in churches and community centers, where they learned Black history and the purposes of the civil rights movement.[82]

On July 29, the Boston School Committee offices were picketed. Protesters demanded that the committee meet with the NAACP's Education Committee, though the event was not organized or endorsed by the NAACP itself. Access to the committee offices was blocked by a human chain for one hour in the morning. The majority of the protesters were white. Throughout the month of August, mainly as a result of the July 29 demonstration, the committee engaged in a series of meetings with the NAACP Education Commit-

This photo is from the Freedom Stay-Out Day held on February 26, 1964. It shows students checking in at the Tremont St. Methodist Church Freedom School, which was set up to support students participating in the boycott. (*Freedom School at Tremont St. Methodist Church in the South End Neighborhood of Boston, Boston Globe* staff photographer, Boston School Desegregation Archival Resources, Archives and Special Collections, Snell Library, Northeastern University.)

tee on Boston school segregation. By August 15, in a turnabout, the committee ceased its meetings with the NAACP Education Committee and refused to discuss "de facto segregation" any further. Meanwhile, on August 19, the Massachusetts Board of Education condemned de facto segregation and urged the elimination of racial imbalance in schools throughout the Commonwealth. On August 20, Gov. Peabody stated that segregation existed in the Commonwealth's schools and that it must be overcome. However, he also suggested that the NAACP stop using the phrase "de facto segregation."[83] On August 29, Kenneth Guscott, president of the NAACP Boston extended an invitation to the Boston School Committee to continue talks and indicated his willingness to reach a settlement by avoiding the "de facto" issue. Superintendent Gillis announced adoption of an "open enrollment" plan, in which students could attend any public school if parents provided transportation.[84]

So many committed individuals with organizing strength were part of this movement—and contributed to its success—with varying approaches. James Breeden and Noel Day of the Massachusetts Freedom Movement—which it should be said was a church-based movement—had their own approach. To dramatize the conditions of Boston's overcrowded Black schools, Breeden and Day asked parents to let their students "stay out" from school and to instead send their students to a Freedom School. As Alyssa Napier writes, "The idea for Freedom Schools originated when social worker Noel Day and minister James Breeden came together to organize the first Freedom Stay-Out, held on June 18, 1963. With students out of school, the organizers needed a way 'to keep them off the streets and to provide an opportunity for them to feel a part of a mass action'."[85] The school Stay Out for Freedom movement took place in the context of the broader civil rights movement nationally. Massachusetts attorney general Edward Brooke had issued an edict that any children who "stayed out" were in violation of truancy laws. Napier continues, "Organizations like the Massachusetts ACLU had attempted to quell these fears by arguing that parents had a right to keep their students from school and thus the stay-out was not illegal."[86]

Another innovative and effective flanking maneuver was the Massachusetts Freedom Movement. Jim Breeden, Noel Day, and a lot of the folks involved were seen as young upstarts. Virgil Wood, as leader of the Massachusetts SCLC chapter, was also a man of the cloth. As men of faith, their overall approach and style was reminiscent of the southern movement. Yet some of the most important actors in this effort were not men. Peggy Trotter Dammond Preacely came from African American and Black Bostonian royalty. She was a descendant of the legendary William and Ellen Craft, who in an extraordinary story used their ability to "pass for white" to escape slavery.[87] Ellen Craft Dammond was Peggy's mother. Peggy's grandmother, Bessie Trotter Craft, was a member of the acclaimed Trotter family. Peggy's great-grandmother was Virginia Isaacs Trotter, the great-great grandniece of Sally Hemings and Peggy's great-grandfather, James Trotter. Peggy's great-uncle was the great William Monroe Trotter, brother of Bessie, Peggy's grandmother. Peggy called him "Uncle Monroe."[88]

Peggy was married to Noel Day during the movement years in Boston and played an extremely prominent role in the coordination of the Freedom Schools, including by doing a fair amount of teaching. She helped write the curriculum for the original Freedom Schools created by the Student Nonviolent Coordinating Committee (SNCC) in the Southern movement. She fundraised for SNCC during her time as a student at Boston University after the summer of 1962.[89] As she stated in a documentary film about the school desegregation movement:

> In the last few days, some people have made a great discovery or, at least, recognized the fact that Roxbury and the South End—in these places we go to segregated schools. These schools are too segregated to be equal. They are not as segregated as Birmingham or as Jackson, but they're segregated enough. They're not segregated by law, but in fact. And this is what "de facto" means—the term you've heard bantered about a great deal. It has been proved, and proved to the satisfaction of the Supreme Court of the United States, that segregated schools, by law or "de facto," cannot be equal schools. We are staying out of school to tell the School Committee and the community that we don't want inferior schools. We want equal schools. Some parts of the program today will give us a taste of what we feel and believe.[90]

And so waves of people would be seen taking part in the walkout, and the power of it—the idea of using children in this case—borrowed a page from the struggle in Birmingham. As Jones recalls, "But this was about the schools, so a school walkout is like, it's not exactly the same as what happened in Birmingham, but it did concern young people, that's the similarity. Because they were punished, the kids were punished, their GPAs were affected. Black students would be punished, and disciplined way higher, and that was of course what they're protesting, but they were also threatened with all kinds of things in the schools, including letters home."[91]

Edward Brooke, the attorney general of Massachusetts at the time—the first Black attorney general—was put in a very difficult position because he was concerned with upholding the law as he understood it and enforcing the law because he was a chief enforcement officer of the state. At the same time, he believed in the right of Black students to fight for their education. His office released a statement saying that yes, while it was legally possible to arrest kids and their parents or guardians for truancy, it shouldn't have to come to that. It should be totally feasible to allow the kids to make up a day's work. And if the kids make a good faith effort to make up the work, that should be sufficient.

Hubie Jones and Mel King decided there should be a general strike to protest all forms of racial discrimination in Boston, something they had been talking about since the spring. Some months passed before their idea came to fruition. On June 13, the attorney general called a meeting at St. Mark's Social Center in Roxbury, inviting the Black leadership to come and tell him about the things that were being planned. Jones, who was then living in Newton, received a call that night. The voice on the other end said, "Hubie, where are you?" It was Jim Breeden, an Episcopal priest and head of the St. Mark's Social Center. "You better get down here," he said. "Ed Brooke is here and the Black leadership is in the room and eventually there's going to be a discussion about STOP."[92] STOP was the name given to the general strike proposed by Jones.

While he hurried to get to the meeting, Jones relied on his co-organizer, Mel King, to "hold this thing until [he got] there." King had been a steady organizing presence, probably the only person who had a hand in almost every important movement in Boston. Frustrated with the lack of Black elected officials in the city, including in matters pertaining to education, King ran unsuccessfully for a seat on the Boston School Committee in 1961, 1963, and 1965. Because the seats were at-large, it was almost impossible to get elected. Meanwhile, he joined Jones in organizing STOP and set the date for the work stoppage as June 26.

Ed Brooke had his suit jacket off and was in his shirtsleeves, sweating as he faced his audience. In their judgment, Brooke had been called in to cool off the Black community. Brooke asked about all the things being planned. Elma Lewis, the legendary cultural educator and community leader who had been a voice for Boston's Black community going back to the 1940s, was there. Challenging the attorney general, she said, "Ed, you don't get it. These people are giving us no choice. They're not giving us any choice but to come to the work stoppage. What are you talking about? You don't know what's going on with us."[93] Brooke responded, asking, "What is this STOP thing I'm hearing all about?" At that point, Jones got up and said, "I'm a part of leading this with Mel King and others and what it's about is basically a general strike to seriously get the attention of the Boston community and particularly its power structure that we're not going to stand for racial discrimination in any form in Boston anymore. That's what it's about. And we have put out a call to folks to stay out of work."[94]

Brooke already knew this because he had been getting calls from business-people, saying things like, "These folks . . . are talking about not coming to clean the John Hancock building on the 26th of June. We can't have that."

Jones continued, "This is what it is. We asked them to stay out."

Brooke said, "Well, wait a minute. Well, you know, it may be a powerful action, but once it's done, it's over. Once you shoot your ammunition, you haven't got anything left."[95]

Tom Atkins, general secretary of the NAACP, initially supported Jones and King's idea about a work stoppage. However, when he went back and talked to his people after a planning meeting, they refused to support it. At the June 13 meeting, representatives from the NAACP joined Brooke in expressing their disapproval for STOP. From their perspective, Jones had come out of nowhere, trying to start a major organizing effort without going through the "accession rituals" in the Black community.

Despite Brooke's and the NAACP's protestations, Jones and King held their ground. Jones told Brooke, "Look, this is what's in play. Now if you're suggesting that we stop this, I couldn't stop this, and Mel couldn't stop this. Nobody could stop this. This has gotten too far for anybody to stop this. This is beyond us. People are saying they want to do this, and they are going to do it. So, there is no way—first of all, we're not going to try to stop it anyway, but even if we wanted to it's beyond us."[96]

Jones later recalled the events leading up to STOP as follows: "So these folks are coming out like this, something's got to happen. So, I suggest we have a Memorial service [for] Medgar Evers who had been murdered in Mississippi on the 14th. . . . So, we can have a Memorial service, at the Parkman Bandstand in the Common. And so, the folks . . . who are going to be staying out can have a place to go." Brooke thought they were "blowing smoke."[97] The memorial service was scheduled for noon on June 26—the same day as the work stoppage—in a park in North Lower Roxbury. Organizers called for all the people participating in the walkout to join them. The plan was to march down Columbus Avenue all the way to the Boston Common.

On the morning of the scheduled work stoppage and rally, Jones woke up with pain in the pit of his stomach. He wondered whether or not people were going to show up. When he arrived at the gathering place, there were at least four hundred people already assembled. Then they had a rally, and by the time the throngs left, with King and Jones leading the line of people down Columbus Avenue, there were about five hundred people. As they came down Columbus Avenue, people started leaning out of the windows waving at them. They waved back and said, "Come on down. Join us."[98]

By the time they got downtown, their numbers had grown to about a thousand people. They marched all the way around Boston Common—winding around Beacon Street, down Tremont Street, and then came in near the bandstand. Finally, the group arrived to where the memorial service had been set up. People stood up on their chairs and clapped.

Tom Atkins was not pleased. During the lead-up to STOP, Atkins and Jones had made an agreement that Atkins was to speak at the memorial service, but they never called on him. After STOP, the NAACP began mobilizing people to go to the March on Washington on August 28 in an effort to recapture its leadership of the movement. The NAACP prepared twenty busloads of people, who left Boston to go to the March on Washington. In her foreword to the classic *Freedom North*, Evelyn Brooks Higginbotham recalled:

> More than 1,000 persons from Boston participated in the March on Washington. Under the leadership of local National Association for the Advancement of Colored People (NAACP) activists, such as Kenneth Guscott and Ruth Batson, the Boston group rode in 30 buses and in private cars. They were in the middle of their own decade-long fight against de facto segregation in the public schools. In June 1963, the Boston NAACP had led a "Stay Out for Freedom Day." Some 8,000 students boycotted their classes, attending instead "freedom schools," which were set up in homes, churches, and other neighborhood institutions. In February 1964, the Boston NAACP called again for a "Stay Out for Freedom Day."[99]

She continues, "The idea for another school boycott, while in defiance of the threats and injunctions by the Boston school committee, won the support of black community organizations. . . . On February 26, 1964, nearly 20,000 students in the city boycotted their classes. Thus, Black Bostonians came to the March on Washington to reaffirm their ongoing commitment and militant position of defying school board orders, disrupting school board meetings, and holding school strikes."[100]

In light of all the organizing energy going into STOP and the March on Washington, the fight with the Boston School Committee took a rear seat during the summer of 1963. This changed with the start of a new school year. In early September, after the March on Washington was over, Tom Atkins, on behalf of the NAACP, presented a new proposal to the school committee in an effort to "get past this stalemate." As a compromise, the plan included voluntarily redrawing a handful of district lines in a half dozen school classes to reduce racial imbalance. No bus transportation would be required. If enacted, it would result in not a single school in the city having a majority of Black students. Even with these concessions, Hicks's school committee rejected the proposal, with only Gartland dissenting. At the time, Hicks stated, "We're not going to do that." She rejected the proposal, saying that it was unconstitutional—that it amounted to gerrymandering. White Bostonians tended to agree. Later that month, during the primary election, Hicks received more votes than John Collins, the popular sitting mayor.

In September 1963, Tom Atkins, on behalf of the NAACP, presented a plan that would desegregate the schools voluntarily by redrawing district lines, which would call for limited busing. But Louise Day Hicks, chair of the committee, said the proposal equated to gerrymandering and was therefore unconstitutional. Hicks apparently believed the NAACP would leave it at that. For its part, the school committee chose to do nothing. The committee's opposition played favorably with constituents, with Jones summarizing it like this: "You stick with us and your children will never have to go to school with Black kids." By September, the movement took more extreme actions, with eight Black and white demonstrators occupying school committee offices overnight while picketers marched outside in support of school desegregation. On September 7, a sit-in was staged by the NAACP at school committee headquarters. By September 11, the NAACP Boston chapter decided to take its confrontation with the school committee to the courts and on September 22, the "March on Roxbury" took place to highlight the unequal educational opportunity and other conditions caused by racial discrimination. At the gathering, Thomas Atkins, NAACP executive secretary, urged Blacks to register to vote. [101]

It was at this point that the NAACP and other Black leadership began to understand. They were hitting their heads against a stone wall, and they had to seek other routes to get quality education for their kids. Among a variety of plans, Ellen Jackson came up with Operation Exodus. Operation Exodus was based on the fact that there were schools with empty seats available to Black children, but these schools refused to take them due to a lack of transportation. As a result, Operation Exodus proposed to provide private transportation for Black students to predominantly white schools where there was underenrollment. Jackson was supported heavily by Muriel Snowden at Freedom House, who was one of her mentors. Prior to her involvement with Operation Exodus, Jackson had worked for Sarah-Ann Shaw in the Northern Student Movement. Now, motivated mainly by her experiences as a mother, she put together Operation Exodus in order to get Black children to predominantly white schools where there were openings. This was a harbinger of the future of integration in Boston.

Student Actors

Many of these activists were young people drawn into the Roxbury orbit from area universities. One such person was Julian Houston, then a student at Boston University, who would go on to become a judge on the Massachusetts Supreme Judicial Court and a well-respected jurist. Like many students at the time, Houston was determined to get involved in the civil rights movement, and within a month he was going to Roxbury every week to work for the Boston Action Group (BAG). Founded in 1962, BAG was "an independent community organization mobilizing for political and economic equality." Like earlier activist groups, BAG attacked systematic discrimination in employment though boycotts of department stores and other businesses. The group also took on a leadership role in the formation of "parent councils to remodel part of the city's public schools," as a way to challenge racial inequality in Boston's educational system.[102]

Many people who would go on to become important figures in the civil rights movement were in some way involved with BAG. Noel Day, for example, who was a social worker, operated out of St. Mark's Social Center, part of St. Mark's Congregational Church. In 1934, under the late Reverend Samuel L. Laviscount, St. Mark's Congregational Church established the first social service agency for children and youth in Upper Roxbury. The center pioneered in youth development, in "getting the boys off the street," in the words of Reverend Laviscount.[103] Day was the coordinator for BAG, and he worked closely with Melnea Cass, who was a member of the St. Mark's congregation and a major figure in the community, especially among the younger members of the church.[104]

BAG was the kind of organization that drew bright, young people into the fold, including Sarah-Ann Shaw, another BAG recruit. Shaw's mother worked alongside Cass, while her father, who was active in the Roxbury Democratic Club, took her to lectures at Jordan Hall, the Ford Hall Forum, and Tremont Temple, where the young Shaw met Paul Robeson. As a student at Girls' Latin School, Shaw was involved with the NAACP Youth Council, comprised of fifty-eight members from twenty-five different community youth groups and Boston-area churches in 1936.[105] Increasingly involved in community activities, Shaw worked with St. Mark's Social Center and as a member of BAG.[106]

As Shaw later recalled, "There was work to be done in the North . . . [though] people really assumed that everything was fine in the North."[107] In one of its first successful organizing activities, BAG staged a boycott of Wonder Bread until the company finally hired Black men as delivery route drivers.[108] Mel King later described the action in the following terms:

> Crucial to the BAG approach was that initial four month information and education stage during which BAG workers knocked on doors explaining selective buying, citing statistics about the economic status of the average Black worker (at the time Blacks made 52% of the average white worker's wage and one out of three Blacks made under $2000 a year), and organizing block captains for future distribution of information. The first target

Students, parents, and teachers on the steps of the St. Mark's Freedom School on February 26, 1964 (*Boston School Boycott—Freedom Day—St. Marks Freedom*, *Boston Globe* staff photographer, Boston School Desegregation Archival Resources, Archives and Special Collections, Snell Library, Northeastern University).

was Wonder Bread. About 12% of the company's sales was made in Black areas of Boston. A meeting with the personnel manager verified that of its 250 workers, the company employed only eight Black people. All eight workers were production employees in the baking plant, with no one in sales, trucking, office demonstration or other customer relations work.[109]

The goal of the protest was to force the Wonder Bread factory to increase their minority hiring for upper-level paid positions. Although they hired route drivers and people to sweep the floor, they had no Black employees in the upper-level positions.[110] Julian Houston recalled, "We would get together every weekend every Saturday and then we would go out and canvass the community, pass out leaflets, and ask people if they were aware of the situation; knock on doors; talk to them. It was a basic kind of community organizing program."[111] "Then the mobilization began," said King. "On the next Saturday, ministers throughout Roxbury, the South End and Dorchester (all areas with strong Black populations) urged their congregations to boycott Wonder Bread; leaflets were distributed through the neighborhoods asking people not to buy 'Jim Crow' bread."[112]

While a seemingly small victory, it was a major success in terms of convincing a large local employer to break its color barrier. Perhaps if they would do so, others might begin to do so as well. This taste of victory whets the appetite of many of the young organizers involved in BAG, and several of them became attracted to a new organization that was forming out of the colleges and universities themselves, the Northern Student Movement (NSM).

As James Breeden, an important voice in the Boston struggle and head of the Massachusetts Freedom Movement, recalled:

> It was a wonderful time. I mean, no one had—no one had tasks and responsibilities—we had these kinds of concepts, right, and my concept while I was there, to organize the parents of the kids who were getting tutored, right. Now, they had a big tutoring program. They must've tutored about five hundred kids a night. . . . And they had centers—the Northern Student Movement had centers in . . . a lot of churches and the kids came there . . . and what [the] Northern Student Movement did was recruit college students to come in and do the tutoring. And so . . . they had these connections with all these families.[113]

Noel Day ran for Congress in 1964, with the idea that all his people would stay together and do community organizing. In addition to the NAACP in Boston, there was also the local branch of CORE (Congress of Racial Equality).[114]

Finally, there was the Massachusetts Freedom Movement, and that was run by Day and Breeden.

Byron Rushing was a preeminent Boston politician, public historian, and inscrutable Black intellectual. As the founding director of the Museum of African-American History, he rescued the African Meeting House from its fate of being forgotten about (having already been a synagogue), then blazed a trail as a state legislator representing the South End, making much history along the way. Eventually, he became the first Black American in the commonwealth's history to be House minority whip. Rushing described his journey:

> I'm originally from New York City, and then as a child my family moved to Syracuse, New York, so I went to high school in Syracuse, New York. That's how I came to Boston—from Syracuse to go to college. I went to Harvard. That was in the 1960s. And I got almost immediately involved in the civil rights movement and began doing work for the civil rights movement full-time mostly in the North. There were two organizations. One was called CORE, the Congress of Racial Equality. And the other was called—everybody called it NSM; it stood for Northern Student Movement. And I did that work here in Boston and also in upstate New York.[115]

Breeden remembers:

> Blue Hill Avenue . . . [by] 1960, was the major place. Blue Hill Avenue and Dudley Station were the major places where black people shopped in Roxbury. Most of the stores on Blue Hill Avenue were not owned by black people. They were owned by Jews because . . . Blue Hill Avenue had been the major Jewish commercial street when that part of Roxbury was Jewish and then the part of Dorchester south of it was still Jewish. . . . But there was also a lot of vacant storefronts, and so it was a place for organizations to—for relatively inexpensive rent, to move their offices. And so . . . NSM, BAG, CORE all had offices on Blue Hill Avenue and then— and then you had a—the few black businesses like Royal Bolling's real estate place was on Blue Hill Avenue. And so . . . people started to call it the strip and when they were referring to the strip, they were referring to all these black organizations that were along Blue Hill Avenue from about, oh, sort of Intervale Street up to Grove Hall. And Intervale Street was, if you turned the corner, Blue Hill Avenue onto Intervale Street, you

got to the mosque, the Nation of Islam's mosque Masjid Al-Qur'an, Boston, Massachusetts where Louis Farrakhan was the minister.[116]

Sarah-Ann Shaw, who called Blue Hill Avenue in those days "Agency row" recalls:

You had Blue Hill Christian Center which was where Reverend Virgil Wood who was the SCLC (Southern Christian Leadership Conference) person in Boston. Blue Hill Christian Center was also on Blue Hill Avenue. The Unitarian Universalists (Unitarian Universalist Association) had an office on Blue Hill Avenue so it was called sort of agency row, we were all in these storefronts. Those were the days when you worked out of a storefront to show that you were indigenous and with the people and among the people.[117]

Byron Rushing's first full-time political organizing work in Boston was working for the Boston chapter of the NSM, headed by Sarah-Ann Shaw. But first he had to have an interview:

While I was there in Syracuse . . . I meet people who were doing similar kinds of work who are connected with an organization called the Northern Student Movement, and I meet a guy named Bill Strickland. He then is working—he's working in New York City—and I go several times to meetings that he's been running about community organizing and how to . . . deal with increasing the power of black communities and not getting into any kind of integration issues. And, and so . . . I'm trying to decide whether I'm gonna come back to school or not and he—and—but I'm gonna—so I come back—so I—so people know I'm coming back to Boston in the summer of '64 [1964], and he says, "Well, . . . you really need to get connected with the . . . Northern Student Movement chapter, in Boston because they have this big, big program . . . of tutoring kids, right, but their politics, they just can't get their politics straight. They don't know what to do with the parents." He says, "You really, you know, with the stuff that you've been doing in Syracuse, you should really get connected with them. So, call up this—call up this girl I know there. She's really slick, right, . . . but she, she—you know, but the thing has sort of grown beyond her and she needs to get focused, you know, so call, call her up." . . . So, I come, I call up Sarah-Ann Shaw and, and say I wanna work . . . , [and] Sarah-Ann says, well, you have to be interviewed. So, I get interviewed, and I go to work for Northern Student Movement.[118]

Ellen Swepson Jackson, who became known for her work later at Freedom House, also worked for Shaw as a parent organizer, after which she broke off and founded Operation Exodus. So, in a sense, the NSM was also dealing with the school desegregation question, because Jackson, according to Shaw, "had cut her teeth" as a parent organizer for NSM.

Conclusion

On June 11, 1963, President John F. Kennedy stated, "Too many Negro children entering segregated grade schools at the time of the Supreme Court's decision nine years ago will enter segregated high schools this fall. . . . The lack of an adequate education denies the Negro a chance to get a decent job. . . . Today there are Negroes unemployed, two or three times as many compared to whites, inadequate in education, . . . unable to find work, . . . denied equal rights, denied the opportunity to eat at a restaurant or lunch counter or go to a movie theater, denied the right to a decent education, denied the right . . . to attend a state university even though qualified. It seems to me that these are matters which concern us all, not merely Presidents or Congressmen or Governors, but every citizen of the United States. This is one country. It has become one country because all of us and all the people who came here had an equal chance to develop their talents."[119] When President Kennedy appointed an Irish Catholic to the office of U.S. attorney for the District of Massachusetts in 1961, he made good on that promise. The U.S. attorney's name was W. Arthur Garrity. A graduate of Holy Cross College in Worcester, Garrity's steady agile mind, studied fortitude, and cautious persistence made him the perfect person for the job.

The headline of an article that appeared on April 5, 1965, in the *Boston Globe* stated the case plainly: "Rights Movement Gaining in Boston" the headline trumpeted. The occasion for the article was the upcoming arrival of Dr. King in Boston to address a rally on the Boston Common on April 23. Only three weeks before, more than thirty thousand people had gathered on Boston Common for a rally in memory of Rev. James J. Reeb, a newcomer to Boston who was slain in Selma, Alabama, while assisting with the civil rights movement. He had gone there, he said, to see the relation between what was going on in Alabama and what he found in substandard housing in Boston. There was a surge of national outrage at Reeb's death, and it was that event, more than anything else, that focused the national spotlight on Selma.

Four days after Reeb was killed, President Johnson delivered the voting rights bill to Congress, famously invoking the language of the movement when he said "we shall overcome" in his televised address to the nation. In a strong show of solidarity in tribute to the slain Reeb was an NAACP float, which was included for the first time in the St. Patrick's Day Parade in South Boston on March 17, 1964. Reeb died of injuries received when he was beaten while leaving a restaurant in Selma, Alabama, only a week before. The inclusion of the NAACP and the larger symbolism of the float was criticized by many. Members of the Roman Catholic Interracial Council marched with a sign reading "Beidh an buadh 'inn," the words in Gaelic for "We shall overcome." They were spat on and insulted by rowdy members of the crowd watching the parade.[120] The article concluded that "the civil rights movement, whose targets have been concentrated in the South, is beginning to take aim in Boston."[121]

CHAPTER FIVE

Say It Loud, I'm Black and I'm Proud, 1967–1970

There are small fires all over the United States and there is a fire here
in Roxbury and nobody is listening, and the fire that consumes Roxbury
will also consume Boston.

—Bill Russell

Around the country I have been doing a lot of things and I wanna bring out
some of the things because I want you to know that I am more than just
an honest man who sings and dance and screams or something on stage;
I want you to know that I am a man, a Black man, a soul brother.

—James Brown

By the late 1960s, James Brown was more than just another Black entertainer; he had become an influencer. By 1968, he had taken the process out of his hair, started wearing an afro, and was talking about Black pride for his people. While most Black Americans were certainly proud of their Blackness, it was James Brown—especially for young people—who made people unafraid to be Black—and proud. Following a string of hits, including socially conscious songs like "Don't Be a Dropout" and "Money Won't Change You," Brown finally began to enjoy crossover success in the late 1960s.

As his reputation grew, Brown became more strident in his language regarding the uplift of Black people—both in his music and in his public utterances.[1]

With the social turbulence of the 1960s, many Black artists had choices to make—where to play, where not to play, how much to address the growing social unrest in their music, thereby risking alienating their white audiences. Brown entered the fray cautiously. Increasingly, Brown felt that because he had such a big platform and a big audience, there was no way that he could just sit back without becoming a voice for his people. He started to tell his story, and he started to tell the story of success and survival in his songs.[2]

Brown's increasing social consciousness became powerfully clear on April 5, 1968, the night after Martin Luther King Jr. was assassinated. Following King's murder, the Black community was not only hurt—it was angry. And many members were ready to take their anger out on the rest of the nation. That night, James Brown was scheduled to perform at the old Boston Garden. To many, this was a powder keg that appeared ready to blow. Indeed,

Boston's newly elected mayor, Kevin White, tried to cancel the concert, citing safety concerns. Tom Atkins, then a city councilor, intervened, making the case for the show to go on with the rationale that if it didn't, "they're gonna try to burn Boston down."[3] Atkins was not the only one. Many members of Boston's leadership structure—both Black and white—believed that if Brown did not perform, rioting, looting, and possibly worse would occur. The main concern was that this mayhem would occur in downtown Boston, where the Boston Garden was located. Brown did not cancel the concert, which has since come to be known as "the Night James Brown Saved Boston," mostly due to a film of the same name, a documentary produced and directed by David Leaf in 2008, which portrays the days following the assassination of Dr. Martin Luther King Jr. on April 4, 1968, when many American cities seethed with rage, riots, and mass destruction of property. But the story of how that happened is one full of twists and turns that could only have been written in Boston. It certainly illustrates some of the peculiarities and paradoxes of race in Boston—especially in the age of Black Power.[4]

James Brown had been booked to perform at the Boston Garden on April 5, 1968, well before King's assassination. Upon hearing of King's death on that fateful evening, Mayor White tried to cancel the concert immediately, fearful that the large Black crowd assembling north of downtown Boston would cause trouble. Instead, it was decided that the concert would be televised, not only to keep people in their homes but also to give the mayor the opportunity to present a message of peace and unity. Leaf's documentary looks at this moment in music history, the politics and money behind the scenes, and the various personalities involved.

While the film presents an interesting moment in music history, it also provides an avenue to understand the unique racial climate in Boston. It introduces and reifies an idea that could be called "Bostonian exceptionalism," meaning the entrenched view that Boston was saved from urban rebellions that occurred in other cities in the 1960s, particularly on the night of Thursday, April 4, 1968—because Boston *did* suffer violence and destruction of property, though it was limited to the Black community itself.

Many commentators reified this myth in the retelling of the legend. One such commentator was James "Jimmy Early" Byrd, who was a disc jockey and the voice of Black radio in Boston, broadcasting from his booth at WILD 1090's offices in Dudley Square (now known as Nubian Square). Despite the mythmaking, this documentary did something interesting, which was to explain how Boston was viewed by the larger Black world. As Cornel West states in the film, "Boston historically has been a liberal city in terms of its intelligencia and self-image, but deeply segregated based on race in terms of its practice."[5]

West continues, "Boston has never been a city that has been highly appealing to Black folk. We don't think of Boston as a center of Black life the way you think of Detroit and New York." And as Jimmy "Early" Byrd states, "Most of the people there did not know what Rhythm and Blues was. They wanted to run me out of town. I understood that they want to run me out of town for playing the jigaboo music. That's what the people outside of town called me; said I was setting race relations back a hundred years."[6] There was a reason Boston did not have a Black-owned FM station. In an interview in the film, Byrd states, "If the concert had not occurred, we would have had the biggest problem in the history of Boston since the Tea Party."[7]

Similarly, the Reverend Al Sharpton, a protégé of Brown's and someone who used to work in his band, says, "If there was a night he had to read the crowd right and use the magnetism of James Brown, that was the night. It was like all his life he was prepared for that night when the world needed him to connect in Boston."[8]

This view that Boston somehow avoided the turbulence around racism has been echoed in other popularized accounts of Boston's Black history. In her 2013 book, *Black Power TV*, Devorah Heitner wrote, "In the week following Dr. Martin Luther King Jr.'s assassination . . . the streets of Boston saw little of the violence that raged elsewhere. City officials ascribed Boston's relative peace to a James Brown concert broadcast live on WGBH, the local educational television station."[9] But this popular retelling of the narrative with James Brown as savior belies the fact that there was rioting in Boston, away from the news cameras and underreported by the media.

The construct of Bostonian exceptionalism is a myth that has impeded racial progress and blocked any real conversation about racial inequity in the city. It has likewise made for an interesting conundrum in Boston's history, one that has largely gone untreated by critical analysis. The myth has stubbornly persisted not only in documentary film but also in the historiography, relatively unchanged since it was crafted and dispatched by the public relations department of Mayor White. The fact of the matter is that Boston not only had rebellions that night (though on a somewhat more limited scale than other American cities) but had a growing Black Power movement as well—one that was galvanized in part by this moment.

The decision was hastily made to go through with the concert, with deals forged and money exchanged to, if nothing else, control Black people from flooding the streets. According to the *Boston Record American*, "A massive mob of youths were milling around the Heath St. housing project in Roxbury wielding clubs and swinging chains."[10] The false alarms started, liquor stores were emptied, a fire blazed in a furniture store, and the crowd began pulling white passersby from their cars and beating them.

Boston's Black community leaders had feared such actions because of the bloodshed they had witnessed and experienced during the welfare riots of 1967, in which volunteer units of young men were formed to cope with inflammatory situations. In 1968, volunteers wearing white armbands went out into the community to cool tempers. Two Black volunteers driving a YMCA truck saved a white motorist from the hands of his attackers by simply carrying him away in their arms. One of the volunteers described the rioters and their anger at the injustice of the system: "It was not safe to be a white man in Roxbury. That's the way it was, and I don't know if that has changed. We will not allow ourselves to be mistreated any longer."[11] Even Black people were in danger. A crowd viciously beat a light-skinned Black man on a motorcycle until one of his attackers recognized him. During the unrest, the police cordoned off a two-mile radius of the Grove Hall section, but looting, arson, and stoning continued until 3 a.m., when rain began to fall. Such actions weren't intended to stop the riots but merely to keep the rioting confined to Black neighborhoods.

While the murder of civil rights leader Martin Luther King Jr. may have provided the spark for the violence that ensued, tensions had been building for some time. The riots around the country were a reaction to decades of injustice and inequality. According to historian Jack Tager, "Boston's violence was more contained and on a smaller scale than in other cities, but it demonstrated the sense of despair and powerlessness of the Black poor."[12]

Other cities burned for similar and varying reasons. As the news of the assassination of King spread, riots broke out in 160 cities, with catastrophic results in the largest urban ghettos. For example, in Washington, DC, there were 11 people killed, 1,113 injured, over 2,000 arrested, and $24 million in property damage. Called in to quell the violence were 12,500 National Guard and federal troops. Similar large-scale violence erupted in Chicago and Detroit, resulting in deaths and damage and leading to a massive infusion of troops. Tager writes, "Every city that contained a Black ghetto, no matter its size, suffered through rioting in revenge for the death of King."[13] Testimony was held about the riots in hearings before the U.S. Senate in September and October 1968. According to the proceedings, during April 4–9 in Boston, five law officers were injured, twenty-nine civilians were injured, and looting and vandalism resulted in eighty-seven arrests, the cause listed as "Dr. King's Death."[14]

Although the rioting in Boston was not on the same scale as that in other major cities, thanks in part to the concert that kept many people in their homes, it would be incorrect to state that Boston was saved from the rioting, which transformed Blue Hill Avenue and other neighboring environs from the once bustling thoroughfares of Black businesses, storefronts, and communities to boarded-up and shuttered housing and businesses that would not rebound for decades. The *Boston Globe* reported that these neighborhoods "seethed with emotion and tension . . . angry bands of Negro youths stoned cars and buses traversing Blue Hill Ave. screaming their vengeance and pathos."[15]

Needless to say, King's death affected people in Boston on a personal level. He had, after all, gone to school in Boston, earning his doctorate in theology from Boston University. Tom Atkins recalled, "King's assassination hit Boston with a particularly heavy impact that there was a sense of loss that was very personal on the part of many people in the city."[16] Another veteran of Boston's school desegregation movement, Ellen Jackson, stated, "We were, you know, naturally all very sad and shocked and frightened, didn't know what was going to happen. And then we heard the smashing of windows and cars with honking going down the street. People were crying and screaming, and it became very chaotic at that point."[17] The net result of the Bostonian exceptionalism narrative is that it only counts violence and destruction of property in downtown Boston a threat; it did not view the many acts of violence and destruction in the Black community as a problem.

The Night James Brown Saved Boston

As previously noted, Mayor White's first instinct was to cancel the concert. Upon hearing this, however, James Brown threatened to sue the city, still wanting to get paid. Brown sent Tom Atkins to speak to the mayor. Atkins countered White's logic, saying, "Kevin, you are doing exactly the wrong thing. If the word gets out in the Black community that the city would not let James Brown come to town and perform in the wake of King's assassination, all hell will break loose."[18] In the end, White conceded and allowed Brown to play the concert. The confrontation did not end there, however.

Still concerned about the potential for a social disturbance, Mayor White decided that the best way to keep people at home and out of trouble was to televise the concert. Atkins stated, "He came up with this idea of trying to get somebody to agree to take the program. Well, that was a big problem. It involved a whole lot of complications that none of us realized at the time."

Ultimately, Mayor White convinced the public television station, WGBH Channel 2, to go ahead with the broadcast live, which it played on both radio and television. This decision was made not only in an attempt to keep people in their homes but also to give the mayor the opportunity to present a message of peace and unity.

Atkins recalled, "The next call I got was from Jimmy Byrd . . . who was the DJ at WILD. He called me at City Hall to say that there was a problem, and that the problem was that a concert scheduled by James Brown for Boston Garden was about to be canceled by the city." Not long after, Atkins received "a call from James Brown, who was calling to complain that somebody had announced that this program was going to be carried out live on television, as a result of which people are lined up at the Garden getting refunds, and then nobody was coming to buy tickets. And that was a big problem. . . . That was the first contact I had with James Brown." Yet there was little Atkins, Byrd, or Brown could do about it. Mayor White had gotten his way. "I'm hoping it's [the concert's] one valve that will let off some steam. And I think it is an appropriate place to happen, because it's a peaceful gathering and that is synonymous with everything that King did," White said.[19]

For Atkins, this posed a problem. "It was also clear that Brown was furious, so nobody wants to meet him. Nobody wants to talk to James. So once again, I'm in the wrong place at the wrong time, I got to talk to James Brown. My first meeting with him is going to be to deal with this man who is going to be livid about all the money he is losing. So, I get in the limousine and I go to the airport, I meet James. Before I can even get him close to the limousine, he is all over me about his money."

According to Michael Ambrosino, "Brown finally arrived in a wonderful dark suit, and a retinue of people. I've never been to a rock concert. I've never seen this kind of entrance, and he looked really fine. And I extended my hand to him and said, 'Mr. Brown, it is very nice of you to allow us to televise this concert tonight because of the situation.' And he looked at me, paused, and said, 'What television?' And I thought, 'Oh gosh, we're now going to have a problem.'"[20]

In many ways, televising the concert proved a clever way to allow white people to quietly avoid having to attend the concert at such a turbulent moment but also to not lose their money and still be able to enjoy the concert on television. With the concert now set to be televised, ticket holders could cash in their tickets for a full refund due to the special circumstances. This was subsidized by the city. Tom Vick was one of the ticket holders who cashed in his tickets for a full refund. He later recalled:

I went to Boston Garden with my tickets in hand just to kind of get a vibe you know, is this going to be cool? Is this okay? So, I go up to the main entrance of Boston Garden and there is this big, burly Irish cop. He said, "Hey, kid, what are you doing here?" And I said, "Well, I came to check out this show tonight. Is it still going to happen?" And he said, "Oh yeah, it is going to happen. But if I were you, I wouldn't come." And I said, "How come?" And he said, "Yeah, I don't know. It could be a little edgy in there. Well, if you want to return your tickets, you can go to the box office, and they'll give you your money back."[21]

The decision to televise the concert was not just about ensuring that white people had a way out without losing money; it was also about controlling Black youth. As Kevin White recalled, "His concert we thought might bring as many as 15,000 or 20,000 Black people from the community, particularly young people into the city, that it just had too much emotion in it not to decide whether that would be a problem."[22] White's description of Black youth with "too much emotion" reveals the racism of city leaders.

White's remarks likewise prompt a question: Was city hall afraid of Roxbury burning or Boston itself? Robert Hall came close to injecting some truth into this narrative:

There was riot in Roxbury. The city fathers and the businesspeople were afraid that the kind of audience that James Brown was likely to attract would come downtown and that that would endanger jewelry store windows and downtown stores down around the Garden. Now they didn't appear to be worrying all that much about the riot, and as long [as] it was happening in Roxbury, Blue Hill Ave, they just want to cordon off the riot here and let it happen. But people got worried when it looked like it was going to spill over and not to be contained. And so, they wanted James to cancel the concert.[23]

This is the critical analysis lacking in many accounts of this misunderstood epoch in Boston's history.

Early on the morning of the concert, White, who had been mayor for only eight months, consulted with Black leaders, including newly elected city councilman Thomas Atkins. The mayor authorized the Black volunteers to continue their efforts and decided that a smaller police presence might help maintain relative calm among the demonstrators. At this point, the riot hadn't started. Atkins and his cohort subsequently roamed the ghetto pleading for peace. Two thousand police officers sealed off the area from downtown.

These actions probably had as much—if not more—to do with containing the level of violence than James Brown's concert.

That same day, the day after King's death, President Johnson issued an appeal to the nation from the White House that stated, "The life of a man who symbolized the freedom and faith of America has been taken, but it is the fiber and the fabric of the republic that's being tested."[24] With violence, vandalism, and smoke from the urban rebellions moving across the nation, late that afternoon President Johnson declared a state of emergency.

Despite the efforts of the authorities, Friday, April 5, 1968, witnessed continued actions against white authority. Roving Black bands in Roxbury, appearing more organized than before, posted flyers on shop doors and windows in the area that proclaimed, "This store is closed until further notice in honor of Dr. Martin Luther King Jr., the fallen martyr of the Black revolution." Another group of four hundred protesters, with walkie-talkies and bullhorns, marched on Roxbury's Jeremiah E. Burke High School. They burned an American flag, then went inside and ripped up a picture of John F. Kennedy, destroyed other displays, and vandalized furniture and water pipes. A member of the crowd stole a white teacher's handbag, another white teacher suffered a head injury, and rioters pulled two white teachers from their cars in the parking lot and manhandled them. The demonstrators demanded that officials close the school to mourn Dr. King. Small groups of Black protesters continued looting stores and stoning motorists, police, and firefighters throughout the day and evening.

With troops protecting the Capitol and the White House, and National Guardsman deployed in other cities, Mayor White asked the governor's office to assemble some guard units to protect downtown Boston as a precautionary measure, though they were never used.

Ultimately, Brown's initial protest about getting paid was resolved due to some behind-the-scenes maneuvering and last-minute negotiations. Brown got his money. White said to him, "I'll give you your money. I'll get you your money. But get up on that stage and I want you to put [on] a performance. And I don't just mean a musical one either."[25] Brown came onto the stage about an hour late due to audio problems and other issues. When he finally did get on stage, he began by paying tribute to King. "First, we got to pay our respect to the late, great, and incomparable, somebody we love very much," he said. "Somebody I have all the admiration in the world for, I've got the chance to meet him personally, the late great Mr. Martin Luther King."[26]

Although Brown's disagreements with King on certain issues, such as nonviolence and Vietnam, were part of the public discourse, Brown put these disagreements aside for the moment, saying, "Dr. Martin Luther King got the nerve, the guts, the drive, the determination, and the wisdom to start something and see it through."[27] According to Charles Bobbit, manager of WGBH at the time, "When Dr. King spoke out against the Vietnam War, Mr. Brown thought he was wrong, because Mr. Brown thought that he is a religious leader. He is not a politician. He is getting out of his bag as we would say, he is getting out of what he stands for. And he can create a problem for himself because the powers that be are not going to stand for this."[28]

As to the matter of nonviolence, this is where Brown as "soul leader" eclipsed his role as mere entertainer. According to Cornel West, Brown was in no way a pacifist: "He disagreed with Martin when he got a chance to talk with him. He said, 'You're a great man. I think you've done magnificent things, but I am not a follower of nonviolence. If somebody hits me, I got to hit him back.'" Al Sharpton further stated, "When we talked about his relation with Dr. King, I think that he respected Dr. King for being sincere. And he has always said to me, 'You can't disregard the fact that this is the man who puts his life on the line.'"[29]

As the word spread of what had happened in Boston, Brown was suddenly thrust into a new leadership role nationally. On the morning of April 6, for example, Washington, DC, mayor Walter Washington told his staff, "Find James Brown wherever he is and ask him to come; he can get through to these people." This was a crucial moment, as it demonstrates that the narrative that "James Brown saved Boston" began almost immediately following the riot. Subsequently, Brown helped to soothe Black people's anxieties through his rhetoric. Brown said, "Education is asset. Know what you're talking about. Be qualified, be ready. Then when you have a problem, be ready, know what you're doing. You know, in Augusta, Georgia, I used to shine shoes on the steps of the radio station WRDW. But today I own a radio station. Now, I say to you because I'm your brother. I know what it is. I've been there. I'm not talking [from] my imagination; I'm talking from experience. Let's live for our country. Let's live for ourselves. Please get off the street."[30] The week following the concert, Brown was basically recruited to become a national spokesperson to Black citizens across the country. His name was read into the *Congressional Record,* and he was recognized with gratitude for his work. This Brown emerged as a national political figure who was becoming known for something other than singing. It was the beginning of Brown as a soul leader. The only problem was that Brown was inexperienced in politics, which later led to endorsing policies such as Nixon's "Black capitalism" and, more importantly, his misreading of the politics of the Vietnam War.[31] In late July, Brown endorsed Hubert Humphrey for president. This produced a backlash from the Black Panthers, who called James Brown "S-O-L-D Brother #1."[32] By the end of the summer of 1968, Brown was under a lot of pressure to prove that he was of the people, that he wasn't a supporter of government policies in Vietnam, and that he was not "some sort of sellout or Uncle Tom or lackey."[33]

On Saturday, April 13, "an uncanny calm settled over the Roxbury-Dorchester district."[34] Mayor White told reporters, "The major trouble has subsided. The city has not undergone the reaction to the degree that gripped other cities in the country. We had communication with Negro leaders, and it is continuing. I feel the worst has already gone by."[35] Ultimately, the King riots culminated in thirty arrests, thirteen injuries, and only $50,000 in reported damages, much less than in other cities. Tensions persisted, however. Later, in September, confrontation again flared up over issues that affronted the dignity of Boston's Black ghetto youths.

In the days following King's death, Black patrols helped to keep the city calm. They wore white armbands, passing out leaflets that said "Cool it" and broadcasting the same message through megaphones and loudspeakers on cars as they drove the streets of the community. Patrol members ranged from "family men and high school students to dropouts, cab drivers, community organizers and the unemployed."[36] These Black patrols were called the Roxbury Youth Alliance. Many of the members of this alliance were the same young Black people who had formed a Freedom Security Corps to protect Rev. King during his march through Boston. They also brought the sick and injured to hospitals, and investigated rumors of fires and disturbances. Following the 1967 riots, these young men, along with other young people, came together to protest police brutality, forming a large security patrol that operated out of the Youth Alliance, its function being to calm crowds and observe arrests. They also set up their own photography and karate classes and provided employment information. When sporadic violence began to erupt following word of Dr. King's murder, these young men, who had once guarded King himself, moved swiftly into action to preserve his memory.

Equipped with walkie-talkies, they fanned out into the streets, talking to other young people. They were supported by the Boston Urban League and organizers from Operation Exodus, distributing survival sheets with emergency telephone numbers of doctors, nurses, and community agencies. For many people, the situation demonstrated the need for more Black police officers and firefighters. Moreover, it showed a level of self-determination that had been previously missing from the dialogue. This lasted well into the following week. Deputy police superintendent Warren Blair told the *Boston*

Globe, "They were asking people to cooperate telling them to go home. If they didn't want to, they'd explain why—'use no force.' They helped the community and helped the police. They were a major reason we didn't have major trouble here in Boston."[37]

In the final analysis, it may have been an interview that Chuck Turner gave in the early 1990s that best explained the rationale for curtailing the violence in Boston after Dr. King's death. Because of the welfare riots, which had just occurred the previous year, there was a strong feeling among the Black leadership in Boston at the time that they did not want a white police presence in the Black community that night. Although they may not have seen this far down the road, there may have also been a feeling about the possible gentrification effects that might take hold in the future. In many ways, gentrification was something that did occur in Roxbury and North Dorchester. As Turner stated in *Say Brother* in 1990:

> In 1967 the year before there had been a demonstration at the welfare
> office added in Grove Hall that . . . had led to a major confrontation
> between the police and the community and there had been . . . what
> people call riots . . . a rebellion after that event, and one of the things that
> happened [in] '67 was the community organizations responded by setting
> up teams that would go out and walk the streets, try to talk to the young
> people, try to create a sense of community that would encourage people
> not to take actions that would be destructive in the community. So the
> same thing began to happen.[38]

Not wanting a repeat of what happened in 1967, after the sit-ins at the welfare office, and not wanting white police officers in the community on the night of King's assassination became a strategic move, designed to avoid the problems and pitfalls of what took place the year before.

While the immediate spark for the riots was King's assassination, the underlying cause was decades of injustice and inequality. It was not that Boston was exceptional or special, save in the way that its Black leadership possessed the skill, ability, and power to steer its people out of harm's way, though even then they were only able to attenuate the race problems that visited many American cities after major race riots—certainly Watts, Newark, and Detroit were examples of what Boston did not want to happen to their city. But in this case it was not white Boston but Black Boston—with their champion James Brown—that spared themselves from this fate. This is not exceptionalism, as many historians came to believe but rather an exercise in that abstract concept of self-determination. Leaders like Chuck Turner used that power to try to create opportunities for the Black community, such as the items on his list of twenty-one demands issued just days after King's death. James Brown could not save Boston from what lay ahead. That would take the expert guidance and strategy of Boston's Black intelligentsia and a cadre of select Black leaders who would navigate Boston through perhaps its roughest waters yet.

Boston after Martin Luther King

On the morning of April 8, 1968, there was a memorial service on the Boston Common attended by some thirty thousand people. On the afternoon of that same day, a rally was held by the Boston Black United Front—an organization created out of the riots and headed by Mel King, Chuck Turner, and Byron Rushing—at White Stadium in Franklin Park, at which a list of demands was presented. These demands included the following: "(the transfer of the ownership of . . . [white-owned] businesses to the Black community, . . . every school in the Black community shall have all-Black staff, . . . [and] control of all public, private, and municipal agencies that affect the lives of the people in this community."[39] Boston Black United Front leaders, including King and Turner, met with Mayor White, who rejected those demands but agreed to others proposed by the NAACP and the Black community patrols formed to keep the peace in Roxbury after King's assassination.[40]

Stung by the blatant racism and lack of opportunity that prevailed in the nation, many Blacks sought to increase their self-esteem by emphasizing their roots and their Blackness. Black students at Boston's English High School on Louis Pasteur Avenue in Roxbury organized an all-Black club. They sought recognition of their club and the right to wear African-style clothing and headdresses to school. Over the objections of the faculty, the headmaster gave in to their demands, only to be reversed by the deputy superintendent of schools. (Boston public schools had a dress code at this time, and it was ties and shirtsleeves for men.) This gave birth to an important student movement.

As Tess Bundy has written, "In September 1968, English High senior Glen Grayson and a group of black students began meeting to discuss their dissatisfaction with the lack of black faculty and staff, the school's shirt and tie dress code, and the absence of black history courses. As a protest against school policies, Grayson and a classmate wore dashikis rather than their school uniform to school on September 19, 1968. It did not take long for Headmaster Joseph Malone to suspend the two young men. Within hours of their suspension, black students formed a BSU."[41]

In protest, five hundred Black students walked out of school on Tuesday, September 24, 1968, and demonstrations quickly spread to six more predominantly Black schools. Some of the more footloose students vandalized cars and stores, set fires, and stoned firefighters who tried to put out the blazes, while others assaulted teachers at two middle schools and threw ammonia bombs and started fires at another school. Next door to the school, a meat market had its windows broken and displays taken. White students streamed out of schools, joining in the vandalism and protesting the dress code given to Black students. The all-white Boston School Committee voted unanimously to request the National Guard be called in. Mayor White quickly rejected this demand, believing it would cause more violence. Black youths were protesting the suspension of one student who wore a dashiki to school, and several white students burned their neckties, on the grounds that if Black student didn't have to wear ties, they shouldn't either. All in all, the protest signaled the new direction that young people's protests took in the wake of the death of Martin Luther King.

The next day, September 25, five hundred Black students from different schools met at White Athletic Stadium in Roxbury. As they left, they clashed with police in a violent melee that lasted thirty minutes. "Police were pelted with bricks, rocks, and beer cans from rooftops and along Columbia Rd."[42] Leaving the area, students wandered down the street, assaulting passersby, breaking windows, and burning cars. The next day, matters worsened near the Orchard Park public housing project in Roxbury. Large gangs of Black youths threw rocks and bottles at passing motorists and police cars. Rioters smashed several store windows, but no looting occurred. On one occasion, police officers fired shots in the air, sending young boys running off. The crowd diminished as evening approached and vanished by midnight. Nine police officers and three volunteers were among the sixteen injured. Police arrested eight youths, and damage to property was minimal. The deputy superintendent of schools capitulated, and Black students won the battle over wearing African dress.[43]

Urban Renewal or Urban Removal

Boston's Black population was never particularly large. Although Boston's total population was close to 800,000 in 1930 and the city ranked as one of the nation's most heavily populated municipalities during that decade, Boston had fewer Black residents percentage wise than did any other urban center with a population greater than 500,000. In 1940, Black residents constituted only 3 percent of Boston's population.

Over one-third of the city's Black residents were born in Massachusetts, giving Boston the distinction among large non-southern cities of having the highest percentage of native-born Black residents. Meanwhile, one-sixth of Boston's Black population was foreign-born, emigrating principally from Jamaica, Barbados, and other small British colonial possessions, as well as from the Cape Verdean islands off the West Coast of Africa.[44] As a result of Boston's increasing population, the Black community slowly began to move from Beacon Hill into the expanded South End area. With the development of an affordable public transportation system, there was a migration into Roxbury and Dorchester, which had previously functioned as suburban bedroom communities.

In the late-1970s, Rev. Anthony Campbell—the pastor of a church in Roxbury, a social activist, and a Boston University faculty member—observed: "You have the most deeply divided Black community in the world in Boston; you have about six different classes. They make war on each other, the Haitian Black and the Puerto Rican Black and the Cuban Black and the Nova Scotia Black and the South Carolina Black and the Yankee Black. And let's throw in the Cape Verdeans." He continued:

> And you have people here who are literally here to work to get a social security pension to go back to the island. So, they don't have any long-term stake in staying in the city. You have their children who come up disciplined by the village and the island community life and the pressure of the city, makes that second generation a dysfunctional delinquent and whatnot with that first generation working hard, buying property and saving up to go back home. The catch was if you stand in Deli Station, you'll hear about 30 different accents, it's cosmopolitan. So, if you look at the Black community, you say, "Yep, they're all Black." But they don't think of themselves as all Black. It's a very divided community. The votes are there, but they can never agree on the issues.[45]

The 1950s and 1960s brought many economic changes and spurred the rapid growth and development in terms of Black migration to Boston as more and more Black people migrated to the city in search of jobs and better political and economic opportunities. Unlike immigrants from Europe, notably Irish Americans, racial bias prevented Black people from securing the government jobs that employed a large percentage of the city's workforce. Of these newcomers, many came directly from the South, while others came after a relatively short stay in one of the other ports of entry to the North, including Philadelphia, New York, Chicago, Detroit, and Baltimore.

As more Black Americans and West Indians arrived in the city in search of jobs and improved political and economic opportunities, they were met with an influx of immigrants from Europe, creating unique pressures and conflicts for the relatively small Black population. Throughout the postwar period, racist hiring practices continued to prevent Black people from reaping the benefits of the financial growth of the city. In the 1970s, Black workers earned only about two-thirds of what their white counterparts earned.

In addition to job discrimination, Black people in Boston, like other cities, faced the challenge of redlining and discriminatory lending practices, which prevented them from moving into outlying areas such as Hyde Park and West Roxbury, where many working-class people owned their own homes. Black people were also kept out of poorer white working-class neighborhoods, such as South Boston, Charlestown, and East Boston.[46] As Black residents were pushed out of the historically Black neighborhoods of the South End and Lower Roxbury, ghettos began to emerge in the areas surrounding Roxbury, Mattapan, and Dorchester. The schools and housing in these neighborhoods were inadequate and lacked basic resources.

At the same time, Boston underwent many structural changes in the name of urban renewal as entire neighborhoods were demolished to make way for the city's expansion. As Lew Finfer, longtime Boston-community organizer, stated, "In 1958 the West End Urban Renewal program began, in which the West End neighborhood was torn down to build Charles River Park luxury apartments. West Enders were promised the right of return, but few could afford the market rate apartments they were offered. Jerome Rappaport, former aide to Mayor Hynes, was picked as developer of the Charles River Park Apartments. Rappaport served as a major power broker in real estate interests in Boston over the next 50 years."[47] A citywide and metropolitan campaign to stop the proposed ten-lane Inner Belt/I-95 Extension highway that was to go from Route 128/Dedham through Boston and Cambridge and connect to I-93 in Somerville (including extending I-95 through Lynn) was soon organized. As part of the campaign, a sign was constructed by organizers on the railroad crossing in Jamaica Plain: "Stop I-95—People Before Highways."[48]

In response to the riots that followed Martin Luther King's death, Mayor White and the Boston business community initiated a program that while perhaps well intended, exacerbated the major problems confronting rioting communities like Grove Hall. In the wake of the passage of the Civil Rights

Act of 1968—specifically the Fair Housing Act, which removed discrimination in the housing market and suddenly made it possible for many Black families to purchase homes—a group of bankers formed the Boston Banks Urban Renewal Group (BBURG), which existed between 1968 and 1972. In this well-intended but ultimately failed initiative, banks promised to give home ownership loans to Black families. However, in this program, Black families could only buy homes in existing Black neighborhoods and in the then predominantly white and predominantly Jewish sections of Mattapan and western Dorchester. This "reverse redlining" led to blockbusting by real estate agents and racial conflict as neighborhoods turned from 90 percent white to 90 percent Black in only four years.[49]

The Boston Panthers

Audrea Jones was born and raised in Boston, as were both of her parents. Her father was of West Indian heritage and very much involved in political activities. Her grandmother and grandfather were Garveyites. Her aunts and uncles, also Garveyites, were involved in various movements, particularly in the 1960s. Jones recalls her early involvement in political activities:

> Like the things that preceded the busing, people were involved in school type stuff. So it was pretty natural for me to become involved in political activity. I went to, actually, interestingly enough, I learned about the Black Panther Party because I went to an alternative high school and the alternative high school, I guess it was, I don't know, it must have been pretty revolutionary. But anyway it was part of the Northeastern University and it was an experimental program and the English course was called "Conflict With Social Change," that was the name of the course. In that course they used the Black Panther Party newspaper so that's how I became involved in the Black Panther Party. Actually that's how I got interested in the Black Panther Party.[50]

The Boston chapter of the Black Panthers was unique among chapters across the country in that much of its membership consisted of students.[51] A storefront office at 375 Blue Hill Avenue, in the Grove Hall section of Roxbury, served as the main headquarters of the Boston Black Panther Party. The area is of particular note since it was (and is) the home of Muhammad Mosque No. 11, organized by Malcolm X—the same disaffected and run-down area that was the locus of the 1968 riots in which looting and burning in the wake of the death of Martin Luther King occurred for two days straight.

Jones, who ran the Boston group for a time, recalls her first encounter with them:

> I joined the Party, I was in the Black Student Union, . . . and I was interested in the Black Panther Party 'cause I had been reading about it and I didn't even know there was a chapter in Boston because the people who actually ran this chapter they were all students at Northeastern basically. The Party didn't function like a community organization 'cause walking down Blue Hill Avenue . . . we used to call this Revolutionary Road in Boston because everybody was located on this street. CORE was on this street, the bus, later the Black Panther Party[,] then just regular community based organizations. So, everybody is on this one street on Blue Hill Avenue and I was going to the bus and then I noticed the office that said Black Panther so I went in. Lo and behold one of the people, the person who was actually running that chapter[,] was a brother that I grew up with because he lived in Ruggles Street Project across the street from where I lived. So I knew him very well.[52]

Like most Panther chapters across the country, the Boston chapter was organized according to a central committee leadership structure, which served as the governing body for Panther chapters across the state, including chapters in New Bedford and Springfield, Massachusetts.[53] Gracing the walls of the office were posters, drawings, photos of Huey Newton (imprisoned Panther minister of defense), Eldridge Cleaver, Martin Luther King, Malcolm X, LeRoi Jones, and H. Rap Brown.[54]

Principal leaders of the Boston chapter at its founding on July 4, 1968, included Deputy Minister of Defense Delano B. Farrar and Deputy Chairman Frank Hughes, both Boston natives, as well as Audrea Jones, who was head of the chapter in the 1970s.[55] According to Farrar, the Panthers' goal was to "educate Black folks to our philosophy and let them see how they are being oppressed by the white man. We also want to stop Black against Black crimes."[56] Like the California Panthers, Farrar said that they planned to inform arrested people of their rights and arm the community so that "pigs" (police) will be held in check. In typical Black Panther Party fashion, "The man," he said, "in keeping Black people in check has used the national guard and police. We feel we must do the same." Hughes outlined some of the party's long-range goals, including patrolling police, establishing a nursery for mothers with young children who cannot afford to hire babysitters while they work, and expanding political education classes. Deputy Minister of Education Wendell Bourne and Hughes taught these classes, which were held at Northeastern Universi-

ty's Ell Center and at 366 Blue Hill Avenue. Their approach to political education required their members to read books by revolutionary thinkers such as
Frantz Fanon and Malcolm X.

The Boston Panthers were very involved in activities at local colleges and
universities, including disputes between students and the administration
and appearing as speakers at colleges for lectures and panels. They assisted
the Black Student Union of Boston, a consortium of several area college student unions, during a citywide boycott of schools in the fall of 1968. They also
formed a security patrol when Stokely Carmichael, prime minister of the
Black Panthers at the time, came to speak at Boston University. Indeed, a
great deal of the membership of this chapter was made up of college and
graduate students, similar to the Oakland Panthers.[57] During its heyday, the
Boston chapter informed arrested people of their rights and carried firearms.
From most reports, attempts were made to patrol the Boston Police, but this
was not carried out to the extent that it was in Oakland or Los Angeles. Although the Boston Panthers used the same ten-point program as the national
organization, they were particularly wary of point no. 7, which called for "an
end to Police brutality and Murder of Black People" and dealt with the Panthers' self-defensive posture and right to bear arms. While gun duels with police in California and alleged sniping of police in New Jersey brought most
Panther chapters under investigation by the government, the Boston Panthers claimed that sniping was not part of their repertoire, although they did
keep an eye on police officers in the Black community.

In one of the most dramatic confrontations with Boston Police, six Black
Panthers were arrested at Dudley Station in the first week of September 1969
"for assault and battery, attempting to rescue a prisoner, disorderly conduct
and trespassing."[58] One of the Panthers arrested included twenty-two-year-
old Eugene Jones, future leader of the Boston Panthers. Describing the confrontation, he stated, "We heard the pigs were pushing students around in the
station. . . . A couple of brothers went in to find out. They were told to get
out . . . then we were attacked."[59] Jones explained that the reason that party
members were at Dudley Station was to protest the construction of the
courthouse–police station complex, now located in Dudley Square.

Perhaps none of the Boston Panthers had as many run-ins with the police
as did Robert "Big Bob" Heard, who was one of the men arrested in the Dudley Station protest. In November 1969, Panthers gathered at the corner of
Warren Street and Blue Hill Avenue in Roxbury to call for his liberation, after
he appeared in court the previous week for a probable cause hearing on
charges of armed robbery. With leaflets, signs, and a speaker-car, Boston

Panthers told passersby and people who joined them, "Free Big Bob or the sky's the limit!" According to their version, the charges Heard faced were a frame-up. Heard was subsequently taken into custody and denied bail reduction by the Suffolk Superior Court.

It is important to note the Boston Panthers' engaging in what was practically a rite of passage for Panther chapters: protesting against political leaders who were framed. It not only demonstrates the unity between the Boston chapter and the national network but also symbolizes a Panther consciousness that legitimized the organization, since it was also protesting fellow Panthers' imprisonments. At that time, the list of imprisoned Panthers across the country included the Panther 21 in New York, Bobby Seale in Chicago, Huey P. Newton in California, Erica Huggins in Connecticut, and many others.[60]

Perhaps more significantly, Boston Panthers joined in the national outcry against the killing of Illinois Panther Party leader Fred Hampton by Chicago police. A rally was held in December 1969 in Boston's Government Center, where city hall now stands. At the rally, an alliance was announced between the Panthers and the Weather Underground, a paramilitary offshoot of the Students for a Democratic Society. Audrea Jones, leader of the Boston Panthers Party at the time, was quoted in a newspaper article covering the event, saying, "We did not come out to mourn the death of Fred Hampton, but rather to pick up a gun and intensify the struggle."[61] According to the article, the crowd, predominately white, responded with cries of "right on" and "power to the people."[62] Speakers at the rally urged that all revolutionary groups in "Babylon" come together to "intensify the struggle." Jim Reeves, a leader of the Weathermen group, urged support for the "revolutionary army," including the Panthers and the Weathermen.[63] Perhaps best crystallizing the chapter's ultimate show of unity was their devotion to Huey P. Newton. As deputy chairman of the chapter Frank Hughes put it, "Huey is a political prisoner and symbolizes racism against Black people by the courts. Black people still believe that they can achieve justice through the law. Huey's being in jail shows them that this is not true."[64] Political rallies were still being held for Huey Newton as late as February 1970, including one of approximately fifty people in Pemberton Square, in front of the federal court building.[65] This is significant, since that year marked the Boston chapter's break with Oakland.[66]

Much of this activism coincided with student activism, which had already been going strong by this time in the city. Walkouts were common and had been a powerful tactic throughout the 1960s and early 1970s. As Tess Bundy has written, "The apex of the Boston student movement came in the spring of 1971 when more than fifty percent of Black students staged a city-wide strike of the Boston Public Schools in protest of endemic racism, system-wide segregation, and poor education. The boycott began on January 22, 1971 when administrators at English High School, located in the city's Fenway neighborhood, suspended five Black students on charges of damaging school property. Within hours 200 Black students occupied the auditorium and walked out."

The Boston Panthers worked on forming alliances with members of the Latino and West Indian communities of Boston. In interviews, Farrar frequently mentioned Marcus Garvey and other Black militants who were deported because of their attempts to unite Black people and stop white racism. According to him, the Panthers were working on an alliance with "our Puerto Rican brothers."[67] Other ways in which the Boston Panthers worked with other constituencies was by planning events. For example, the Boston Panthers helped plan a panel discussion in December 1969 at Boston College in which Masai Hewitt of the Black Panther Party, Roy Wilkins of the NAACP, Roy Innes of CORE, and Dr. Ralph Abernathy of the SCLC shared a platform together, perhaps for the first time ever.[68] The event, occurring only weeks after police attacks on Panther headquarters in Chicago and Los Angeles, was marked by a certain uneasiness and urgency, which put the Panthers at center stage.

The Boston Panthers tried to reach every age group in the Black community. Political education classes for teenagers and adults were held regularly, and a Junior Black Panther Party was created for young boys. According to Farrar, the junior group was formed to teach culture, economics, and politics to youngsters, as well as to provide a positive male image, especially for fatherless kids.

The Boston chapter included several women.[69] Audrea Jones was head of the organization during its first few years, until she left the city to run Elaine Brown's unsuccessful 1972 bid for a seat on the Oakland City Council.[70] Jones recalls those early days:

When I first joined the party . . . you know Chico Neblett was the field marshal, the brother who was in charge of that chapter, Deleanor Para, was someone who I grew up with. He actually lived in Ruggles Street Projects. He was like a friend of my brother's; they all went to school together. He was like an older brother; we were all cool. Then we got Susan and a few other people joined the party. Then we got into this issue of nationalism vs. Marxism. The national head of the Party was coming across with a different line than that local chapter. And that chapter was very much influenced by Stokely Carmichael. He basically organized all the people. I think most of the people first started off at Northeastern University. . . . We would literally put out leaflets saying, "Off the Pig."[71]

Chico Neblett was eventually kicked out of the Boston Panthers by Jones and others. At that point, Doug Miranda became in charge of the chapter. As Jones recalls, "I am not sure how we actually did it, but at some point we were in control of the office. We wrote a letter to David Hilliard and we signed it (all six). The letter stated that 'we are the remaining members of the Boston Chapter; we kicked out Chico.'"[72] Hilliard was shocked and came to Boston for about a month to do political reeducation and to make sure the Boston group was "on track." He and others stayed at Jones's apartment, which became the unofficial headquarters for a while:

> My house was the "Panther pad" at that time and he came to my house and stayed there. . . . That is, when we first started the breakfast program; we upped the scale of the newspaper two three four five folds, etc. I don't know how long he stayed with us, but he stayed a few weeks or maybe even a month. That is when Doug Miranda became in charge of the chapter. I was like the communications secretary. So it was cool. . . . When we w[ere] in my house, at the Panther Pad, we used to have to go open up the office in the morning. We didn't even stay in the office 24 hours a day. . . . It wasn't as if someone said to us that the Black Panther party is a communal organization so therefore you know we are going to live together. Prior to us taking over this chapter, people just lived their lives in their own apartments; people didn't live together. You would have maybe a few people living together because they were students. But it just naturally evolved where people started collecting at my apartment and then just being there more and more.[73]

As with the Oakland organization, by the late 1970s the Boston chapter began to wane in membership. By then, the chapter had renounced all ties with the Oakland chapter, which they termed "Black Panther Party II." They also changed their modus operandi with regard to paraphernalia and the policy of open confrontation with Boston police. Gone were the days of berets, leather jackets, and other recognizable aspects of the Black Panther Party. The chapter also moved its headquarters from Roxbury to the Dorchester section of Boston. While the Dorchester group did not have any ties to Oakland, there was no conflict between the Oakland Panthers and the Boston organization according to an article in the *Bay State Banner* from 1977.

According to one party member, Ali Lumumba, "The Black Panther Party II drew its main body of political principles from the Constitution and looked at the struggle of Africans in America as part of an unfulfilled American revolution. We have a Pan-Africanist view," he explained. "For example, we consider the struggle of Blacks in South Africa to be one in the same as the struggle of (colonized) Blacks in America." Asked if they considered themselves to be Marxists, he replied, "We are not Marxists . . . we are not (practitioners) of any of the prominent ideologies. . . . If anyone wanted to categorize our way of thinking, they could say we are Black-nationalist free thinkers."[74]

Conclusion

The period between 1965 and 1980 saw Black Americans shifting their goals and tactics in the civil rights movement, while also witnessing some significant gains. As with other periods, these gains were tempered by white backlash. Even after his death, Malcolm X proved a great influence on the emerging Black Power movement of the late 1960s. Led by young Black men like Stokely Carmichael and H. Rap Brown, Black Power activists advocated Black pride, militancy, and separate institutions. The Black Panther Party, the most militant of the Black Power groups, suffered increased repression by police and other authorities, while implementing useful programs for poor inner-city Blacks. The late 1960s also saw large numbers of urban areas erupt in violence as Black residents became increasingly frustrated by economic disparity and discrimination by police. Some politicians, including Lyndon Johnson, worked to improve conditions for Black people. Johnson's War on Poverty, dramatically reduced and eventually destroyed by the war in Vietnam, provided numerous useful programs for Black economic, social, and political opportunities. The riots and continued problems also forced Martin Luther King to reevaluate his tactics and ideas. Shortly before his death, he focused his energies on economic issues as well as opposition to the war in an effort to maintain gains for Black people.

Black people did, however, make some gains politically, including election to political office in greater numbers. The civil rights movement in the 1970s, in fact, moved away from direct-action tactics and more toward the electoral process as a way of change. Students also played an increasing role in civil rights from 1968 to 1975, protesting continued racism but also pushing universities to accept Africana studies as a legitimate scholarly endeavor. The presidents of the 1970s would prove less helpful than Johnson. Richard M. Nixon proved a mixed bag, pushing some beneficial programs but also opposing desegregation through busing. Jimmy Carter appointed many Black people to government positions, but despite the administration's best efforts, the economic downturn of the 1970s hurt many poor and working-class Black people.

Meanwhile, the Boston chapter of the Black Panthers became for all intents and purposes a reformist organization working within the system. The Boston Panthers served in a social services capacity in the Black community through their free breakfast programs, clothing drives, and schools. The Panthers now had to work with other Black community groups to help solve problems in the Black community, such as unemployment, crime, and poverty. The organization had a school to aid in political education as well as a private health clinic. The clinic had been established very early on, and in 1970 it was mentioned in a news article as the "Franklin Lynch Health Clinic on Tremont Street, operated by the Black Panthers with the assistance of individuals from the medical community," where they dispensed health-care services to the community.[75]

The white working-class responded by electing leaders who defended white neighborhoods at all costs, including the right to retain their own neighborhood schools. In the face of municipal power and the federal court, antibusing extremists resorted to violence to protest against school desegregation, which led to violence in the streets and nearly daily fights in the hallways and classrooms of Boston's public schools.

Competition around jobs was a main source of tension in the city, where the contestation over de facto residential segregation and urban renewal had far-reaching consequences. Although increased opportunity led to some occupational and economic gains for Black community members, compared to whites, those figures remained low. Unlike other cities that had sustained periods of Black migration, Boston's Black community continued to have difficulty achieving political parity with the long-established white ethnic population due to its relatively small numbers.

In spite of the victory of Thomas Atkins for city councilor in 1967, Black Americans were unable to win many seats in local and state government. Without a political voice, municipal jobs, which were often reserved for the relatives of white elected officials, continued to remain elusive to Black Americans. This situation would improve somewhat in the 1970s with the advent of school desegregation.

The riots of 1967 and 1968 gave voice to the discontent of the Black poor. Feeling betrayed and excluded from the American system, angered by their sense of impotence, and demanding to be heard, Black plebeians chose direct-action communal social violence to redress long-held grievances. In choosing rioting to make themselves heard, they joined with a long line of Boston's poor, who for three centuries broke the law rather than suffer in silence. Racial tensions remained high in Boston. While no more ghetto riots took place, poor Blacks turned to violence in retaliation for what they considered to be white provocations.

Ultimately, Black Bostonians were fighting the system, but they were also fighting against multiple myths, one of the most important of these being the myth that Boston was a milder sort of racism than that found in the South—another form of Boston exceptionalism. Racial violence in Boston was a real phenomenon. It was not uncommon for people to be caught after dark and get badly hurt by hurled glass bottles or worse. Like other northern spaces that had seen racial violence—including Chicago, Detroit, and Philadelphia—Boston was supposed to be liberal, a home for higher learning and intellectual thinking. Boston had found a way to become synonymous with these platitudes in the minds of many Americans while keeping its relatively small group of Black citizens under control, and the night of King's assassination is one great example. Indeed, it was King's assassination that led to the rise of Black militancy and calls for Black Power in Boston.

Clashes between Roxbury citizens and Boston police and lawmakers manifested the development of a militant wing of Black politics in Boston that included local and national Black Power organizations. SNCC, the Black Panthers, and other local Black cultural and educational groups developed a significant following in Boston in the 1960s.[76] These clashes likewise placed an emphasis on interracial cooperation. The major issue in Boston has not so much been organizing only for Black advancement but organizing to improve "race relations."[77] This of course is a weighted term that derives from social science and has somewhat negative associations in that it was often deployed as a way of sidestepping questions of injustice. It was particularly effective in Boston.

Mel King's words are instructive about the elusive nature of the seemingly good race relations in Boston: "What people are saying when they say their race relations were good is that Black people kept their mouth shut and stayed in their place." But Black Bostonians did not stay in their place. They fought Jim Crow racism both tooth and nail. But despite these efforts, they could not change the entrenched nature of Jim Crow in Boston. That would have required much more of an acknowledgment of said racism by *all* parties in Boston and a profound transformation in the city's political economy, educational structures, and job market. Judge Garrity's decision forced the city to begin that reckoning.

In the late 1960s, groups like the Boston Black United Front—which was formed after the 1968 assassination of Martin Luther King by Chuck Turner, Byron Rushing, Mel King, and others—would find the delicate balance between militancy and mainstream political leadership. These groups were the embodiment of the true ideal expressed by Black Power advocates of effectuating power in all areas of American life—especially elected office. As Kwame Ture (Stokely Carmichael) and Charles V. Hamilton define it in their classic 1967 work *Black Power: The Politics of Liberation in America*, "Black Power means proper representation and sharing of control. It means the creation of power bases, of strength, from which Black people can press to change local or nation-wide patterns of oppression—instead of from weakness."[78]

Because of Boston's many colleges and universities, Boston activists became insurgents in the vanguard, remaking and rethinking race, inequality, and injustice in the grand experiment of American democracy. Many of them had a ready-made and much-needed constituency right outside the university walls in Roxbury and Dorchester, where the Black community was sorely in need. The Northern Student Movement, which was conceived by Yale undergraduate Peter Countryman and William Strickland (who attended Harvard), became a force to support and bolster the emerging civil rights movement in the South.[79] Often referred to as the "SNCC of the North," the NSM is a good example of the kind of critical organizing that took place in the student movement to reshape the real world. So many of the students, like Robert Hall, Chuck Turner, William Strickland (a Roxbury native), and Byron Rushing, made lasting contributions to the struggle for civil rights in the "cradle of liberty."[80]

SNCC, the Black Panthers, and other local Black cultural and educational groups developed a significant following in Boston in the 1960s. As Black Bostonians turned toward more militant action, they received more and more of the support and attention of Black radicals and community leaders. Roxbury and Dorchester citizens saw the likes of Malcolm X, Stokely Carmichael, and Elijah Muhammad each espousing their own position on Black Power and calling them to join in Black revolt. Black Bostonians' avid support of these radicals led local civil rights leaders like Reverend Virgil Wood, head of the local chapter of the SCLC, to proclaim in 1965 that "the Negro Movement in Boston is beyond the Civil Rights phase."[81] Based on his lifelong commitment to the freedom movement in Boston, he was well qualified to judge.

CHAPTER SIX

Boston, Not Birmingham

Busing as Boston's "Reconstruction," 1965–1988

In the fifties people opposed to our activism would say, "This is Boston, not Birmingham." Yet, in fact this city is to be compared in every way to the most entrenched opposition to civil rights in the South or anywhere else.
—Mel King

When we fight about education, we're fighting for our lives. We're fighting for what that education will give us, we're fighting for a job, we're fighting to eat, we're fighting to pay our medical bills, we're fighting for a lot of things. So, this is a total fight with us.
—Ruth Batson

Okay, now you hear a poor white would call you nigger, but very seldom do you see a white they roll down the window of a Mercedes and yell out, nigga.
—Anonymous Black Bostonian

On the weekend of March 10, 1972, eight thousand Black delegates convened at Westside High School in Gary, Indiana, for the National Black Political Convention. Attendees included such prominent Black leaders as Gary mayor Richard Hatcher, Congressman Charles Diggs, Black Panther Party cofounder Bobby Seale, scholar-activist Vincent Harding, and Cleveland mayor Carl Stokes. The convention focused on the lack of political power and economic opportunity for Black people in America. Touting the slogan "Unity without uniformity," the delegates formulated a political agenda that attempted to address their communities' needs—a national Black political agenda that became known as the Gary Declaration.[1] Poet and activist Amiri Baraka (also known as LeRoi Jones) presided over some of the most contentious sessions and helped diverse delegations unite behind a common political program.[2] The agenda described an America in 1972 vastly in need of reform:

> Our cities are crime-haunted dying grounds. Huge sectors of our youth—and countless others—face permanent unemployment. Those of us who work find our paychecks able to purchase less and less. Neither the courts nor the prisons contribute to anything resembling justice or reformation. The schools are unable—or unwilling—to educate our children for the

School Committee picket in the summer of 1963 (*School Committee Pickets, Boston Globe* staff photographer, Boston School Desegregation Archival Resources, Archives and Special Collections, Snell Library, Northeastern University).

real world of our struggles. Meanwhile, the officially-approved epidemic of drugs threatens to wipe out the minds and strength of our best young warriors. Economic, cultural, and spiritual depression stalk Black America, and the price for survival often appears to be more than we are able to pay.[3]

At the Gary convention, a resolution against busing was passed. It stated, "Busing is not the real issue in American education today, and we condemn the dishonesty of the Nixon Administration and other forces in making busing an issue when, in fact, busing has officially been used to maintain segregation for many years in many sections of the country. The real education issue for the Black community is how do we get supreme quality education for all our youngsters."[4]

The fact that busing was raised at all was a surprise to many in the media, as well as the country at large. What organizers at the National Black Political Convention were advocating for was a more independent approach to Black education, which emphasized the principal of self-determination—a strong feature of the civil rights and Black Power movements of the 1970s. This put the delegates of this convention in conflict with the NAACP and other organizations that had come out in favor of busing, including many Black parents and teachers in Boston. Busing was also very much in the public narrative because the previous year, the Supreme Court had ruled that busing was a lawful remedy for segregation in public schools following *Brown*.

The Boston School Committee

In 1965, the Massachusetts legislature passed what became known as the Racial Imbalance Act, which "evolved from a report in April 1965 by an advisory committee appointed by the Massachusetts Board of Education and the Commissioner of Education to study racial segregation in the public schools of Massachusetts generally and of Boston, Springfield, Cambridge, Medford and Worcester individually."[5] The report is often referred to as the Kiernan Report, because it was authored by then commissioner of education for the commonwealth, Dr. Owen B. Kiernan. "The report concluded that racial imbalance was educationally harmful and should be eliminated."[6] Ruth Batson recalls that time:

> When we would go to white schools, we'd see these lovely classrooms, with a small number of children in each class. The teachers were permanent. We'd see wonderful materials. When we'd go to our schools, we would see overcrowded classrooms, children sitting out in the

corridors, and so forth. And so, then we decided that where there were a large number of white students, that's where the care went. That's where the books went. That's where the money went.[7]

These were the days when the Boston Public Schools were still a creature of the white working-class ethnic enclaves of Boston. They served white students and families and were at the same time controlled by them. In a city where the Irish themselves could be the victims of discrimination, it was a way to control and dole out jobs to friends, family, and political allies. As such, the Boston School Committee refused to comply with the Racial Imbalance Act. They disagreed with it in toto, the superintendent responding with his own study, which the school committee endorsed without question.

Ruth Batson chaired the Public Schools Sub committee of the NAACP Boston branch.[8] According to Tom Atkins, legal counsel for the chapter, "We just want[ed] them to say yes there is segregation in the schools, and we wanted them to acknowledge that the problem exists and to commit themselves to do[ing] something about it."[9] To the activists and parents, the request seemed rather humble. As Ruth Batson recalled, "The statement that we made to the school committee said that where there were a majority of Black students, there was not concern for how these kids learned, that there were crowded classrooms, temporary teachers, not enough books and supplies were low and all of that kind of thing. Even physical conditions were poor."[10] Many of the schools Black students attended were old and in disrepair. Some of the buildings dated back to the nineteenth century and were falling apart. The school committee budgeted less to them, and they were on the verge of crumbling.

In a complete denial of the problem, the school committee stubbornly refused to acknowledge the issue. They used trickery and sleight of hand—twisting the words of the activists in ways that made them seem stupid and yet made the larger point: that they did not have to do anything to fix the problems. Parents responded with a variety of strategies throughout the mid-1960s. They organized one-day school boycotts, and the Northern Student Movement set up Freedom Schools, with curricula that focused on Black history and emphasized the importance of Black accomplishments. But short-term protest was not enough. Candidates were run for the school committee, but they usually lost. Eventually the state got involved and passed the Racial Imbalance Act of 1965, which outlawed racially imbalanced schools in the Commonwealth of Massachusetts. The school committee not only refused to enforce it but actively defied it. In their intransigence, the school committee left parents and students little choice. By refusing to make even the slightest accommodation, it pushed parents and activists to seek ever more extreme tactics to fight the school committee.

As Ruth Batson recalled, "We decided that where there were a large number of white students, that's where the care went, that's where the books went, that's where the money went. So therefore, our theory was move our kids into those schools where they're putting all of the resources so they can get a better education."[11]

A line had been drawn in the sand. Black parents, teachers, and families knew that without an education, one could do nothing in life. So it became an all-or-nothing fight for the Black parents and children, who saw their very lives at stake. As Ruth Batson put it so succinctly, "When we fight about education, we're fighting for our lives. We're fighting for what that education will give us, we're fighting for a job, we're fighting to eat, we're fighting to pay our medical bills, we're fighting for a lot of things. So, this is a total fight with us."[12] And fight they would.

Because they were too small of a minority in the city to affect the kind of real change they hoped for through voting, parents took matters into their own hands—and as they did so, they became stronger. Some parents, like Ellen Jackson, set up voluntary programs that moved children to empty seats in Boston Public Schools in white neighborhoods. The schools themselves did everything possible to discourage this phenomenon. Even though many of these schools were under-enrolled, principals and teachers did their best to make the students feel unwelcome and, in some cases, even used extralegal means to prevent them from enrolling.

Kim Archung was one of the Operation Exodus kids. When Ellen Jackson first started Operation Exodus, Kim was going into fourth grade, and her brother Lee was going into sixth grade. Known as young prodigies from a very well-regarded Black family in Boston, the Archungs went to the Sarah Greenwood School. The neighborhoods of Roxbury, North Dorchester, and Grove Hall, which had once been Irish, Catholic, and Jewish, were changing, due to the increase in Black migrants from the South and from the Caribbean. And certain schools like the Christopher Gibson and Sarah Greenwood in the Black neighborhoods were overcrowded. As Archung recalled, "The rule on the books was, if there isn't a seat in your neighborhood school for your child, but there's another neighborhood school in Boston that has empty seats, you can put your child in those schools." Archung went on to graduate from Hampshire College and become a teacher in one of the most prominent of Boston's Black independent schools, Paige Academy.[13]

In the late 1960s through the 1970s, Archung was connected to people in the Black Panther Party, the Highland Park Free School, the Bridge, and other community-based organizations that worked on Black educational advancement. During her high school years, she worked with other high school students attending independent schools to establish Black student unions at their various private schools. With these other Black students and those attending METCO, she established a community-based theater company, which produced consciousness-raising theater and put on performances for the various independent schools in Roxbury. As a high school student and young adult, she worked with Joe and Angela Cook to help found Paige Academy, an independent community-based preschool and elementary school based in Roxbury, where she later became head teacher and educational director. Paige Academy was established to combat the lack of quality educational experiences for young children, particularly Black children, in the Boston area. The school was founded on the Nguzo Saba—the Seven Principles of Kwanzaa—which undergird the school's culture and curriculum, and provide a framework for celebrating and honoring the legacy of its African roots. Archung later earned a PhD.[14]

Other parents established their own parent-run, independent schools or sought a safe haven by working with the Archdiocese of Boston to create Black parochial schools. Mary Gunn was such a teacher, who worked at a Catholic school in Cambridge in 1977. Many of her students were Haitian and lived in Boston. As she explained, "Their parents sacrificed everything to send them to private school because busing was a violent experience in Boston." She spent forty years in Boston's nonprofit sector, working with families and children from underserved communities and working directly with schools to provide after-school programs and literacy programs, namely as the executive director of Bird Street Community Center, which provided much needed after-school services in the Uphams Corner neighborhood of North Dorchester.[15]

Besides Operation Exodus, there was METCO, which formed relationships with suburban school districts like Brookline and Newton in its early years, due mainly to the efforts of Hubie Jones, who lived in Newton at the time. METCO was founded in 1966 as a voluntary school desegregation program. As Boston's longest-running such program, it is a direct legacy of these years of school desegregation and has become a national model. METCO bused students outside the Boston district altogether, into the metropolitan area of Boston and its suburbs. As such, it has not been without its controversies, mainly because it has been such a success—a success due mainly to one of its original founders, Jean McGuire, who was featured prominently in the

Eyes on the Prize episode "Keys to the Kingdom." McGuire came from an extraordinary family and grew up partly in Roxbury, partly in Washington, DC
(where she was educated for a time), and partly in Boston's suburbs:

> I went to the Holden School for kindergarten. . . . I went to first grade and
> second grade at the Kimball and the Campbell in Stoughton. I went to the
> third grade at the David Ellis down the street and I went for two weeks to
> the fourth grade at the Higginson and then we moved to Canton. . . . Then
> I went to the Elliot School in Canton on Washington Street . . . and then
> we moved into town during World War II and I went to the Dearborn.
> I went to the Dearborn School and then I went to girls—I went to the
> Dearborn in the class of '44, went to the girls Latin School in '45 . . . and
> then that summer, because we had so many substitutes, it was World War II
> 1945, and I went to some school at English high school with all the kids
> who got bad marks. It was crowded and school was a full school. It was
> mostly boys but all the girls in Latin school were there.[16]

In understanding McGuire's background, it becomes clear that how and why
METCO started, and the way it was designed, came straight out of McGuire's
experience. She recollects, "I have [Route] 138 in my mind and all the years we
would take the bus to go into Boston. I have so many stories about what it was
like to be Black, waiting on the side of 138 and we have the Canton, Stoughton
cops come up by the Sunoco station on 138, shining their lights on you. The
lights that are on the top of the police car. They knew who we were. We're the
only three families in Canton."[17] McGuire essentially came from a family of ge-
niuses. She remembers, "My father subscribed to newspapers and every week
in the mail, we got the *Boston Guardian.* That's a precursor to the *Bay State Banner.* We got the *Pittsburgh Courier;* we got the *Baltimore Afro American* and we
got to learn the constitution every week. And then we had of course the *Christian Science Monitor.* Because if there was an editorial in another language,
which they always have French, German, Latin, you name it, my father made us
translate it if it was in those languages we were taking in school."[18]

METCO drew some of the brightest Black students from Boston, giving
them a real opportunity to gain a very good education. Patrice Shelbourne
was one such student. While students had widely divergent experiences de-
pending on which school they attended, Shelbourne recalled the horrific
treatment of Black students in Swampscott Public Schools. As she explained
it, with a very low rate of college-educated parents in Swampscott, "intelligent
Black children were perceived as a threat." However, her siblings, who attended METCO in Brookline, were treated much better.[19]

Mrs. Joyce Scott Wife Of Liberation School Temporary Principal Teaching 3rd Grade Children At Freedom House, Crawford St. Dorchester

Joyce Scott teaching a 3rd grade class at a temporary Freedom School held at the Freedom House (*Liberation School Class at Freedom House*, Richard Chase [photographer], *Record American* [later *Boston Herald*], Boston Public Schools Desegregation Project, Archives and Special Collections, Snell Library, Northeastern University; courtesy of *Boston Herald*).

The school desegregation period was ushered in by federal district judge W. Arthur Garrity Jr. in 1974, when he ordered the Boston School Committee to develop a school desegregation plan that would require the citywide busing of students. Roberta Logan began teaching in Boston Public Schools that same year. Before that, she taught in the Massachusetts Experimental School System, an alternative school located in Dorchester from 1972 to 1974. This was one of several initiatives begun in Boston as a viable alternative to Boston Public Schools. At that time, Mel King's son, Michael King, was a student at the school. Logan herself had attended Philadelphia Public Schools, graduating from the Philadelphia High Schools for Girls in 1964, which at the time was a predominantly white school. From 1974 to 1976, she was employed as a teacher at Michelangelo School, a middle school in the North End. During the first year of busing, most of the students who were bused into the North End were Asian students from Chinatown and a significant number of recent immigrants, who were English-language learners. According to her recollection, during her second year at Michelangelo School, students from the Orchard Park neighborhood were bused to the North End also. From 1976 through 1989, Logan was a teacher at Phyllis Wheatley Middle School (no longer in existence), one of three schools that were voluntarily integrated, the others being the William Monroe Trotter School and Copley High School, which was eventually renamed after Muriel Snowden. Logan's impact on generations of her students was significant. She later went on to teach at Northeastern University.[20]

This narrative of Black independent schools represents a little-known phenomenon. While it was advertised to students and legally regulated, it was very much under the radar and the noses of the Boston School Committee—but not under their jurisdiction. It became a matter of survival and a fight for the minds of Black children in a school system that abused and mistreated them and did its level best to destroy their spirits at their most vulnerable points. It also became a matter of Black pride and dignity. Instead of begging the school committee to integrate white schools, Black independent schools took matters into their own hands—much like the resolution of the National Black Political Convention, manifesting the ideal of Black self-determination that was a bellwether of the 1960s and 1970s. This different approach bore much fruit.

Independent Community Schools

During the academic year 1964–65, Jonathan Kozol found himself teaching in a segregated classroom of the Boston Public Schools. With no training in education and no experience as a teacher—though highly educated—he was sent into an overcrowded ghetto school on a substitute basis and given a yearlong assignment. However, he was put on a day-to-day salary to teach a fourth-grade class within a compensatory program that had been designed for Black children.

He was later fired because he refused to stop teaching a Langston Hughes poem, "Ballad of a Landlord," which was not an "approved publication" in his fourth-grade class. As he wrote in his now classic *Death at an Early Age*, "The room in which I taught my Fourth Grade was not a room at all, but the corner of an auditorium. The first time I approached that corner, I noticed only a huge torn stage curtain, a couple of broken windows, a badly listing blackboard and about thirty-five bewildered-looking children, most of whom were Negro."[21]

As a result of his firing, the New School for Children was conceived. Jonathan Kozol's firing and the uproar that accompanied it caused many parents to become involved in the development of indigenous community schools. There were three community schools that were associated with one another: Highland Park Free School, the New School for Children, and Roxbury Community School. They received a charter from the state incorporated as the Federation of Boston Community Schools. Dr. Philip Hart served as its first superintendent. He recalls, "I was recruited then to run the Federation of Boston Community Schools. These were alternative schools that black parents had founded in the 1960s because essentially, the Boston Public Schools were racist. So, the black parents came together and formed these alternative schools called the Federation of Boston Community Schools."[22]

Philip Hart and his wife of television fame, Tanya Hart, were also members of the parent organization for one of the schools, the Roxbury Community School, which their daughter Ayanna attended briefly.[23] He recalls, "So, '72 [1972] is when I started running these alternative schools, and they were primarily black schools in the African American community, and I was like the superintendent of schools. I was about twenty-seven, twenty-eight years old. They were the largest budgeted nonprofit agency, if you will, in the city." The schools were truly independent, not funded at all by the city of Boston. "So, part of my job was I had the development office; we raised money. So, it was private foundations, Ford Foundation, local—the charitable community in Boston is very strong. You know, we had a—we were—federal—we had a lunch program, which was federally funded."[24] Hart went on to become a professor at the University of Massachusetts in the College of Public and Community Service, which he helped design and get off the ground.

When Judge Leslie Harris, a legendary presence in Black Boston, graduated from Northwestern University in 1970, he came to Boston and ended up teaching at the New School for Children in 1971. Harris had been offered a teaching job at the University of Japan, which wanted him to teach American history. Then the New School called. "I got asked to teach at this little community school. And they said they needed a Black male teacher. They wanted a Black male teacher, and would I consider doing it," he said.[25] The school offered half the money that Japan was offering, and Japan was giving him a free place to live, but Harris turned the Japan job down. When he took the job with the school, it was for $8,500, which was then reduced to $8,000. He said yes anyway; he hadn't taken the job for the money. He started teaching third and fourth grade to a mixed group. It wasn't structured like the regular Boston public schools.[26]

Unfortunately, Harris's stay at the New School wouldn't last: "New School went broke in December of '71. And what happened was they couldn't pay us. They couldn't pay the teachers. So, I got $25 a week as a stipend to try to live off of. And I lost my apartment because I couldn't pay rent. . . . But at the end of that year, I went to Highland Park pre-school to teach because middle school couldn't afford new teachers anymore. Taught for two years at Highland Park pre-school, then what did I do? Oh, I ended up working for METCO."

Jean McGuire was the head of METCO by that time, and she wanted Harris to go and help establish a new program in Melrose. Harris accepted and gave her a two-year commitment. Harris recalls:

> I respect the people who had the vision. The problem was they had to raise funds and rely on grants. I know that the Ford Foundation was one of the early supporters. But when they changed their focus, or when the grants ran out, the schools couldn't survive because they had no income. The parents couldn't pay tuition. Not enough to pay the teachers, you know. And believe me the teachers, I still respect them because they were paid less than one third of what Boston public school teachers were getting and they end up spending a lot of their own income right back into the school. I got to school between 7:00–7:30 every morning and sometimes didn't leave until midnight. And you know, when I was in New School, we redid the auditorium which also doubled as the gym. . . . My class and I built a science lab in a basement. We had to paint our own classroom and build our own bookcases out of our own money, you know. But those teachers stayed and did that. And it was commitment from the teachers that allowed those schools to survive. It was the commitment of . . . a number of people. It was a wonderful experience for me. You know someone who came from a community where some of the adults mentored me and you know, to come to a community where I got that same opportunity to do it for other people.[27]

Juanita and Ken Wade were two of the people in the community who also led these kinds of efforts. As Juanita Wade would later note, "Parents saw that public education was not offering young people not only the strong education they needed, but the social relationships or recognition of who they were as African-Americans, just wasn't happening in the Boston public school system. So there was a real move, community-wide, to develop institutions that would meet both of those needs."[28] In many ways, the Wades' point of view was in line with the resolution of the National Black Political Convention in the sense that they did not see busing as a school desegregation measure as a good thing for the Black community. Nor were they the only ones. According to Juanita Wade:

> Boston parents had had a taste of controlling their own institutions, and in fact the struggle to desegregate the schools in the manner that the NAACP was putting forward diluted that struggle, was in fact taking power away from parents in their own neighborhoods and saying, "These young people will go all over the place. We will disperse them." So, parents were in fact powerless, in South Boston, in Hyde Park, in Roslindale. Not only were they not able to organize with their neighborhood for quality education in their local schools, but they could not even go in those neighborhoods in safety to organize with those parents. So, the power that they had been able to amass, particularly through the community control struggles, was totally diluted and dissipated.[29]

Wade had a particularly distinct way of characterizing the issues facing the community, and where people stood ideologically, politically, and intellectually:

> We know in the mid '60s, if you think back, many teachers in the Boston Public School System limited our options, told us we were going to be menial laborers, that we were not going to be professionals. . . . I think the struggle in the '70s could have been different if the NAACP and those who supported the suit . . . began to, ah, reframe the question around what parents really want, and not what the lawyers and the legalists saw as important. Parents demanded quality education, the opportunity to determine for themselves what was best for their children. That required a certain amount of political power in Boston, which we didn't have in the late '70s. . . . While a few Blacks held political office on the state level, . . . we did not hold political power in the city, and in fact had no political power as it related to public education. . . . So it could have been different had we been able to change the direction of the struggle.[30]

Joe and Angela Cook, the founders of Paige Academy and other schools, pursued the Black private school route, which was a newer concept in Boston at this time because the students paid tuition. Dr. Angela Cook had been part of the Black Power movement during the 1960s, becoming active during her undergraduate years at Fisk University. Working alongside a group of students, they opened one of the first Freedom Schools in Nashville, which taught young Black children who lived in the inner city. "My colleagues and

I taught them their history and helped them develop a sense of pride in themselves and the work of their ancestors because public education did not teach these concepts." The Freedom School was located in a small storefront on the main dirt road in the Black community and only met on Saturdays. "We served the children a nutritious hot breakfast and taught them among other things the alphabet—A is for Africa. B is for Black. C is for colored, at this time an appropriate label, as well as Negro spirituals and civil rights songs. We took great pride in our Freedom School and worked hard to make it reflect the pride and self-determination we felt in being Black."[31] One of the few original independent schools still in existence, the Paige Academy's impact on Black education in Boston cannot be overstated. Generations of Black students have benefited from this impact and met the goal of the school, which was to produce Black scholars.[32] Juanita Wade echoes these sentiments:

> The implementation of the desegregation plan was very difficult on the Black community. The burden of desegregating the schools fell on Black families from Roxbury, the South End, Dorchester, and Mattapan. Our young children had to ride the buses into communities, into violence, anger, every day. . . . It was uncomfortable, and it was difficult. Many parents at that time said, "I will not do this to my child." Many parents rode in their cars behind the buses so they could escort their individual child through the doorway, through the police barricades, around the angry . . . residents of those neighborhoods. . . . That was a time for, particularly the Black parents, where desegregation, it wasn't worth it.[33]

Tallulah Morgan et al. v. James W. Hennigan et al. (1974)

Despite these efforts, the main battle would have to be fought within the Boston Public Schools itself. In 1972, Black parents, under the direction of NAACP leadership, filed a class action suit against the school committee in federal district court. No one could have predicted what would happen next—a showdown with the Boston Public Schools in federal court. Thomas Atkins was an attorney working with the Boston NAACP. Atkins served as associate trial counsel for the plaintiffs in *Morgan v. Hennigan*. Tallulah Morgan was the named parent in the suit. The class action comprised fourteen Black families in Boston: the Morgans; the Purcelles; the Yardes; the Wheatons; the Reeds; the Vaughns; the Eskews; the Phillips; the Pruitts; the Reeds; the Burdettes; the Crocketts; the Murphys; and the Means. Atkins recalls the beginning of the fight:

When the decision was made to file the lawsuit in the first place, there was no agreed-upon strategy as to what the solution, what the remedy, was going to be. The NAACP did not have a remedy. It didn't have a proposal in its pocket or stashed away in a drawer somewhere as to what the judge ought to do if he agreed with the lawsuit that was filed. And as a matter of law, the nature of the remedy that you get, says the Supreme Court, must be tailored by the scope of the violation you've proven in court. So, you can't really start putting a remedy together, a solution together, until you have proven the dimensions of the problem you've described.[34]

Atkins was also a good friend of Nathaniel Jones, who was general counsel for the NAACP during this time, handling most of the northern school desegregation cases. (Atkins would later succeed Jones as NAACP general counsel, and Jones would become a judge.) Speaking in reference to remedy, Jones explained:

It's part of the remedy at times if necessary, to transport the students. The transportation came about usually because of state law—state law required that when students had to travel a certain distance, it was the responsibility of the school officials to see that they got to the new schools. And that if it's over a mile and a half or two miles, whatever the state law was, they're obligated to transport them, and that's where—that's it. . . . When the court ordered desegregation, oftentimes, the students were assigned to schools somewhat remote from their former school or segregated schools and in every assignment process, they were reassigned to schools some distance from where they had been going . . . and state laws kicked in . . . well, you must transport them.[35]

He continues, "And they didn't know what the plan was. . . . When the court found the segregation, when the court found a violation that the policies— this is particularly in the north—when they found the policies pursued by the school district whether it was a pupil assignment, zoning, housing, what they generally did in the north was to—their defense was, 'Well, we just assigned the kids of where they are—where they live.'"[36]

As Thomas Atkins stated, "We filed a lawsuit in the federal court because there was no other place for us to go. It was literally the court of last resort."[37] Adding to the problem was the fact that because Boston's neighborhoods were separated by race, desegregating the schools would require busing children from one neighborhood to another. For years after busing first began, the anti-busing opposition talked about the value of neighborhood schools. Although some people may have liked their neighborhood schools—the convenience of them and the peace of mind of knowing their children were close—this discourse ignored the fact that there were many who did not like their neighborhood schools and would prefer to go to another school but could not, because they lived in the wrong neighborhood due to the color of their skin. As Jones explains:

> Restrictive covenants, line drawing, the way the school district drew the school district lines, those are all official acts they created or they built upon the segregated pattern of living . . . and if you could show as we did in those cases, we can show that they had options. If they drew those lines east and west instead of north and south, they could have minimized segregation and enhanced desegregation, but that was—that was what he had to prove to the court. If he proved those things to the court like we did in Detroit, Boston, Cleveland, and these other cases in combination, the school board's policies and housing policies which went to restrictive covenants, banking and lending practices, mortgage problems, all those things were—when they were added to the decision of the school board to draw the lines, the court found that those are causative factors. And being causative factors, they were held to violate the Constitution.[38]

Jeanne Theoharis explains school conditions at the time of movement:

> Six of the city's nine predominantly Black elementary schools were overcrowded. Four of the district's thirteen Black schools had been recommended for closure for health and safety reasons, while eight needed repairs to meet city standards. Per pupil spending averaged $340 for white students but only $240 for Black students. Teachers at predominantly Black schools were more likely to be substitutes and often less experienced than those assigned to white schools. The curriculum at many Black schools was outdated and frequently blatantly racist, and the school district overwhelmingly tracked Black students into manual arts and trade classes, rather than college-preparatory ones. The school district also segregated through pupil assignment policies that fed Black students into high school in ninth grade and whites in tenth—and often into different junior high schools before that . . . in addition to the racial gerrymandering of attendance zones (many schools were located at the edges of irregularly shaped districts.[39]

On June 21, 1974, federal district court judge W. Arthur Garrity ruled that the Boston School Committee "was guilty of consciously maintaining two separate school systems, one Black, one white."[40] The remedy was citywide busing to start that September. Less than a mile separated Roxbury—the heart of Boston's Black community—from South Boston, the home of Louise Day Hicks, William Bulger, and other politicians and activists who constituted the bulk of white resistance in the city. South Boston had an Irish lore that was fascinating and full of history but one that also harbored a long and deeply held racism toward Black Bostonians. Black parents held their breath as students were to be bused between these two very different ethnic enclaves.

As Ruth Batson recalled, "When Garrity's decision came down in June of 1974, we were sunk when we heard some of the remedies, the one of busing to South Boston because those of us who had lived in Boston all of our lives knew that this was going to be a very, very difficult thing to pull off."[41] Ellen Jackson provided leadership and resources to the parents, children, and residents of the community through Freedom House. However, no one was prepared for the level of violence that was to come. According to Jackson, "The mood in the community was one of confusion, concern, and fear because the elected officials during that summer of 1974 after the order had been given by Judge Garrity were very often making statements that this would not happen."[42] Batson explains the mix of reactions at the time:

> There were black people and a lot of our friends who said, "Ruth, why don't we get them to fix up the schools and make them better in our district?" And, of course, that repelled us because we came through the separate but equal theory. This was not something that we believed in. Even now, when I talk to a lot of people, they say we were wrong in pushing for desegregation. But there was a very practical reason to do it in those days. We knew that there was more money being spent in certain schools, white schools—not all of them, but in certain white schools— than there was being spent in black schools. So therefore, our theory was move our kids into those schools where they're putting all of the resources so that they can get a better education.[43]

In a series of coffee hours set up in homes throughout the city, Mayor White met with white parents opposed to busing. While he heard them out, he made some very interesting observations, stating, "It'll be a painful process going through it because the South didn't just slide through it, it tore them apart as it'll help to tear us apart."[44] In the spectrum of reaction, White represented the moderate view. His concerns were those about public safety and the city's mandate to comply with the court order. As he explained, "The first recognition is that it's a court order, it has to be enforced by the city, but it's a final decision, that it's irrevocable and that I'm going to be responsible at a minimum for public safety and at a maximum for the social health. In a way it's a little exaggerated, but the morals of the town, it's a moral question as well as a political question. What I did was respond politically."[45]

Batson recalls the response—or lack thereof—of the city:

> As a child I had encountered the wrath of people in South Boston. And I just felt that they were bigoted. I just felt that they made it very clear that they didn't like black people. And I was prepared for them not to want black students coming to the school. Plus, which, they said it. I mean, they made it very clear. The other thing was that there was absolutely no preparation made for this transition. There were a couple of athletes and other people who would go on TV and they would say, you know, "We have this thing that we have to have happen in our city. We're going to be busing kids and so forth and so on. And we have to be brave about it." And you say to yourself, Well, what are they expecting? Here were little children that were going to a school and they were talking about being brave as if some alien from some planet was coming into the school. I never heard any public official on the state level or on the city level come and say, "This is a good thing. We should all learn together."[46]

Three days before school was due to start, a mass rally was held in front of the federal building to protest Senator Edward M. Kennedy's support of desegregation. The crowd pursued and chased Kennedy to the doors of the building, breaking the glass in the process. Kennedy was the target of jeers, boos, and genuine rage. J. Anthony Lukas, author of *Common Ground*, recalled getting the idea to write his magnum opus on busing based on this incident, having read the story in the *New York Times* with amazement.

September 12, 1974, the first day of school, began quietly enough. Under federal court order, and against the wishes of the Boston School Committee, the integration of Boston schools became a study of opposites. A committee of Black parents waited to greet the few white students who came to Roxbury High School. Conversely, in Southie, crowds of whites began gathering outside South Boston High School in the early hours of the morning. Many of the white students were absent, due to an anti-busing boycott. By the close of the school day, more trouble was waiting outside. School buses were attacked as they left South Boston.

The level of racial violence in Boston shocked many Americans and made headlines across the country and around the world. This was not the city known as the "cradle of liberty" that most Americans recognized or had been taught about in their American history textbooks. As Alan Lupo, a columnist for the *Boston Globe* during busing, later commented, "The real story of Boston is the story of two Cities. It's a story of the traditional, alleged liberal, abolitionist Boston, the progressive Boston, the folk who sent Cesar Chavez money for his grape union. The folks who supported the Hungarian revolution in 1800 something." He continued:

> But the other Boston is a very hidebound distrustful, turf conscious, class-conscious, parochial city, full of people who did not make much progress over the years. I'm talking about white folks. They were not middle-income people. They were poor folk and they were running hardscrabble operations. And they were scared folk. And they had had plenty of things done to them. Highways had come through their living rooms. Nobody bothered to ask. Airports expanded into their neighborhoods. Nobody bothered to ask. Some of their neighbor-hoods had been torn down totally, two of them integrated neighborhoods. Nobody bothered to ask them. By the time busing came around, these people were ripe for revolution.[47]

One of the most interesting things about the anti-busing opposition was the number of tactics whites borrowed from the Black freedom movement. Whites staged a citywide school boycott, a tactic they unapologetically borrowed from the civil rights movement. This is interesting not least because of the many ways that poor whites in Boston simultaneously reviled Black Americans and imitated them. Perhaps it is not that much of a stretch to consider that when one group is looked down on—indeed, seen as less than Black in many ways in the strange hierarchy of whiteness—said group will become the most racist toward Black Americans. This particular example was simply one of the many instances of cultural and racial borrowing that speaks to the deeper, more complicated relationship between Irish Americans and African Americans in Boston specifically.

Michael MacDonald writes in *All Souls*, his memoir of growing up in the Old Colony projects in South Boston: "Danny told me that the people who ended up in D Street were 'white niggers.' I'd never heard the term before; and I ran it around in my head over and over again, trying to picture what it might mean, and wondering whether white niggers were friendly with the Black niggers over in Columbia Point, where we were also never to cross through. I didn't hear the term 'white nigger' again until I passed through City Point and found out that I was one myself."[48] The passage continues:

Of course, no one considered himself a nigger. It was always something you called someone who could be considered anything less than you. I soon found out that there were a few Black families living in Old Colony. They'd lived there for years and everyone said that they were okay, that they weren't niggers but just Black. It felt good to all of us to not be as bad as the hopeless people in D Street or, God forbid, the ones in Columbia Point, who were both Black and niggers. But now I was jealous of the kids in Old Harbor Project down the road, which seemed like a step up from Old Colony.[49]

As a result of the boycott, more than 50 percent of all white students stayed home. Jane Duwors, one of the parents from the anti-busing side, recalled, "The boycott was that if there were no children in school, they couldn't implement the plan. So, we decided to—and it came from another thing, it came from the Freedom Schools in Roxbury in the '60s. We had a community meeting, asked the parents, explained what we thought and asked the parents if they would go along with the boycott. The majority of people did."[50]

Luis-Orlando Isaza offers another perspective:

As a student leader in Colombia, prior to my entering the United States in 1965, I was intellectually aware of the tragic history of racism in the country. But I was not really prepared for the emotional impact of witnessing the neglect and insults propelled in the South at a dear Black friend, Marcos, a fellow student immigrant. Once at Brandeis I was glad to hear of the Massachusetts School Desegregation Act and appalled by the often cited racist, vicious and malignant statements of Louise Day Hicks, whom I believed was then the chair of the Boston School Committee, in opposition to any implementation efforts. Sometime in the early seventies the NAACP brought a class action suit to Federal Court demanding implementation of desegregation plans, which resulted in Judge Garrity issuing a plan and ordering its implementation. The opposition and disobedience to implementation of the plan was most pronounced in South Boston, the home of Louise Day Hicks. As riots and protests developed, involving injuries and arrests, I heard of the Progressive Labor Party organizing "non-violent" marches in support of school busing. I decided to participate in one of the marches at South Boston High School, only to witness mayhem. The school appeared to be occupied by state troopers, insulted and assaulted with all kinds of objects hurled at them by white youth and adults, while they were seemingly trying to protect black students entering the school. It was chaos. At some point there were people wrestling in the street and others trying to flee the scene. I was one of the ones to flee, in terror.[51]

Finding "Common Ground"

On September 28, 1985, a conference was held at the John F. Kennedy Library
in Boston, called "In Search of Common Ground: A Town Meeting on Race
and Class in Boston," for which J. Anthony Lukas provided commentary. Lew
Finfer, a longtime community activist in Boston, was there.[52] At the gathering, Lukas made some very telling remarks that help to elucidate the discussion on race and class—some of which can be regarded as major admissions
that pave the way forward for a potential rapprochement between the two
ends of the Boston school desegregation debate. For example, "I am not urging class as the only analytical prism through which to view such events. I
advocate not class instead of race, but class and race. . . . Boston's school system was flagrantly segregated by a School Committee, which repeatedly and
blatantly flouted State law and the United States Constitution. Arthur Garrity
had no choice but to order a far-reaching remedy of that segregation. In so
doing, he upheld the law. He deserves our gratitude and respect for that.
Nonetheless, there was a pervasive class bias in his orders."[53]

As in any lawsuit, a suit that is brought to the court can only be adjudicated
within the confines of the law. Lukas conceded that in *Milliken v. Bradley*, the
court overturned a federal district court ruling that required cross-busing between Detroit and its surrounding suburbs. Since the lower court had found
de jure segregation in the city but not in the suburbs, the Supreme Court held
that a metropolitan-wide order "would impose on the outlying districts, not
shown to have committed any constitutional violation, a wholly impermissi-
ble remedy."[54] Surely the suburbs contained the constituency that the court
would least wish to alienate. But whatever the justices' motives, *Milliken v.
Bradley* makes metropolitan remedies very difficult to achieve throughout
the industrial North. The consequences of limiting school desegregation to the
city proper were grave indeed. It meant that the sons and daughters of metropolitan Boston's businesspeople, engineers, lawyers, physicians, professors, ac-
countants, and journalists were, with few exceptions, exempt from Garrity's
orders. Lukas went on:

> I believe in such lawsuits by minorities. That is one of the central roles of
> the law: to preserve the rights of minorities against rampant or tyrannical
> majorities. We must jealously preserve that recourse, what such lawsuits
> can accomplish. The adversarial system, I'm afraid, is simply not the best
> way of making progress in the social arena. Lawsuits can accomplish
> specific limited ends but can rarely resolve social conundrums. In the
> case of the Boston schools' case, for example, Arthur Garrity's orders

desegregated the city's schools. They gave Boston's Black plaintiffs the rights so long denied them by Boston's politicians. That is important. But, in my view, they did not achieve social justice.[55]

This is a view that has been adopted by most Bostonians. They blame Garrity. They blame the suburbs. They blame everyone but the Boston School Committee, who had almost ten years to get it right but whose immovability forced the hand of Boston's movement.

As Lew Finfer has written, a major influence on the school desegregation decision happened during a September 20, 1971, meeting at the Patrick O'Hearn School (now called the William Henderson Inclusion School) in the Field's Corner section of Dorchester. Some four hundred parents, most of them white, filled the school auditorium, while several hundred more listened outside. Finfer writes, "The impetus for the gathering was a vote taken by the School Committee that year to overturn a vote it had taken in the late 1960s involving the construction of a new school on Talbot Avenue named after a longtime school committee member, Joseph Lee. The school had received special state funding on the condition that it be opened as an integrated school, and the School Committee had agreed to this at a time when the neighborhoods around the Lee School were overall somewhat integrated." [56] James Vrabel also concluded the same thing:

> On the very warm night of September 21, 1971, more than 500 parents—most of them white—filled the auditorium of the O'Hearn School for a special school committee meeting in which the board was to discuss reconsidering its vote. . . . The size and the mood of the crowd had a particularly strong effect on school committee member John Craven, who had already announced his intention to try to advance his political career by running for the city council in the next election. When Craven switched his vote that night, it caused the Lee School to become racially imbalanced and the Massachusetts Board of Education to withhold $14 million in state aid due Boston schools that year and freeze some $200 million that had been set aside for the construction of new schools in the city.[57]

The change would also prompt the state board to stop waiting for the Boston School Committee to come up with an acceptable racial imbalance plan and develop one of its own instead.

The *Boston Globe* chronicled the moment, "Bowing to the will of hundreds of Dorchester parents, the Boston School Committee last night reversed itself and voted, 3–2, to abandon a plan to racially balance the new Lee

School in Dorchester." The vote, which allowed about 225 white children to continue attending their traditional neighborhood schools and officially admit more than 200 black children to the Lee, was "greeted with cheers and applause from more than 400 parents packed into the sweltering O'Hearn school auditorium."[58]

The takeaway point from this is that, as Vrabel and Finfer contend, the school desegregation court order never had to be; there was already progress being made, and it was all tied to the construction of new schools. Monies were being made available by the state, which administrated the federal money for schools. And in large part, the state was sympathetic to the concerns and complaints of these parents and of the issue. Although the Racial Imbalance Act passed the legislature, it didn't mean that everyone voted for it or that everyone supported it. As Vrabel points out, there were several attempts—some nearly successful—to overturn the Racial Imbalance Act: "From the day the Racial Imbalance Law was signed, Hicks and the other elected officials who got in line just behind her did everything possible to keep it from succeeding. Every year, Hicks and the school committee submitted imbalance plans they knew wouldn't satisfy the requirements of the law. And every year, the Massachusetts Board of Education rejected those plans, and eventually began withholding millions of dollars in education aid from Boston's already financially struggling public school system."[59]

It would not be until 1970 that Hicks was no longer on the committee, as by then she had won a term in the U.S. House of Representatives. With different leadership, the Boston School Committee began to entertain the possibilities of self-desegregation, but the damage by Hicks had already been done, and it was too little, too late. As Vrabel explains, "The school committee finally seemed ready to comply with the law by accepting state funds to build a new Lee School in a racially diverse part of Dorchester, with the understanding that the school would be racially balanced. By the time the school was ready to open in 1971, however, the area had become a predominantly minority neighborhood. So in August 1971, the school committee voted to bus some 400 white students from the nearby Fifield and O'Hearn Schools so that it could meet the requirement for those state funds."[60] The solution was one that dictated that if the state held this money for new school construction, it could work with different communities in the problem areas to try to create new schools that would be racially balanced—and the state was pretty lenient, as the "Lee School" episode suggests. In ignoring the obvious effects of segregation that were happening, the anti-busing advocates lost the thing they cherished most: the "neighborhood school" concept. This change hurt those neighborhoods, and really hit them where they lived. High school athletics were affected. Classrooms were affected. Lives and careers changed. For some, opportunities that they felt ought to have been theirs were taken away—a severe punishment for the crime of racial exclusionism and an unwillingness to share the wealth of the City on a Hill. Vrabel writes, "In 1963, when the much more modest Atkins Plan was proposed, there were only 16 segregated schools in Boston, and they could have been desegregated by redrawing a few school district boundaries and without resorting to any busing at all. But by 1965, the state classified 45 schools in Boston as being 'racially imbalanced,' and compliance meant that thousands of students would have to be bused."[61]

It is true that the growing movement was originally proposing very modest ways of addressing the segregation of the schools, and as Vrabel accedes, Tom Atkins himself had proposed a simpler plan at first, and perhaps it could have been done quite simply that way. Almost everything that would have come from what Ruth Batson calls the Black educational movement would have been very mild or would not have caused as much disruption as the court order ended up doing.

But of course if you have a bill due and you never pay it, you most likely missed your chance to do it the easier way and now collections is involved and there are penalties and fees. Much like the "Lost Cause" interpretation of the Civil War by the American South, which began to refer to it as the "war of Northern Aggression," ROAR (Restore Our Alienated Rights) and other anti-busing elements chose an intransigent path and would have none of it. By digging in so early and not being willing to budge, they left it to the court to decide. The court happened to draw the name of Judge Arthur Garrity, an Irishman who was friends with the Kennedys and who apparently had a burning sense of justice on many issues. The sense of betrayal that many whites felt toward Garrity—Irish Americans in particular—is impossible to overstate.

Unfortunately for the anti-busing forces, Garrity handed down a strong, practically unimpeachable legal decision. One of the reasons why it was so strong is because of the timing. Remembering that *Brown v. Board of Education* made an exemption for de facto segregation, Garrity essentially waited for two Supreme Court cases to be tried: *Swann v. Mecklenburg* in Charlotte, North Carolina, and *Keyes v. School District Number 1* in Denver. Those decisions—which stated that de facto segregation can be remedied and is unconstitutional, just as is de jure—was a major change in the law that made *Morgan* possible.

As Lukas writes in *Common Ground*, "Lacking a definitive Supreme Court precedent on which to rely, Garrity studied the Gary, Cincinnati, and Kansas

City cases on the one hand and the Hillsboro, New Rochelle, and South Holland cases on the other. But the case which weighed most heavily on him was the only school desegregation suit tried by a federal court in Massachusetts since the *Brown* decision."[62] Lukas continues: "In *Keyes*, seven justices put the capstone on the evolving doctrine of Northern school desegregation. Denver's schools had never been officially segregated—their segregation probably grew out of relatively innocent housing patterns. But henceforth the origin of segregation—whether by law or by residence—would not matter. What would matter was the immediate cause. In cities like Denver, the issue would be whether local authorities had maintained, reinforced, or expanded residentially based separation by covert techniques, and then whether their actions were guided by 'segregative intent.'"[63]

Those cases formed the protective constellation around *Morgan v. Hennigan*. There was no denying the clarity of implication of a segregated school system, and the particular pieces all moved into alignment. Many often asked, Why does it only apply to Boston and not the suburbs? Why is it that it only focuses on the city of Boston, for a judge that lives in Wellesley? That's a misunderstanding. The case in Detroit says very clearly that one couldn't do that and is very clear on the question of "metro" versus city. That would not have been legally acceptable ground—and moreover, it didn't meet Garrity's standard. Lukas writes:

> Boston seemed to him [Garrity] an infinitely more compelling instance of intentional segregation than Denver had been. But the judge was determined to produce such a tightly reasoned decision that it would satisfy even Justice Powell, whose opinion in *Keyes* had outlined a rigorous standard of proof for such Northern school cases. So Garrity worked hours each day at the long table in his chambers, beneath the signed photographs of Jack and Robert Kennedy; then, after a quiet supper at home, he worked well into the night in his second-floor study. But the job went slowly, partly because he was burdened with several other major cases, partly because his diligence required that he personally examine each of the thousand-odd exhibits—depositions, minutes, charts, computer printouts.[64]

Garrity's 152-page opinion came on June 21, 1974. He found that "all of the city's students, teachers and school facilities have intentionally brought about and maintained a dual school system. Therefore, the entire school system of Boston is unconstitutionally segregated."[65] As Lukas notes, "In producing such a document, the judge had two principal objectives: first, to ensure against reversal on appeal, and second, to overwhelm Boston's persistent opposition to desegregation by the sheer weight of evidence and the power of his logic. He achieved his first goal. Six months later, the Court of Appeals upheld Garrity, noting, 'In the light of the ample factual record and the precedents of the Supreme Court, we do not see how the court could have reached any other conclusion.' And six months after that, the Supreme Court itself let that ruling stand."[66]

Losing Ground

In 1994, another gathering was held at Northeastern University, this time organized by Ruth Batson, an instrumental activist in the fight for school desegregation in Boston. The goal of the conference was to provide a forum for individuals active in the Black educational movement in Boston from 1954 to 1975 to detail the events of that period as well as their contributions and experiences in improving educational opportunities for Black children in Boston. The larger goal, however, was to respond to the book *Common Ground* by J. Anthony Lukas.

Lukas's book placed poor and working-class white families at the center of the story of school desegregation, while giving short shrift to Black activists, parents, and children. In Lukas's and others' telling, including that of popular writer Alan Lupo, busing was a story about the white working-class families in places like South Boston and Charlestown who were "running hard scrabble operations" and "had not progressed very much economically." These "white working class" people, according to Lukas, were likewise victims of urban renewal and economic displacement amid the transition to "the new Boston." Lukas thus portrayed these pro-busing advocates as "victims" at the same time as he argued that they demonstrated some sort of symbolic class solidarity with Black people because they both occupied the economic bottom rungs of Boston society. This false dichotomy, in which all whites are working-class laborers and all Blacks are poor, misses the fact that neither group was monolithic in this way. Such is the way, however, that the story of busing in Boston is told—in generalities.

As Lew Finfer wrote in an article celebrating the fortieth anniversary of the 1974 federal court decision, "Busing and desegregation. People who were there then use only one of those terms to describe what happened. African-Americans and liberal whites called it desegregation, as in court-ordered desegregation, and poor and working class whites called it busing. This divergence of words symbolizes the division that racked Boston then and continues, to some extent, to this day."[67]

This myopic view does something more: it removes race from the discussion and effectively erases the vibrant parent-led movement to rid Boston of Jim Crow education in its school system. In the quest for healing and reconciliation, it is this kind of position that writers have settled on because it represents a middle ground, or a "common ground," effectively dismissing race from the conversation. It also represents an assumed class solidarity that was clearly not there. No class solidarity, for example, stopped white people from yelling racial epithets or holding bananas as the school buses arrived or shouting, "Go home niggers." Obviously, there was no class solidarity happening there. Nor did Irish Americans own feelings of inferiority stop them from looking down on Black Americans. Rather, it seemed to only accelerate such emotions. The truth is that class does play a major role in this story—just not in the way it has been popularly depicted.

Lukas attended Harvard University, where he majored in government. He was the editor of the *Crimson*, Harvard's daily newspaper. He served in the U.S. Army and wrote for the *Baltimore Sun*, eventually joining the *New York Times* in 1962. He was an award-winning writer, winning the Pulitzer Prize in 1968. Before writing *Common Ground*, he wrote three other books, in addition to founding and editing a magazine. Lukas spent more than seven years researching and writing *Common Ground*. From Lukas's point of view, the struggle over school desegregation was not simply about race but about economic class.[68]

In looking at the crisis, there are several questions that have not been fully explored: How can we understand the resistance to busing by people on all sides of the issue? As Jeanne Theoharis has written, "The 1986 publication of J. Anthony Lukas's Pulitzer Prize–winning book *Common Ground* . . . galvanized many in Boston's Black community to put forth their own histories of Black families, community organizing, and the city's turmoil surrounding school desegregation. The dismissing of three decades of Black activism and the dysfunctional portrayal of the book's main Black family in Lukas's book was galling to local activists like Ruth Batson, who had spent the better part of their lives fighting for educational equity in Boston and against these pathologizing images of Black families."[69]

For years after its publication, Batson, James Green, and many others wrote reviews from the perspective of the Black community and were completely ignored. In addition to Batson, who declared, "Lukas hijacked our movement," James Green wrote: "Common Ground is a classic example of how history can be distorted. Since it continues to be touted as the book of record of this era, I feel compelled to correct the record and, in the words of the great historian and creator of Black History Month, Carter Woodson: 'TO FILL IN THE MISSING PAGES.' Many Black people have been education activists, workers in the equal rights vineyard. We were educational patriots loyal to our cause." He continues, "In *Common Ground*, the debate over desegregation is conducted largely among Harvard social scientists; it is a dialogue between white liberals and neo-liberals, not a dialogue within the black community where there was an important discussion over community controlled schools. The others become central figures in the struggle, Ellen Jackson, Mel King and Paul Parks are ignored." In all its many pages, Ruth Batson is mentioned only twice.

Jon Hillson, an education activist and author, wrote in a review that *Common Ground* "negates two things. First, the rich and powerful record of grassroots Black community activism that marked the fight for school desegregation starting in the 1950s and continuing through the climactic years after the Garrity order. . . . The efforts during the 1960s by Boston Black figures such as Ruth Batson, Ellen Jackson, and Mel King are given little or no mention. Projects and activities on behalf of Black rights are written out of history. . . . Central Black leaders like Boston NAACP President Thomas Atkins disappear from this history."[70]

In 1985, Thomas Atkins himself reviewed *Common Ground*, writing in direct tones: "Inexplicably missing from Lukas' collection of 'notables' are all of the many Blacks, whose roles in Boston's desegregation saga dwarf that of the White, Hicks, Winship or Medeiros. The absence of a credible Black leader permits, or forces, Lukas' narrative to ignore the broad unity that characterized the Black community's search for a way out of the substandard system of educational apartheid fashioned by Boston school officials." He goes on to say, "Missing from *Common Ground* is the Black community effort that included establishing Operation Exodus (sending Black students to other Boston public schools through open enrollment), METCO (sending Black students to other public schools in suburban communities), The Bridge (sending Black students to private schools), Catholic Bridge (sending Black students to parochial schools), and a variety of private or experimental schools started by the Black community and their white allies."[71]

But the argument was often made about the pathology of the Black family that he chose, the Twymons. Although that was a long-standing critique, it appears that it was never quite compelling enough. *Common Ground*, draped in its Pulitzer Prize–winning glory, became the favorite of the literary establishment. So, while people were often making the claim that this book did damage, they couldn't quite explain how. And then there was an article that appeared in the *Boston Globe* on April 14, 2021. Tito Jackson, who had served as a city councilor from the Roxbury district, mounted a mayoral campaign against the incumbent Marty Walsh, which was ultimately unsuccessful. It is, however, an important Black mayoral campaign, to be placed with the likes of Mel King's unsuccessful bid in 1983. Jackson's life was altered, not only by the events depicted in *Common Ground* but by the book itself.

Jackson, who was a METCO student at Brookline High School, recalls, "I was going to school in Brookline and seeing what opportunity and affluence looks like and then I went back to Grove Hall and seeing the impact of poverty and there's visible prostitution and the like. So, there was always that kind of day–night continuum and then I got to college, and this correlates with how I got to this place about looking for my mom." Upon finding out about his birth mother and that she was a Twymon, Jackson immediately thought about *Common Ground*: "I literally rushed home and grabbed a copy of the book." He continues:

> I have like four or five copies and I just started reading and I got to the chapter that little Rachel has a baby. And you read it and it's totally a paragraph that I'm in there. And that paragraph actually changes Rachel's life also, because the characterization of Rachel by Lukas in the book was that she was a 12 year old slut. That she was loose and that she was out there. Never putting into context 1975, never putting into context that it makes no sense for this mom who was heralded for being so strict, that her 12 year old daughter ends up in this situation.[72]

We know how many lives were hurt or affected by school desegregation and busing in Boston. What a lot of people have been claiming for years is that the Pulitzer Prize–winning book, *Common Ground*, was damaging to the story of school desegregation in Boston. It has been accused of distorting and pathologizing history, of fetishizing in so many ways whiteness and the Harvard-educated white male alongside the Boston ghettos, which Lukas spends just as much time in. *Common Ground* has a rape scene and makes many off-color comments; even for the time it came out in the 1980s, *Common Ground* took liberties. But now, for the first time, is physical living proof of the damage of this particular book. Jackson notes, "I went from having no history to there's a chapter in the Twymon section that goes all the way back to Africa that put my family through slavery. So, I literally went from having no history to instantly having some of the best researched genealogy that they had at the time." Asked what he made of Lukas finally, Jackson remarked, "I think he meant well, I do. I think that he failed my mom and failed that family for several reasons; one, when they spoke, my uncles and my mom said that they started reading it and like this, Lukas characterized their conversations in a very Ebonics like fashion. And it turns out that my family actually speaks proper English. So, this component of the difficult broken black family and all that stuff. But I think they liked him. My mom spoke at Lukas' funeral."[73]

Finally adding a real-world example of how damaging Lukas's book could be, Jackson's story is just the beginning. So many people who were interviewed or featured in *Common Ground* say that when it came to the chapters on the Black community, Lukas employed hyperbole and an insufficient amount of restraint concerning his own prejudices, biases, and fantasies about Blackness and the all-mysterious ghetto. Jackson's final analysis bares out this truism:

> But Lukas is an enigmatic character in that he[,] I think, was trying to shine some light and some truth on what was happening, I think he got lost in the sauce in many regards. I feel like . . . the story and some of the realities that people [are] shining are very important. But I think the characterization of the family was really harmful and I think the most harmful part was he dealt with little Rachel's pregnancy and my birth on one paragraph. But then I was gone from the rest of the book. He failed, just as so many adults fail[ed], my mom, to ask her, how did this happen to you? Her pastor never asked her that. He was accusatory. . . . The school failed her because they didn't seek out that information. Social services failed her because they didn't figure out how this happened at the time. The community and the structures that were supposed to take care of her and in this case, this is [an] exceptional writer who had ten years to write this book. So, he failed there.[74]

In the final analysis, this class and white ethnic element of Boston's busing story, made so popular by books like *Common Ground*, needs to finally be addressed. Again, Sugrue is helpful here:

> The Manichean narrative—elitist social engineers versus long-suffering working-class whites—downplays everyday racism, marginalizes the Civil Rights activists and Black parents who fought for decades against Boston's separate and unequal schools, and draws a false dichotomy between urban and suburban whites. Urban whites in Boston and throughout the North were not racial innocents. Their neighborhoods were segregated as a result of long-standing public policies, real estate practices and everyday violence that restricted Blacks' freedom of choice in the property market. A Black person who made the mistake of crossing one of the city's invisible racial boundaries would be beaten or worse.[75]

Racial violence was a fact of life in Boston, often parceled out in the most arbitrary ways for those who violated its invisibly drawn borders.

Examining and repositioning the Boston busing crisis of the mid-1970s within the broader context of the long history of civil rights activism helps us to see the school desegregation struggle in a different light. Instead of a narrative focused almost exclusively (and somewhat sympathetically) on white reaction, Black agency and activism take center stage, situating the busing program as the culmination of nearly three decades of consistent political organizing by Black Bostonians. In addition to community organizing and protest politics, this is also the story of a decades-long legal battle, pressed by community activists like Ruth Batson and championed by Black lawyers like Nathaniel Jones in the NAACP and their allies. The ultimate result was the historic 1974 decision, which would define the busing controversy in the city for the next decade and a half. In this light, Black Bostonians were not merely pawns of Judge Garrity's "judicial activism," as has often been suggested, but engaged participants in the unfolding drama.

Busing as Boston's "Reconstruction"

The notion that busing was Boston's version of Reconstruction is part of an inclusive historical vision that unifies notions of Black competency, agency, and civic participation with what happened in the South a century before— the birth of a centralized, activist government, a nation-state in the modern sense of that term. In order to imagine new ways of seeing what Boston underwent in the 1970s, we must make solid theoretical, scholarly, and logical connections between what was happening on a political and economic plane and how that translated into policy, paradigms, and life for freed men and women in the South shortly after the Civil War and to the end of Reconstruction in 1877.

Reconstruction had profound implications for freed men and women in the South, transforming the lives of Black Southerners "in ways unmeasurable by statistics and in realms far beyond the reach of the law."[76] For a brief shining moment, it seemed that America would finally make good on its professed ideals of "liberty and justice for all." The North's priorities after the Civil War included making money and getting back down to business in the wake of the redemption of the South and the converging of both Northern and Southern ambitions toward reunification.

There are widely diverging opinions as to what freedom meant during this period. However, the dominant notion of freedom for Black people was defined as the vendors of their own labor in the marketplace. Although slaves were freed by the Emancipation Proclamation, it is not clear in what sense they were free. Before passage of the Fifteenth Amendment, they were not able to vote. However, Black Americans were active agents in their own liberation during this period. They struggled for their citizenship through the use of violence and force, methods that the American military state respected. Du Bois wrote, "How extraordinary, and what a tribute to ignorance and religious hypocrisy, is the fact that in the minds of most people, even those of liberals, only murder makes men. The slave pleaded; he was humble; he protected the women of the South, and the world ignored him. The slave killed white men, and behold, he was a man."[77]

Of course, the primacy of land and property in the history and development of the United Sates cannot be overstated, but Black Americans were keen to that too. What else can account for the rapidity with which they organized themselves to stake their claim to the land on which they had toiled for generations? Reconstruction was so many things, but the greatest challenge it posed was to build on the shaky foundation of generations of slavery and a way of life that had developed very differently from that in the North a great experiment in biracial democracy.

The idea of what Reconstruction attempted to do is staggering, and yet it has been viewed by many historians, including Eric Foner, as failing to live up to its potential. It is ironic that the interpretations of Reconstruction by contemporary political figures of that day, such as the racist interpretations of the Dunning School, and those by historians such as Foner conclude that it was a failure. Of course, they all had vastly different interpretations of this time and judged it as a failure for very different reasons, but it is this remarkable moment in the American past that continues to haunt us today. It is America's unfinished revolution.

In thinking about Boston as a southern space in the North, with the ushering in of Irish control of the city following the election of the city's first Irish American mayor, Boston politicians began to align themselves with southern racialized viewpoints by the 1920s. This retrenchment of progressive politics in Boston created the space for the resurfacing of redemption and reconciliation ideologies through the early twentieth century in cities like Boston.

Mel King writes in *Chain of Change*, "Boston also has the reputation of being one of the most racist cities in the country. The racist violence of white people in Boston has been intense in part because the Black community has taken forceful steps to secure its freedom. The struggle by the community of color has been actively opposed by the cornerstones of white Boston society including the Catholic church, the Brahmin power structure and white politicians. As always, from Reconstruction to present, when people of color threaten to become too effective, violent retaliation is carried out."[78]

Marc Schneider's *Boston Confronts Jim Crow* makes the point well. Carefully detailing the ways in which Boston fought off attempts to institute southern-style Jim Crow laws, Schneider portrays Boston almost as "an unreconstructed space." One thinks of Kevin White, Boston's mayor during the busing era, who attended teas to discuss the problem with residents of South Boston and who remarked plaintively about the racial violence then spilling out into Boston streets, saying, "The south went through it, and so must we."[79]

Had Boston dealt with its Jim Crow patterns itself, the federal court order that created school desegregation might not have been needed, but no one seized the opportunity. Boston, in essence, failed to begin the process of Reconstruction until the mid-twentieth century, in part because of its ingrained myths of progressivism. And like other sites of covert and overt racial inequity, it took a long time to both come to grips with the problems and undo the deleterious effects of racism and Jim Crow. Bostonians didn't want to change, but they had to. And ultimately, they paid a heavy price, in ways similar to the South after the Civil War, when the federal government intervened in the enforcement of the Reconstruction Acts.

If there was progress to be made, it would happen locally. And it was all tied to the construction of new schools. The solution, from a top-down perspective, became one of control of the purse strings and money for new school construction. If they could work with different communities in the problem areas to create new schools that would be racially balanced, that may have solved the problem.

Legal and de facto policies and practices with regard to race reveal Boston as a city of contradictions, which remained so for decades without any serious and widespread public discussion until the busing crisis. Despite its representation in history as a site for progressive ideas, the patterns of segregation and racial discrimination that existed in the areas of jobs, housing, recreation, and education continued unchecked well into the twentieth century. Indeed, Boston's active promotion of its image as the "cradle of liberty" and reputation as a bastion of liberalism served as a veneer to hide the real and ever-present racial tensions in the city and its role as the original site of "separate but equal." Rather than presenting this city as the bastion of progressivism by the mid-twentieth century, it is more accurate to identify it as a space that was more segregated, more prone to racial violence, increasingly regimented in terms of its invisibly drawn borders, and more insidious in the subtle and not-so-subtle ways in which race, class, and gender lines were drawn.

Boston was not merely a "southern space" ensconced in the North but rather the original template for segregation in the nation.[80] When considered in this light, the notion of Boston as the "cradle of liberty" appears as a mere myth. Engagement in Boston's historic struggle with race relations presents a much more accurate picture of the importance of this local fight for racial justice. To understand it, one must go back to a campaign not in the twentieth century but in the nineteenth. Jim Crow in the "cradle of liberty" was no simple matter, not so much a legal practice but one of tradition and custom.

Because of the widespread inequality and white intransigence to these myriad protests, Boston did not begin its Reconstruction until the late twentieth century. And still, its Reconstruction remains unfinished. The words of John J. McDonough, head of the Boston School Committee during the time of busing, are instructive here. On December 30, 1974, in the midst of railing against Judge Garrity's decision, he stated: "Reconstruction has finally come to the North, with a vengeance."[81] Busing *was* Boston's Reconstruction—and it has been rebuilding ever since.

Black Churches in Boston

When Virgil Wood first came to Boston in the 1960s, he had already worked with Martin Luther King Jr. for about six years, and he would continue to work at his side for the whole of his national work. In his conversations with him toward the end of his life, his lament was that the movement had not gotten to the economic issue. That was one of the issues that Wood was most interested in. When King gathered twelve hundred urban pastors five weeks before his death at the Sheraton Four Ambassadors Hotel in North Miami, Wood had been harassing him about going to Washington with the Poor People's Campaign—seeking an extension of the welfare state, more food stamps, and so on.[82]

Martin Luther King was about to implement it on behalf of all the poor of America when his life was snuffed out. Virgil Wood always posed a challenge to the Boston community from his post in the Blue Hill Protestant Parish. During the days of the migration of Blacks from Beacon Hill to Lower Roxbury and eventually to Roxbury Highlands, Grove Hall, and parts of Dorchester, Mattapan, and communities along Blue Hill Avenue, there was no community center of any significance in the Grove Hall area, nor were there churches of color. Dialogues between settlement house leaders and Michael Haynes, Virgil Wood, and other ministers began to focus on development, concentrating on the Grove Hall area. Out of that came the Blue Hill Protestant Center, which was pivotal in the civil rights movement during the 1960s and 1970s.

It was the Twelfth Baptist Church, under the sage stewardship of Rev. Michael Haynes specifically, that led the way through the "powerful days" of the civil rights struggles of the 1960s and 1970s. With the massive school desegregation organizing that took place within its walls, the Black church in Boston functioned much as an incubator for social change and justice in the Judeo-Christian sense. It was that kind of fervor and pride that brought Martin Luther King to Boston University, which at that time thought of itself as being the school of prophets who would transform the nature of the society and the way one understands the obligations that a religious person possesses. By being on the hunt for "prophetic" students who might one day create social change, the university built up, over the years, an impressive roster of not only students but faculty, who left a major impact on the city, the country, and the world.

Conclusion

Boston in the 1970s came to embody all the ambiguities, tensions, and social problems in American society of the 1970s that were happening across the country. A civil rights movement that was beginning to grow in Boston and raising important questions about the nature of justice and power—who should have it, who decides, and who can get it. This accompanied a major economic shift in the country, with more money being poured into the Vietnam War than was being spent on schools and domestic concerns. Boston was no exception to all the craziness, violence, and social turbulence of the 1970s that was happening nationally.

In the 1970s, during the years of Boston's busing crisis, the products of those early efforts by traditional civil rights groups to organize along the lines of Marxist theory and dogma reached their fruition in the formation and activities of groups like the Weather Underground, which covered the issue of busing extensively in its journal *Osawatomie*. The question of busing also made its way into the pages of the *Militant*, a weekly socialist newspaper, and the monthly *International Socialist Review*, which offered a socialist analysis of the issues posed by the struggle over busing in Boston. While each approached the issues somewhat differently, they all presented proposals for a campaign of action to "stop the racists."[83] The *Militant* assessed the situation in an editorial written at the height of the struggle: "A victory for the racist mobs in Boston would also give the capitalist government an excuse to retreat on enforcing other laws against discrimination, and would encourage it to deny further concessions to Blacks."[84] These radical anti-capitalist organizations stemming from Marxist-Leninist thinking were an important bridge during the years of the Great Depression. They filled in the vacuum left by the inactivity of the more nontraditional civil rights organizations at the time.

Despite the various campaigns that broadly attacked racial inequality, most of the city's white residents and those in positions of power refused to acknowledge Boston's past investment in segregation. While the issue of education was the lightning rod for the busing crisis, the decades of activism demonstrated both the depth and the breadth of the problem. It would not be until the 1980s, when Mel King ran for mayor, that Black Bostonians would fully enjoy freedom in the city heralded as freedom's birthplace.

By the 1970s, America was already beginning to turn away from the symbolic commitment to civil rights and was less willing to put its money into educational opportunity programs. Affirmative action became a flash point, and people began to hear more and more about reverse discrimination. This was the principal response to school desegregation efforts. This backlash informs the school desegregation story in Boston. It is not a stretch to say that the 1970s were marked by a backing away from the gains of the 1960s. Some might even say that the 1960s were to Reconstruction what the 1980s were to the nadir period. Busing and the Bakke case became signposts for the more conservative rollback of the 1980s that would characterize the Reagan years.

The role of Black student organizations at Boston area universities drew a cadre of Black leadership to Boston, many of whom ended up staying and becoming part of the movement as well as taking on roles in organizations such as the Urban League of Boston, the Boston NAACP, the League of Black Boston Workers, Boston CORE, BAG, the Freedom House, and the Black church in Boston.

Epilogue

On September 28, 1979, Darryl Williams, a Black high school student, was shot by two snipers during a football game in Charlestown. As a result, he was paralyzed for life. That incident along with others gave neighborhoods like Charlestown, East Boston, the North End, and South Boston the reputation of being racist. Race relations in the "post-busing" period, which we can call 1980–95, were bad. Although they were never very good in the twentieth century, they became much worse after the most difficult years of the school desegregation struggle.

The notion of Boston as a "divided city" offers up a way of understanding Boston as a place with many divisions, not only between Black and white but between rich and poor, Protestant and Catholic, Irish and English, African American and West Indian, southern and northern. Black Bostonians saw themselves as being imbued with the same Yankee spirit as other New Englanders but expressed in a different way. During this period, Black Bostonians were largely conservative, concerned with creating positive race relations. They attempted to lead and maneuver through white patronage. They forged an alliance with the Boston Brahmin upper class, whose common enemy was the Irish, and other ethnic whites.[1]

James Loewen's groundbreaking work *Sundown Towns: A Hidden Dimension of American Racism* features compelling examples of thousands of communities that kept Black Americans (or Chinese Americans, Jewish Americans, and so on) out of their towns by force, law, or custom.[2] These communities were sometimes called "sundown towns" because Black people were told—often by signs that used racial epitaphs to make the point not so gently—that they were not to let the sun go down on them and still be in town. As Loewen painstakingly details, Black people could work in these towns, but they would have to be gone by sundown. Besides the signage that warned of this, some communities even had foghorns or whistles that blew to remind people to clear out.

This framework becomes useful in understanding a city like Boston as well. If some of the states "from Maine to California" that Loewen discusses in his book had sundown towns, then Boston could be said to have "sundown neighborhoods." South Boston, Charlestown, the North End, and to a lesser extent East Boston were places where Black Bostonians did not want to be found after dark. They could work there during the day, perhaps drive through there in a work-related vehicle during business hours, but in almost every instance they would have been chased out by the police—but more likely by roving gangs of white vigilantes, who policed their own neighborhoods and meted out a form of street justice that was at once violent, menacing, and in some cases deadly.

This is the living manifestation of "the divided city" that Black Bostonians know only too well. Almost without exception, Black Bostonians above a certain age carry a similar kind of painful story, or memory of an incident, in which they were the subjects of racial violence, taunts, or threats of violence in Boston. These attitudes carried over into the schoolroom, the cashier's table at department stores, banks, restaurants, movie theaters, and just about every other institution and business establishment in Boston. It took the form of a peculiar kind of bitter, hateful, meanness that only Black Bostonians can truly understand, giving rise to a very strange New England racial etiquette, unique to Boston but perhaps only rivaled by southern-style racism, which one could argue is probably its closest counterpart. Black Bostonians became used to this climate, perhaps stronger because of it, but also immune to the daily indignations, personal slights, and painful blows to their self-esteem, which began at birth and continued into adulthood. Perhaps they reasoned that these affronts to their dignity were a small price to pay to live in a city with such educational advantages, supposed employment benefits, and a past rich with history—the city where freedom was born. They may have dismissed such racist attitudes as ignorance, or as desperate acts of a people who themselves were oppressed, considered "white trash" in the strange racial hierarchy of whiteness that had been constructed in Boston, in which not all groups were equally white.

In Defense of Busing

Why isn't the school desegregation struggle in the North looked upon as a functional, continuing wave of the civil rights movement and Black freedom struggle? In *From Brown to Boston*, Leon Jones writes, "Boston—thought to be the hub of libertarianism by some people, may be unique in some ways, but with respect to public education it is no different from cities in the South and elsewhere which have had to face court-ordered desegregation. Indeed, the people who have struggled and demonstrated the stamina to make school desegregation a reality in Boston—namely, Black parents and Black children and Federal District Judge W. Arthur Garrity, Jr.—are deserving of the same high praise as similar pioneers of the South."[3] The civil rights struggle in Boston that resulted in court-ordered segregation was an organized effort by Black parents, families, and teachers to break the back of Jim Crow education in the North. It took different forms in different cities, but we always discuss this as if busing were a top-down governmental program that was "popular" or "unpopular." The conventional wisdom is that busing failed, even though it transformed cities like Boston into more democratic and racially open spaces (after much turmoil, of course). It was painful for Black children.

One way to think about this is to compare it to the campaign in Birmingham in 1963. There, James Bevel and other organizers in that struggle made the decision to involve the children in the movement because of their independence—not being tied down with a job, not having a family to rely on them for economic survival, and less able to be co-opted. It was a very controversial decision (and remains so for many to this day). The Black children who were bused should be seen in this light—as freedom fighters and hostages to fortune in the struggle for Black liberation. At such young ages, of course it is hard on their spirits. Birmingham had its Bull Conner; Boston had Louise Day Hicks.

Make no mistake, many still carry those internal bruises. But they are heroes who, at least in the case of Boston, literally changed the city in terms of race and racism. In 1977, after the implementation of busing in Boston, the first Black member of the Boston School Committee was elected, longtime school guidance counselor John D. O'Bryant.[4] In the 1980s, a Black school superintendent Laval Wilson was appointed. This would have been unthinkable before the court order.

As mentioned in chapter 6, even J. Anthony Lukas had to concede that the law worked to provide justice to the plaintiffs—in this case, Black families and students—as represented by the NAACP. The school board, by violating the Massachusetts Racial Imbalance Law of 1965 (and *Brown v. Board of Education*), forced society's hand. There were a lot of other ways to solve this; people could even have kept their neighborhood schools. However, the problem was that Black neighborhood schools were deeply substandard. Running an illegally segregated (de jure) school system left the parents and courts little choice in Boston. Judge Garrity wrote of the school desegregation struggle: "As for the defendants' asserted neighborhood school policy, findings heretofore may prove that it was so selective as hardly to have amounted to a policy at all. . . . When the defendants have emphasized considerations of distance and safety, it has usually been when they could be used to maintain segregation; students have seldom been the benefactors of this concern when there was no prospect of integration. The neighborhood school has been a reality only in areas of the city where residential segregation is firmly entrenched." According to Garrity, "The Court concludes that the defendants have knowingly carried out a systematic program of segregation affecting all of the City's students, teachers, and school facilities and have intentionally brought about and maintained a dual school system. Therefore, the entire school system of Boston is unconstitutionally segregated."[5]

The BPS lost its funding from the federal government for this in 1973, and it still didn't make a difference. Just like anything in life, there is an easy way to do it and a hard way. When you have broken the law, you put yourself at the mercy of the courts. Busing was not popular, but it broke the back of Jim Crow education in Boston.

In thinking about a conceptual framework for understanding the freedom movement in Boston, one needs to consider the idea of Boston not as a southern enclave ensconced in the North but as the template for segregation for the entire country—as begun in the North. Some historians, including this author, call this "the Deep North."[6]

Drawing from many of them, especially Jason Sokol's formulation of the northeastern United States as an important unit of analysis, this framing becomes helpful in carving out regional niche differences within the larger "North." As our understanding of the "Strange Career of the Jim Crow North" has been more clearly sussed out by Jeanne Theoharis, Brian Purnell, and Komozi Woodard—indeed, as the field they created has broadened—this is the natural future course for this kind of work. As Sokol points out in his wonderful treatment of the Northeast, *All Eyes Are upon Us*, the Northeast is an area that has cherished certain triumphs in equality, civil rights, and integration. It is a complicated and contested space, home to important reform traditions, such as abolitionism and school desegregation, and serving as a historic space of refuge for Black Americans from the time of slavery through the twentieth century, with people migrating from not only the southern United States but also the Caribbean and other parts of the diaspora. Just like the Deep South, what scholars are calling the Deep North has embedded traditions of white supremacy—a long history of de jure racial liberalism that hides its de facto segregation and white supremacist political leanings and origins.[7] (Possibly the first attempt at a history of the Northeast since Sokol's is *Sweet Land of Liberty* by Tom Sugrue, which takes on the entire "conceptual North.")

Despite the various campaigns that broadly attacked racial inequality, most of the city's white residents and those in positions of power refused to acknowledge Boston's past investment in segregation. While the issue of education was the lightning rod for the busing crisis, the decades of activism demonstrated both the depth and the breadth of the problem. In the words of the late Reverend Anthony Campbell—pastor of a church in Roxbury, social activist, and Boston University faculty member—"I think what busing did was to make a lot of people who are concerned about turf and neighborhood and who made their whole lives never leaving that neighborhood all of a sudden becoming afraid that their neighborhood was going to be invaded by a group of people who may want to stay. I think the threat was a threat of real estate and turf and not necessarily a threat about integrated schools or even interracial marriage. And I don't think it brought to the surface anything more than was already here."[8]

The Divided City

At the close of the twentieth century, many Americans, particularly Black Americans, formed a distinct impression of Boston as a racially hostile city prone to ethnic strife, racial violence, and residential segregation. Headlines and images that proliferated in American newspapers from the period in the 1970s known as busing in Boston did much to burn this image into the collective memory of many Americans. Ironically, for this reason, Boston has been thought of as a city hostile to Black Americans.

As a symbol, Black Bostonians have always been emblematic of that distinctly American of dilemmas—the curious conundrum of what it means to be Black in the "cradle of liberty." Boston was the first city in the country to integrate its public schools, yet Boston literally tore itself apart during the turbulent busing crisis of the 1970s. Perhaps for this reason and above all others, Boston's civil rights movement has not received nearly as much attention as the school desegregation period that led up to and reached a crescendo in 1974. Both popular and scholarly attention, where it has been paid, has focused on the busing crisis of the 1970s, ignoring Boston's civil rights activities in the postwar period that paved the way for the educational equality movement to come and focused mainly on issues of employment, housing, educational equality, and quality of life.

By the 1970s, Boston has undergone a major urban renewal, but it was also largely in financial crisis. It could not afford to fund all of its schools or to provide city services to all its neighborhoods. The busing riots that ripped through the neighborhoods of Boston in the 1970s took a heavy toll on the city's national reputation and caused many to question Boston's reputation as the "cradle of liberty."

While the perception of Boston as a place of racism lingers, the reality is more complicated—and even optimistic. The election of Deval Patrick in 2007, only the third Black governor in the history of the United States, is emblematic of change. Growing numbers of Black professionals are settling there, and with the recent election of Linda Dorcena Forry as the first Haitian American state senator from the so-called Southie-seat, claims of the "New Boston" can finally start to be substantiated. Perhaps this is the signpost for Black Bostonians to write a new chapter in the turbulent history of Black Americans in Boston. While many strides still need to be made, the twenty-first century has thus far ushered in some promising developments. Ayanna Pressley, having served as the first Black woman elected to the Boston City Council, made history again when she became the first Black woman in Massachusetts to be elected to Congress.

More scholarship is needed to bridge this historical gap by examining the wide range of Boston's civil rights activities in the earlier period that paved the way for the educational equality movement to come, which focused on issues of employment, housing, educational equality, and inequality. Furthermore, scholars need to relocate Black Americans to the center of the discussion of civil rights in Boston and consider Boston's "hidden-in-plain-sight" legacy of racial violence and Jim Crow–style racism in the North as a starting point for debunking Boston's myth as the "cradle of liberty."

Exploring Black Americans' long movement for racial justice and educational equality in Boston, Massachusetts, allows scholars to highlight the critical roles this community played in the broader national movement. A larger goal of this new scholarship should be to document that history, rethinking the Boston school desegregation crisis and the parent-led movement by relocating Black people back to the center of the busing discussion. By exploring the history that led up to the school desegregation decision, this work traces the development of the Black activist community in the inter- and postwar period and highlights the importance of this work in laying the foundation for the parent-led education movement to come. The presentation of a counternarrative that foregrounds Black community agency and activism helps to construct a more complete historical understanding of the role played by those residents who were most affected by the resistance to the court order and least mentioned in most accounts of school desegregation—Black Bostonians.[9]

Throughout the twentieth century, Black Bostonians, with the support of white allies, have fought, through power and protest, for civil rights, equal employment, and equal educational opportunities. Boston has been the site of often vigorous and vibrant protest activities ever since African Americans' arrival in Massachusetts. Since the 1930s, the decades leading up to the city's infamous busing controversy have been marked by local, national, and international economic dislocation, by the ravages of world war, and by other issues that marked the mid-twentieth century. Throughout this period, Black activists from a variety of protest organizations mounted campaigns in support of national and local initiatives calling for racial equality, racial justice, and economic opportunities.

The history of busing in Boston is as much about Black working-class people as it is about white working-class people.[10] The multiple issues engaged by Boston's freedom movement and the accompanying challenges that reside deep within the city related to race are worthy of deeper study and scholarship.[11] Yet in order to fully answer these questions, we need to explore the decades before the busing crisis for Black Bostonians.

Part of the problem with the narrative of Boston's busing crisis is that the city has been romanticized as a bastion of racial liberalism, linked to the fact that Boston served as the headquarters of the antislavery movement in the nineteenth century and home to the most famous white abolitionist, William Lloyd Garrison.[12] The mythologies of abolitionist Boston and the fact that the city served as the headquarters of the antislavery movement have made it easy not to truly see and reckon with this story. In this period, Black Bostonians lived on the North Slope of Beacon Hill and established some enviable institutions, such as the African Meeting House and the Abiel Smith School for Black children. These and other notable accomplishments have been further romanticized over time. Perhaps more importantly, the city was ambivalent about abolition as it unfolded but would in later years claim that history with a pride that was not necessarily evident in the earlier days of the abolitionist movement. The moniker of "birthplace of abolition"—not to mention the myth of the "cradle of liberty"—has thus served to limit later discussions about the dug-in nature of racism in Boston. As such, the emphasis on Boston as a hotbed of abolition comes to mean very little and is somewhat undermined by the facts. In reality, the city was ambivalent about abolition. Many of those abolitionists now claimed by the city with pride in reality held less progressive social views about Black Americans, with at least one example, Wendell Phillips, not willing to socialize with them. In addition, the moniker "birthplace of abolition" served to limit later discussions about the ingrained racism of Boston.

Legal and de facto policies and practices with regard to race reveal Boston to be a city of contradictions that remained so for decades, without any serious and widespread public discussion until the busing crisis. Despite its representation in history as a site for progressive ideas, the patterns of segregation and racial discrimination that existed in jobs, housing, recreation, and education continued unchecked well into the twentieth century. Indeed, Boston's active promotion of its image as the "cradle of liberty" and reputation as a bastion of liberalism served as a veneer to hide the real and ever-present racial tensions in the city and its role as the original site of "separate but equal." Rather than presenting this city as a bastion of progressivism, in terms of the mid-twentieth century it is more accurate to identify it as a space that was more segregated, increasingly prone to racial violence, highly regimented in terms of its invisibly drawn borders, and more insidious in the subtle and not-so-subtle ways in which race, class, and gender lines were deployed. When considered in this light, the myth of the "cradle of liberty" is debunked, and Boston's historic struggle with race relations presents a much more accurate picture of the importance of this local fight for racial justice.[13]

Acknowledgments

A landmark accomplishment in the understanding and depiction of some of the years discussed in this book occurred with an episode of the documentary *Eyes on the Prize II*, produced by Henry Hampton's company Blackside. The episode, "The Keys to the Kingdom," skillfully documented the years of school desegregation in Boston. Over the years, my colleagues and I have often wondered what that title meant and where it came from. For myself, I had generally assumed it meant that education and learning were the keys to the kingdom. The other alternative was that it must be a passage from the Bible, and it is, in the Gospel of Matthew, chapter 16, verses 18–19.[1] However, I was still not convinced that was its origin. Then I heard a story in Evelyn Brooks Higginbotham's classroom at Harvard University, where she teaches in the History Department. Through our work together with the HistoryMakers, this story was shared with others of our "teaching fellow" cohort during a discussion on the school desegregation story in Boston. Higginbotham shared an observation that many of the students in METCO wore their house keys on a chain around their neck. The keys that Higginbotham spoke of added a new layer of meaning to the ongoing mystery of "The Keys to the Kingdom," the title that Henry Hampton in his sage wisdom chose and, in so doing, made a major contribution to our understanding of this epoch in Boston's history. This title could also be used to describe my own experience in writing this book. The many people documented in that episode and those I am thanking here gave me the "keys to the kingdom" through their love, support, and learning. As such, the first person I would like to thank is Evelyn Brooks Higginbotham, who has been in my corner all the way on this project. I thank her for her mentorship, level of scholarship, and support.

The next person I would like to thank is Jean McGuire, who ran METCO for many years, was an elected member of the Boston School Committee—and a featured participant of that legendary episode on Boston—and reminded me of the specialness of the METCO opportunity. I would call it the METCO miracle, really, as it so deftly made the point about the importance of school desegregation and then modeled how it could work—could have worked all along—had there been more support for change in Boston. METCO has literally brought so many Black Bostonians and their families into the middle class, creating lasting changes and providing advantages, that it cannot be overstated. As such, I'd like to thank the current leadership as well.

Naturally one incurs a great many debts in the completion of a book, and this project is no exception. The ever-winding path toward building enough expertise in any given area to write a book is filled with ideas, people, influences, and experiences. If I had to pinpoint the beginning of my own intellectual awakening it would be when I first arrived on the campus of Boston College in 1992. I had no idea about the world I was entering, but the way was made much smoother by a series of devoted Black faculty members and staff who served as key mentors to me at that tender age. This was made possible by my uncle, V. Paul Deare, who, through his involvement with Concerned Black Men of Massachusetts, introduced me to a universe of people I had never met before, like Dr. Donald Brown, who connected me with Steve Pemberton, the admissions officer who accepted me to Boston College, and therefore the first of many I must thank. Today Steve is an author and wrote a beautiful book about his life called *A Chance in the World*, which recounts some of the history at play here. In addition to being such a moving, life-changing memoir about Steve's life, it is also one of the best treatments of Black history (during some crucial years) in New Bedford and greater Boston that I have read in a long time. By February of my freshman year, I had gotten involved in writing for the school newspaper, the *Heights*. Steve encouraged me to submit some of the articles for a scholarship given every year by the Boston Association of Black Journalists (BABJ), which I did, and I won the scholarship.[2] There was a special reception at the John F. Kennedy Library to which my family and I were invited. The guest of honor was none other than Henry Hampton himself, the director of *Eyes on the Prize*. I have to thank Sarah-Ann Shaw (who was head of the BABJ at that time and has known my family a very long time) as well as Elaine Ray, Barry Lawton, Robin Washington, Leonard Greene, Derrick Jackson, Liz Walker, Don West, Kenneth J. Cooper, Melvin Miller, and many others who sowed a seed in me at an early age. Words cannot fully describe the feeling of pride and joy I felt that night, flanked by my family—including my mother, father, and grandmother—accepting an award in front of some of the most influential Black people in Boston.

In addition to the scholarship funds, all the winners were given a condensed version of *Eyes on the Prize* and a signed copy of the companion volume, *Voices of Freedom*. There's no way to explain how important that gift ended up being in my life, and I have certainly made good use of it. I must have shown that video to thousands of students over the years. *Voices of Freedom* has been an indispensable resource for my research and writing about the period.

I would like to thank the late Andrew Buni, professor emeritus of American history at Boston College. He taught the popular History of Boston Neighborhoods course. I consumed courses in history and Black studies as an undergraduate at Boston College, taken with the broad range of faculty that taught during those years. Those of us who were educating ourselves in such things at the time read many books with great enthusiasm, and my studies there have become the cornerstone of much of my work on Boston. In my sophomore year, I enrolled in my first Afro-American history class, taught by Karen Miller, who would later become a friend and mentor to me. Professor Miller, along with Buni (and many other excellent faculty), offered a solid foundation for work in African American history. I thank her for everything that I am because she was literally my first mentor in the history profession. I would also like to thank the late Amanda Houston, a leader in Boston's Black community, who inherited a disorganized, virtually nonexistent Black studies program when she took over in 1979, turning it into a vibrant and successful place of learning by the time she retired in 1993. I also thank her replacement, Frank Taylor, a Jamaican scholar who was also very helpful in my development in Black studies. Moving to the other side of campus, I'd also like to thank Donald Brown, who was a mentor and father figure to me, as well as Dan Bunche, Paulette Durette, and Janet Costa-Bates.[3] By my senior year at Boston College, I'd begun serving as an editorial assistant for an academic journal called *Transition*, edited at the Du Bois Center, in conjunction with the Department of Afro-American Studies at Harvard University. I'd like to thank Henry Louis Gates Jr. for that opportunity as well as Michael Vazquez, managing editor. I also wrote for the *Encarta Africana Encyclopedia* (in print as *Africana*), and so I'd also like to thank Patricia Sullivan and Richard Newman, who were there at that time. This was an amazing entrée into the field as an undergraduate and would prove important to my later work. Along the way, I also met David Blight and the late great James Horton, who wrote a very important book on Black Bostonians at a Gilder Lehrman–sponsored summer teacher's workshop at Amherst College in 1999. He became a person that I stayed in touch with over the years.

I would like to thank all the professors of the Department of Afro-American Studies at the University of Massachusetts–Amherst, where I attended graduate school. I am particularly indebted to Manisha Sinha, who took special care and time to guide and help me formulate my studies on Boston and New England, which in many ways gave rise to this book. Special thanks go to Manisha for all her advice and for her high standards of scholarship and professionalism. Special thanks are due to my mentor and graduate adviser and all-around guru John H. Bracey, whose encyclopedic knowledge of the Black experience is the foundation of the field. Professor Bracey's guidance about this book has been nothing less than central to its development, as he helped me to situate Boston into the larger Black experience. John Bracey's genius is well known to those of us in the field of Black history. To have studied with him is to have touched the holy grail and the soul of the race. He taught me a system of Black ethics, what some might call a Black sensibility—what one might do or not do if the generations of ancestors were "looking on."[4] Because so many students from the Boston Public Schools attended UMass Amherst over the years, and so many—both Black and white—took courses in African American studies, many of the professors in Western Massachusetts took a certain interest in the school desegregation process in Boston. Of course, a similar process occurred in Springfield, just down the road. I benefited greatly from that collective analysis of the educational problems in Boston. When I arrived in fall 1999, there was much to say, learn, and hear—and read.

My graduate education was the key lesson in unlocking the true heart of the proud and vulnerable Black community of Boston, in the last outpost of the Deep North and its attendant liberal biases. For this I also must thank Ernie Allen. Serving as a teaching assistant for his courses established foundations for a clearer understanding, such as the many documents we scanned together, which included hundreds of pages of Black Student Union newspapers, including those at English High School during a key moment in students' revolt against the racial tyranny of the Boston Public Schools. For an extended tutorial on this, I would also like to thank Leon Rock. Much of those digital gems have served as crucial data sets for this book and much of the work and teaching I've done since then. Our many engaging conversations helped me to formulate an interdisciplinary approach to Black history. His mentorship over the years has pushed me to become a better student, researcher, writer, and teacher. Recognition is also due to Esther M. A. Terry, whose institutional leadership as chair of the W. E. B. Du Bois Department at the time made my doctoral education possible. I would like to thank Professor Michael Thelwell, professor emeritus and founder of the Afro-American Studies Department at UMass. I had the distinct honor of serving as a graduate teaching assistant for his course History of the Civil Rights Movement in fall 2002. There was no better teacher of the movement.

I have to say a special word about Bill Strickland, who helped me with this project in its earliest incarnations. He was one of the first professors I met at UMass, by phone. Studying with him and everyone else was one of the smartest moves I've ever made. Bill, in addition to being from Roxbury and attending Boston Latin School, was the pride of his community when he entered the ivy-covered walls of Harvard University. Strickland, in all the places he traveled in the world, never forgot about Boston—not as a major leader of the Northern Student Movement (NSM) or as one of the founders of the Institute of the Black World in Atlanta. Strickland—or "Strick," as we all called him—was the linchpin of this entire project. With his memories of Roxbury and vast network of colleagues, friends, admirers, and compatriots from NSM—Vincent Harding, Chuck Turner, Sarah-Ann Shaw, Malcolm X, and so many others—I literally needed only to utter Bill's name and doors were constantly opened.

I owe a lot to Jim Smethurst, whose recollections of his years in Boston and vast knowledge of both the Old and the New Left added much insight into the book. A special thanks to Agustin Lao-Montes, who is the real deal. He is a brother and a friend, a true theorist, and one of the most brilliant lecturers I have ever heard. I thank him for being a role model and an encouraging supporter in the early days of my graduate studies.[5]

I would also like to thank my fellow graduate students at UMass Amherst, particularly David Goldberg and Shawn Alexander, who have probably done the most to support my writing over the years, as they have read the majority of my work and offered invaluable feedback and resources. Stephanie Evans and Dan McClure also deserve special mention for their support. I also must thank David Lucander, who really went to bat for me early on with this book, sending me documents over the years and reading a very early version of my book proposal. His insights, time, and labor will always be appreciated. Thanks also go to Tricia Loveland, the departmental secretary, who has been a miracle worker over the years.

I wish to thank all my classmates at UMass Amherst, with a special thanks to my cohort of Stephanie Evans, Trimiko Melancon, Adam Linker, and Catherine Adams. I learned so much from each of them. I would also like to thank Ernest Gibson III, McKinley Melton, Markeysha Davis, Jamal Watson, Kabria Baumgartner, Jonathan Fenderson, Jacqueline Jones, Christopher Tinson, Alesia McFadden, Anthony Ratcliff, Thomas Edge, Michael Forbes, Ousmane Power-Greene, Rita Reynolds, Lindsey Swindall, W. S. Tkweme, Paul Udofia, Andrew Rosa, Tanya Mears, Kelli Morgan, Jennifer Jensen-Wallach, Francis Njubi Nesbitt, and Christopher Lehman. There were also students who came after me that I got to know over the years, and I thank H. Zahra Caldwell, Julia Charles, Trent Masiki, Peter Blackmer, Crystal Lynn Webster, and Johanna Ortner. UMass Amherst Afro-Am is like a family, and I'm proud to be a member of it.

Lastly, I am indebted to Robert Hall, who is now retired from Northeastern University, for being especially supportive of my efforts over the years and for being a pillar in the community and my model for engaged, activist scholarship. Bob Hall has known me since I was an undergraduate and gave me a teaching job in 2006. I learned so much from that experience, not only about teaching but about life. For the continuation of those lessons, I would like to thank David Coleman II, Kwamina Panford, Ron Bailey, and the late Leonard Brown. I am also especially indebted to my very good friend Kerri Greenidge, now of Tufts University. Kerri and I were both adjunct instructors during the academic year 2006–7, and I learned so much from her expert teaching. From Boston Technical High School, now the John D. O'Bryant School for Math and Science, I'd like to thank Mr. Weiner, my high school U.S. history teacher, and Mrs. Holland, the librarian. In addition, I must thank Mr. Lyons, Mr. Hecht, Ms. Doran, and Ms. Nevins, who were wonderful teachers, as well as Mr. Belle, who was always there for me. I also must thank Mrs. Roberta Logan, a noted Boston educator who taught at the Phyllis Wheatley Middle School for many years, as well as at Northeastern University, and Mrs. Zuhaira Bilal, also of the Phyllis Wheatley Middle School. They both had a profound impact on me. During those years I was personally mentored by Mr. John D. O'Bryant, and so I must thank him for that early intervention. He seemed to think I had it in me to do something good with my life, and I cannot put into words how important that early intervention was. Lastly, I would like to thank Mr. Adam Artis, Mr. Sampson, and the late Mrs. Barbara Jackson, teachers and headmaster of the Trotter Elementary School, respectively, in the 1980s. Very special thanks go to Robert C. Hayden, the dean of Boston's Black history. Bob Hayden is actually someone I've known since high school, when I was a student in the Massachusetts Pre-Engineering Program (Mass PEP) he directed. Reading his book *African-Americans in Boston: More Than 350 Years* is what sparked my interest in Black history as a young person.

An especially powerful thanks goes to the late Gerald Gill of Tufts University. I first met Gerald at the first American Historical Association (AHA) meeting I ever attended. Later, having read a chapter from my dissertation, he met me at a gathering of the Mass Historical Society to provide his feedback verbally. The original marked copy ended up in the Gerald Gill Papers at Tufts University. The next time I saw him would be at Boston College, where he gave a lecture about racial politics in Boston in the 1950s titled "No Time for Banqueting," where he signed my copy of his book with a beautiful note of encouragement that I never forgot. Professor Gill examined an early version of my doctoral dissertation and provided feedback and encouragement that led directly to the publication of this book. The next time I saw him would be at the Power and Protest Conference in 2006, put on by the Kennedy Library and curated by Julian Houston. He was the keynote speaker and gave a rousing address that left a profound impact upon me. When Professor Gill passed away, I felt an urgent need to try to fill the void left by my friend, mentor, and colleague, first with a conference paper at the Association for the Study of African American Life and History (ASALH) and then at other conferences and academic meetings, because I felt it was so important for the historiography. That led to a collaboration with many amazing colleagues, all of whom had a similar goal: seeing Gerald Gill's particular approach come to life. As Dr. Gill was such a mentor to me, I was glad to see that a collection of his work had been created at Tufts, archived for all to use. His unfinished project on Boston, "Struggling Yet in Freedom's Birthplace," was the major inspiration for this book. His wisdom, approach to Boston, and insight is on every page of this book. It is my hope that more people will turn to his powerful unpublished pages for the incredible insights they contain. Gill was a mentor to many people, and I would like to thank one of his students, Max Felkor-Cantor—who also happens to be one of my favorite historians—for all of his support and for sharing the unpublished manuscript pages with me before I was able to see them at Tufts.

I would also like to thank the AHA, the Organization of American History (OAH), and the *Journal of American History* for opportunities to publish my work. I'd also like to thank the New England Historical Association (NEHA) and its many leaders over the years who invited me to present. Particular thanks go to Mark Herlihy of Endicott College, a friend and colleague, who made space for the earlier iterations of this work when he was president of NEHA. One of my first jobs was at Endicott College, and Mark was a supportive presence.

I want to thank Judge Leslie Harris. We met once a long time ago at Boston College when I was an undergraduate there. Henry Hampton was given an honorary degree, and I was his usher for the day. This was in 1993, my freshman year. I also met Ruth Batson there, who was Hampton's guest. There is a great photo that I still treasure, which captures this moment. Boston College, in general, was a great place to attend school. It provided special moments and opportunities like this, and for that I'll always be thankful.

Much of the interest in and new scholarship on the Black freedom movement in the North came in the wake of the publication of *Freedom North: Black Freedom Struggles Outside the South, 1940–1980*, edited by Jeanne Theoharis and Komozi Woodard. This groundbreaking work opened the door to new dialogues about the racial histories of twentieth-century northern cities that challenged both the chronology and the territorial limits of the civil rights movement in the "urban North." I must pause at this point to make an expression of gratitude to Jeanne Theoharis, whose work on Boston appeared in *Freedom North* and was very influential. We organized a panel together at the OAH, which resulted in a special issue on busing in the *Journal of Urban History*, coedited by Jeanne Theoharis of Brooklyn College and Matthew Delmont of Dartmouth University, which came out in 2017.

I thank Shawn Alexander for being a steadfast and unfailing champion of this work. It was through our many discussions and conversations that this book became a reality, and that is a tradition that my friend Shawn and I have been engaged in since our graduate school days at the UMass Amherst. Few words come close to describing how instrumental his steady encouragement and constructive feedback has been for the development of this work. He has been my tutor for intellectual history, and our many conversations about William Monroe Trotter were critical for gaining a fuller understanding of Boston.

I would like to thank Tomás González, who is one of the most knowledgeable people I know about Boston's history. He also happens to be one of my oldest and closest friends *y mi compadre*. He and I went to high school together and have been friends ever since we reconnected during our years at Boston College. We wrote a piece for a special issue in the *Trotter Review*, published by UMass Boston's William Monroe Trotter Institute and edited by Kenneth J. Cooper. "'Separatist City': The Mandela, Massachusetts (Roxbury) Movement and the Politics of Incorporation, Self-Determination, and Community Control, 1986–1988" appeared in the 2016 issue, coinciding with the thirtieth anniversary of the referendum to create a separate municipality. I would like to thank the González family—Daila, my goddaughter Taina, Tomás Alejandro, and Solina—for their support over the years. Their homes and various summer cottages made many a writing space for me. I cannot think of anything that makes me happier than writing in these surroundings—sharing my drafts, getting feedback, with the whole family contributing and editing.

I would also like to thank Lew Finfer, an important protector and guardian of Boston's historical legacy, especially where progressive history is concerned—both the writing of it and the living of it. Karilyn Crockett has been such a wonderful friend and colleague, and so supportive that it requires special mention. Professor Crockett of the Massachusetts Institute of Technology wrote a master's thesis on the Mandela movement before publishing her wonderful book, *People Before Highways*. She is also a member of one of the *Morgan v.*

Hennigan families. Her work, in tandem with that of Lew Finfer, has set the bar high for work on these areas. I am glad to be carrying this forward with their support from the very start. Thanks also go to Jim Vrabel for taking the time to speak with me not only about the Mandela project but also about this book project. His expert advice, support, and encouragement were very much appreciated. Thank you to James Fraser, formerly of Northeastern, now at NYU. The ongoing work at Northeastern, both in the archives and as a critical organizing space—not to mention the university-wide efforts to preserve this history—was apparent to me (and anyone who knows this struggle) from the very beginning. Most of it—including the publication of Ruth Batson's seminal work *The Black Educational Movement in Boston: A Sequence of Historical Events; A Chronology*—he arranged personally. The leadership Jim Fraser provided as the founding dean of the School of Education was instrumental in the documenting of this history. In fact, I think it's fair to say that Northeastern University as a whole has been central to this, and so I would also like to thank Joseph Warren, Robin Coleman, and Richard O'Bryant.

The article I coauthored on the Mandela movement prompted my involvement (along with my co-collaborator) in a peer-reviewed digital forum on race, capitalism, and property, and the first piece I ever wrote for the African American Intellectual History Society (AAIHS) blog site *Black Perspectives*. The article was titled "How Gentrification and Displacement Are Remaking Boston." I'd like to thank Walter Greason for curating that series and for being a steadfast colleague through the years, Duke economist William Darrity, and Paige Glotzer. I would also like to thank Keisha Blain, Chris Cameron, J. T. Roane, Tyler Parry, Chris Tinson, Quito Swan, Ashley Farmer, Robert Greene, and Charisse Burden-Stelly (Dr. CBS) from AAIHS and many other friends and colleagues who have written for *Black Perspectives* and attend its yearly conference. I would also like to thank Jarvis Givens, who has been very supportive, as well as his graduate student Alyssa Napier, who is at the Harvard Graduate School of Education.

As many of my colleagues know, so many important connections and relationships are formed at the annual ASALH conferences. I cannot think of a grander or more important professional space for the Black historical profession and those of us who work in it. We are all indebted to this thing that Carter G. Woodson built. It can be truthfully said that this book would not exist had it not been for the association. So much of the material and so many of the chapters were first presented there and had to withstand the peculiar scrutiny of the brilliant minds who attend the ASALH conference. The feedback I received and the opportunity for scholarly exchange cannot be overstated. I am particularly thankful to V. P. Franklin, Sundiata Cha Jua, Clarence Lang, Brenda Stevenson, Gerald Horne, the late Rosalyn Terborg-Penn, and Darlene Clark Hine. I'd like to make special mention of Willard R. Johnson and Vivian Johnson, who always appeared at my presentations. Seeing their familiar faces from year to year as a graduate student did something for me that I cannot explain. They lifted me up with their support. Their insights about Boston were instrumental in shaping this work, and I thank them both for their support and stewardship in Boston through the years.[6] I'd like to thank Lou Moore, Diedre Hill Butler, David Goldberg, and Dan McClure for one of the first panels I ever participated in that I actually enjoyed. I thank Bob Hayden for helming several of them, either as chair or chair extempore from the audience. I would also like to thank Sylvia Cyrus, Lionel Kimble, and my fellow members of the executive council for their support while writing this book.

An article titled "Before Busing: Boston's Long Movement for Civil Rights and the Legacy of Jim Crow in the 'Cradle of Liberty'" was published in a special issue on "Rethinking Busing" in the *Journal of Urban History*. I would like to thank Jeanne Theoharis and Matthew Delmont and my co-contributors, Tess Bundy, Tatiana Cruz, and Lynnell L. Thomas, for that wonderful experience of presenting, work shopping, and publishing the work. Mark Schneider's book *Boston Confronts Jim Crow: 1890–1920* has had a major influence in my approach to this work. Although Schneider and I were both at Boston College at the same time—he being a graduate student and I an undergraduate—our paths never crossed. I would not meet Professor Schneider until 2006 at the Power and Protest Conference at the Kennedy Library. I'd also like to thank Stephen David Kantrowitz, specifically for his work *More Than Freedom: Fighting for Black Citizenship in a White Republic, 1829–1889*. I would also like to thank Davison M. Douglas, whose work *Jim Crow Moves North: The Battle over Northern School Segregation, 1865–1954* was very helpful and persuasive in making my own argument about the dug-in nature of Jim Crow in Boston. *Before Busing* would not exist were it not for *Up South: Civil Rights and Black Power in Philadelphia* by Matthew Countryman. I thank Martha Biondi, whose work on New York and campus organizing in the 1960s and 1970s was crucial to my own understanding of this project. Brian Purnell's *Fighting Jim Crow in the County of Kings: The Congress of Racial Equality in Brooklyn* became a model as to how to go about framing Boston. I also thank Jason Sokol, whose *All Eyes Are upon Us: Race and Politics from Boston to Brooklyn* is a very important work and a signpost to the future of this subtopic of the larger Jim Crow North project. This work is in deep dialogue with the wonderful *Sarah's Long Walk: The Free Blacks of Boston and How Their Struggle for Equality Changed America* by Stephen and Paul Kendrick, who are worthy of thanks. I would also like to thank Shannon King, Mary Barr, Tom Sugrue, Laura Warren Hill, Devin Fergus, Jake Dorman, and Kristopher Burrell.

I want to thank Lyda Peters, who is one of a handful of people who not only became scholars of this movement but also lived the movement. Her help and support over the years have meant everything, and I hope I did justice to what her mentor, Ruth Batson, would have wanted to see on these pages. I would also like to thank another movement veteran, Malia Lazu, who has been a steadfast supporter of my work. She organized the HUB Week Boston 2018, which took place in Boston's City Hall Plaza on October 11, 2018. I was encouraged as the opening speaker to help frame the discussion. I gave a talk titled "The Deep North: Boston's Racial Paradox," in which this idea of "the Deep North" became a way to understand Boston's backwardness with regard to race. For that inspiration, I need to thank the other veterans of the Boston movement who also performed, presented, and were in attendance.

I would like to make a special thanks to Patrick Jones, who patiently read the early stages of this manuscript and offered expert advice and steady support. In addition to his many accomplishments and thoughtful leadership, one will never find a better friend than Patrick Jones. He brings people together and is a solid humanist, in the greatest sense of the word. I would also like to thank Ibram X. Kendi, who has always been an encouraging colleague and is doing amazingly important work at Boston University. He participated in a public conversation I led on his book *Stamped from the Beginning*, which won the National Book Award for Nonfiction. It was a delight to share the same stage with him.

I have amassed a number of friends and colleagues who have been near and dear to me in various ways. We may only see each other at conferences once a year, but they are all people whose work I respect tremendously. For this, I thank Hassan Jeffries, Peniel Joseph, Jeffrey O. G. Ogbar, Stefan M. Bradley, Fanon Che Wilkins, Johanna Fernandez, Paula Marie Seniors, Treva Lindsay, Sowande Mustakeem, Cornelius Bynum, Aminah Pilgrim, Derrick Alridge, Barbara Ransby, Violet Showers Johnson, Shannon King, G. Derek Musgrove, Zoe Burkholder, Jeff Hegelson, Maurice Hobson, Jessica Milward, Keona Irving, Scot Brown, Tiffany Gill, Curtis Austin, Jakobi Williams, LaShawn Harris, Dierdre Cooper Owens, Simon Balto, Dan Berger, Daryl Scott, Jelani Cobb, Mark Anthony Neal, Jakobi Williams, Walter Greason, Fanon Wilkins, Amrita Chakrabarti Myers, Amani Marshall, Yohuru Williams, Robyn Spencer, Donna Murch, Jessica Millward, Tiffany Gill, Allison M. Parker, Jessica Marie Johnson, Dawn-Elissa Fischer, Markeysha Dawn Davis, Paula Marie, Sowande Mustakeem, Shannon King, Brittany Cooper, Keeanga-Yamahtta Taylor, Douglass Flowe, Martha Biondi, Lionel Kimble, Randal Maurice Jelks, Charles McKinney, Tanisha C. Ford, Tammy L. Brown, Kelli Morgan, Maurice Hobson, Larry Lee Rowley, and Nishani Frazier. I would also like to thank the following people who influenced me through their work, though they may not have known it: Imani Perry, Farah Jasmine Griffin, A'Lelia Bundles, Charles McKinney, Crystal Sanders, Erica Armstrong Dunbar, Koritha Mitchell, Robyn Spencer, Carl Suddler, Danielle McGuire, Emily Crosby, Marcia Chatelain, Shennette Garrett-Scott, Dwight D. Watson, Kellie Carter-Jackson, Theresa Runstedtler, Khalil G. Muhammad, Cherisse Jones-Branch, Crystal Moten, Nell Painter, Julianne Malveuaux, Crystal Lynn Webster, Martha S. Jones, Le'Trice Donaldson, Andre Johnson, Mary Phillips, Craig Wilder, Nathan Connolly, Miriam Harris, Marshanda Smith, Sherie Randolph, Noliwe Rooks, Siobhan Carter-David, Kendra Boyd, Jennifer Guglielmo, Barbara Krauthamer, Jamon Jordan, Alondra Nelson, and Whitney Battle-Baptiste. I would also like to thank Davarian Baldwin, Khalil Muhammed, and Pero Dagbovie. Thank you for your time and support; you have helped me more than you know.

I must take a moment to thank my brother, my friend, who also happens to be one of the most noted thinkers on Black internationalist thought, Minkah Makalani. He gave me some of the best advice I have ever received about writing, and truly set me on the course to do the actual work itself. I value our friendship and the good work that has come out of it. I thank him for showing me around Brooklyn and being so welcoming to me and my family. He is the man.

I would also like to thank Michael Eric Dyson for being a friend and mentor. I must thank Cornel West just for being who he is. His humanity and warmth have influenced me greatly. I thank Mark Naison for being a man among men, who is always willing to stand up for the underdog, and for teaching me that inspired teaching will always be done with a heart of true love for the people. I thank him for inviting me to speak to his class when I was going through a tough time. We shared an experience that will always help me remember to put the people first. I thank him from the bottom of my heart. I thank Sonia Sanchez, who always spoke to me at conferences. I never got over the shock of being taken completely seriously by someone like her. I cannot recall the few times I ever cried at a public lecture, but it happens almost every time I see her speak.

I'd like to thank David Roediger, who spoke to me when I was in graduate school like I was a human being, and never thought for a moment that I did not belong at some of the table discussions that often take place in academia. In fact, he invited me to many of them.

In 2010–11, I had the distinct honor and privilege of serving as the postdoctoral fellow in African American studies in the Department of History at Case Western Reserve University. This fellowship supported me in the writing of this book manuscript, which was loosely based on the dissertation. Naturally, a great deal of my efforts that year were focused on making major strides in the research and the initial phases of the writing.

I believe it is imperative to bring about the triangulation of the academy and the community in the best traditions of academic and community partnerships. Having had a chance to work closely with an activist scholar such as Rhonda Y. Williams, the director of the fellowship, gave me an opportunity to witness up close the power of African American studies to effect change in a city like Cleveland. Dr. Williams deserves special thanks for making the space for this opportunity, which has led to this book being part of the Justice, Power and Politics series, of which she is coeditor with Heather Ann Thompson.

The fellowship allowed me to make several research trips to Boston in order to collect oral histories for this project, giving me my first opportunity to interview people involved in the Boston struggle, such as Mel King, Lenny Elkins, and Sarah-Ann Shaw. I would also like to thank Dottie Zellner, James Breeden, Bob Phillips, Hubie Jones, Owen H. Brooks, Byron Rushing, Chuck Turner, Vernon Carter, and many others. It was my belief then (and still is) that the strongest, and really only, existing work we had to date on Boston's Black freedom movement was Mel King's book *Chain of Change*. I would like to thank Mel King, who helped me with this project from the very beginning. He was beyond generous, and I thank him, his wife and daughter, and the entire family. They are beyond meaningful to me. I would also like to thank Judge Julian Houston and especially Topper Crew, and so many other people who spoke to me because of Mel King's support of this project. The fellowship gave me the opportunity to investigate the origins of the movement and illuminate the myriad factors that gave rise to the unique nature of civil rights organizing activities in Boston. It was with the support of my uncle, V. Paul Deare, that many of these interviews were able to be conducted, and I don't believe that would have happened without the special friendship, which I want to honor, between Mel King and the older members of my family. My grandmother used to send me news clippings of his articles when I was in graduate school. It is amazing what can happen when intergenerational dialogue and education is allowed to find its way. Along those same lines, I would like to thank Joe and Angela Cook, Ken and Juanita Wade, and Kim Archung.

As part of the fellowship, I was asked to choose a guest speaker to deliver the annual postdoctoral fellowship guest lecture and serve as a reader of my work in progress, as well as to serve as a potential future mentor. The scholar I selected was Jeanne Theoharis, professor of political science and endowed chair in women's studies at Brooklyn College of CUNY, coeditor of *Freedom North*, and author of several articles and essays on the Boston freedom struggle. As a noted historian, her work has been extremely influential in establishing a framework for an understanding of the Boston freedom struggle. The foundation that her work established on this important if neglected area of study cannot be overstated. I had a chance to meet with Dr. Theoharis for an extended dialogue and critical feedback session on my work-in-progress essay at the time titled "Fighting Freedom in the Cradle of Liberty," which was worked on and written principally during my fellowship tenure. The feedback I received was absolutely invaluable and contributed greatly to the book manuscript project. An added bonus was the somewhat serendipitous timing of her visit, which coincided with the news that I had just been offered a visiting assistant professor position in Department of Africana Studies at Stony Brook University in New York. As a neighboring colleague at Brooklyn College, Dr. Theoharis offered the added perspective of advice and tips on serving in such a position in the New York City area, including colleague introductions, suggestions for further reading, and an overview of the landscape, which was extraordinarily helpful.

It was also in Cleveland that I first met the brilliant and amazing Heather Ann Thompson when she came to speak at a conference put together by Rhonda Williams. Thompson is a scholar's scholar, and one I can only hope to emulate. Her book *Blood in the Water: The Attica Prison Uprising of 1971 and Its Legacy*, which won the 2017 Pulitzer Prize for History, was an inspiration for "doing hard history."[7] I am just so grateful for her and the door she opened for me during the conference on social justice, of which she was one of the main speakers. It was during the dinner afterward when I first had the idea of writing my book on this topic. Dr. Williams deserves special thanks for making the space for this opportunity.

Many other friends and colleagues came to Ohio for that special gathering, including two key individuals who had so much to do with the development of this project: David Goldberg and Daniel McClure—two great friends, colleagues, compatriots, and everything in between, who both attended UMass Amherst with me. We used to talk late into the night at bars, in each other's apartments, and whenever we would get together about the Boston struggle and its uniqueness. At the same time, those discussions allowed me to see the universality of the situation in Boston, and how it was connected with struggles in other American cities, like Detroit, where David grew up, and New York, where Dan had lived and also the city that David wrote a brilliant book about: *Black Firefighters and the FDNY: The Struggle for Jobs, Justice, and Equity in New York City*. David Goldberg deserves special mention as well. It was he who first introduced me to Rhonda Williams at an ASALH meeting in 2008. Williams was so gracious, inviting me to share my postdoc statement with her. Later, at another ASALH meeting, David mentioned the work I was doing on Boston casually at the hotel lounge—with Rhonda, Heather, and Derek Musgrove all in attendance. Anyone who knows David will understand that this gathering was not entirely coincidental, nor was it planned. This book would never have happened without David Goldberg, and I can never thank him enough.

One of the benefits of the postdoctoral fellowship was an opportunity to work in a history department with so many esteemed historians, many of whom took the time to read my writing in progress. Stephen Hall and Renee Sentilles deserve special mention in this regard. Stephen, who was in residence as a visiting assistant professor, deserves special mention for both reading my work and providing feedback during our many chats throughout the year. He gave me some very good advice about how to position my work, which proved to be indispensable later on. Thank you to Marixa Lasso, who has continued to be a great friend and supporter and more recently served as a DuBois fellow at the Hutchins Center before returning to her native Colombia to take a job. Likewise, Miriam Levin, who was a fellow alum of UMass Amherst, was also a very supportive colleague, opening her home to my wife and I and our new baby at the time.

As part of my fellowship duties, I developed an Advanced Readings in African-American History course, based on the civil rights and Black Power movement in the North. The texts included Jeanne Theoharis's *Groundwork*, Peniel Joseph's *Neighborhood Rebels* and

Waiting 'Til the Midnight Hour, Komozi Woodard and Jeanne Theoharis's *Freedom North*, Clarence Lang's *Grassroots at the Gateway*, Martha Biondi's *To Stand and Fight*, and Patrick Jones's *Selma of the North*. If anyone had told me then that I would get to meet and work with almost all of those people one day, I would not have believed it. Patrick Jones also covered the course for me when my oldest son was born in February 2011. Speaking of Cleveland, I'd like to thank Todd M. Michney and many others who keep the wheels moving at the Urban History Association. I'd also like to thank the editors of the *Journal of Urban History*. It is perhaps impossible for me to fully put into words what this experience has meant to my life and career. I have been forever changed by my experience at Case Western Reserve University, and it is something that I will carry with me for the rest of my career. I remain proud to have been the 2010–11 postdoctoral fellow in African American studies and am deeply grateful for the opportunity.

I came to Case Western Reserve University from the University of Nebraska at Omaha, where I was an assistant professor in the Department of Black Studies. I must thank my old colleagues there, especially Omowale Akintunde, Peggy Jones, Sekhmet Ra Em Kht Maat, Bob Armstrong, and the late Larry Menyweather-Woods, as well as Adam Tyma. I would also like to thank the late Robert Chrisman, Nathan Hare, Floyd W. Hayes III, and John Grigg.

I would like to thank Brian Purnell, who read an early draft of the book proposal (and a lot of other things over the years), and Adrian Burgos, who was very supportive of my work early on and remained so throughout the years. I would also like to thank Kevin Powell, who is a great writer and the author of fourteen books. He was very supportive as a fellow scribe and encouraged me to believe in my own writing, among other work that we did together. I thank him for his friendship. I would also like to thank filmmakers Spike Lee and Ralph Celestin.

I would like to thank the many talented archivists in Boston and other New England area archives and special collections repositories, where much of my data collection was derived, including the Massachusetts Historical Society, the Bostonian Society, the Boston Athenaeum, the Boston Public Library, the Social Law Library, the Healey Library at UMass Boston, and Harvard University Libraries, including the Harvard-Radcliffe Schlesinger Library. I did a tremendous amount of work at Boston University's Howard Gotlieb Archival Research Center, which was absolutely crucial to my research, so I must thank Sarah E. Pratt and Laura Russo. I have a special place in my heart for Archives and Special Collections at Northeastern University, where I probably did the vast majority of research. In addition to the collection being absolutely unparalleled for work on this topic, it employs the nicest people. This archive is exceptionally important to the Black freedom movement in Boston. I am particularly indebted to Giordana Mecagni and Molly Brown. I would also like to thank Michelle Romero, who is now at Emerson College Special Collections. I also worked extensively at the Joe Moakley archives at Suffolk University, and I thank the staff there as well.

I was able to do some of the best research right at my home campus of Stony Brook University through its excellent library staff. They include Kristen J. Nyitray, Janet H. Clarke, Giuleta Stoianov, Jennifer A. Devito, Kenneth O. Doyle, Diane E. Englot, and Kenneth Schaal. I thank the expert staff at the Harvard-Radcliffe Schlesinger Library, especially Jennifer Fauxsmith, Erin Weinman, and Jane Kamensky. Speaking of research, I want to say thank you to my friend, my sister, and my trusted and able research assistant, Susan Paul, whom I have known for some time, going back to our days at Bird Street Community Center. Susan worked on this book project and did an incredible job helping to spread the word for the questionnaire that we distributed. She made it available to churches, community centers, and libraries and the word began to spread. She also worked with the Grove Hall Branch of the Boston Public Library, which I would also like to thank. In addition, I would like to thank the Uphams Corner Branch of the Boston Public Library, Salvation Army Kroc Center, the Church of St. Augustine and St. Martin, South Street Church, and Twelfth Baptist Church for help in distributing questionnaires and flyers. This was a group effort. I would also like to thank my former undergraduate and graduate student Sushank Chibber. I know we say it a lot, but I also don't think we say it enough sometimes, especially these days. He was one of the original research assistants on the book. I want him to know I really appreciate his labors, which have been so key to the completion of this work.

Furthermore, the travel and research funds made available to me from a number of sources made it possible to visit private libraries and archives throughout the Boston area, such as the New England Historic Genealogical Society. These include funds and grants from Stony Brook University; the Special Media Collections of Washington University in St. Louis, particularly the Henry Hampton Collection; and Emory University Libraries.

I would like to thank the College of Arts and Sciences at Stony Brook University for sabbatical time, which was of great assistance to me not only in publishing my book manuscript but also as I worked toward gaining tenure at Stony Brook. By providing much needed time to write and do research, the sabbatical allowed me to make the necessary revisions and conduct the final research I needed to complete my manuscript. I thank Dean Nicole Sampson, Associate Dean Amy Cook, and former dean Nancy Squires, who did so much for me and my family.

I would like to thank the HistoryMakers for a teaching fellowship in 2020–21. The opportunity to receive any fellowship award is cause for joy and pride in communities and families alike, and my experience in this regard was no exception. The HistoryMakers documented and recorded many of the voices that fill the pages of this book, and so I owe it—we all do, really—a special thanks for its wonderful oral history collection. Teaching fellowships such as these reflect very well on the recipient's home institution, as they add to the richness and prestige of faculty offerings. I can attest that the fellowship was certainly seen in that light at Stony Brook University. The scholarly exchange that I benefited from, through discussions and collaborations with other teaching fellows, as well as opportunities for feedback, was unparalleled.

I don't think it would be an exaggeration to say that the Department of Africana Studies at Stony Brook University is known and respected throughout the field and discipline of African American studies, owing to the fact that Amiri Baraka and later Peniel Joseph taught there. I want to thank both of them. I first met Baraka as an undergraduate at Boston College, and he was a frequent visitor to UMass Amherst. A nationally known poet, thinker, humanitarian, and social activist, his credentials are well documented and do not need to be repeated here. Above all, I would like to thank my colleagues in the Department of Africana Studies, including Abena Ampofoa Asare, George Aumoithe, Mark Chambers, Crystal Fleming, Georges Fouron, Shimelis Gulema, Adryan Wallace, and Jarvis Watson. Very special thanks go to Tracey L. Walters, who served as chair during most of the completion of the manuscript, and to Patrice Nganang, the current chair. Thanks also to Ann L. Berrios, the departmental secretary, as well as Anthony Hurley and Les Owens.

I would also like to thank my colleagues in the Department of History, particularly Robert Chase, fellow recipient of the fellowship at Case Western, whose work I admire greatly. I send very special thanks to Christopher Sellers, who read one of the earliest finished copies of this manuscript and offered amazingly valuable feedback. Thanks also to Lori Flores, Paul Gootenberg, Shobana Shankar, and Jenny Anderson. Having such an intellectual circle at the same university has created a very rich experience from which I have benefited greatly. I'd also like to the Humanities Center, which has been supportive of my scholarship and intellectual work.

I would like to thank the membership and clergy of Calvary Fellowship AME Church in Brooklyn, New York, especially Rev. Dr. Lisa Williamson. She has been a constant source of encouragement, inspiration, and hope. Calvary Fellowship has many members who hail from the state of South Carolina, including Rev. Joseph A. DeLaine, who pastored Calvary during the 1950s and was a key leader in the struggle for integrated schools in Summerton, South Carolina. I was able to interview some of its members who were involved in *Briggs v. Elliott*, and their testimonies and wisdom are in every part of this book, and I thank them for their selflessness. Thanks especially to Francena Simmons and Lula Mae Caldwell, who shared their stories with me. Their testimonies, wisdom, and fortitude helped me to better understand the Boston situation.

I need to make a special thanks to Jessica Levy, who read every single page of this manuscript and offered thoughtful and critically important notes, edits, and suggestions that literally made this book possible. Some people have an eye for editing, and she is definitely one of them. I simply cannot thank her enough. Having to read through my sometimes disorganized manner of writing is no easy task, and many of my (thankfully not former) friends can attest to this. Jessica Levy can be categorized in a multitude of ways—rising historian, professor, colleague, fellow urbanist, editor—and I'm happy to add friend as one of them.

I have to thank Brandon Proia for being an amazing editor, as well as Andrew Winters and everyone at UNC Press for the expert copyediting, textual analysis, advice, and support. I extend a very warm thanks to Rhonda Y. Williams and Heather Ann Thompson for believing in this project from the very beginning, and for their support of me as a scholar, a historian, and an author. I need to thank my parents, who sacrificed so much to help provide for my education. This book is a dedication to their faithfulness. I also thank the rest of my family, especially my grandfather for his infinite wisdom. I also wish to thank my brother, Jamie, for his steadfast support over the years. Finally, I would like to thank my wife, Karla, for all her help and dedication to this project as an expert editor. She helped raise our family while I was off "working on the book" and missing infinite precious moments with our children, Zebulon Jr., Saúl, and Marc, whom I also thank for their patience, love, and support. They believed in me before this project began, and I thank them for their love, faith, and perseverance over all these years. I thank my beautiful and brilliant mother, Veronica Miletsky, whose many recollections as a girl fill the pages of this book. Somehow, she was in attendance at many of the events depicted herein. These include the Stay Out for Freedom Days and the James Brown concert at the Boston Garden. As a little girl, she attended the

Harriet Tubman Settlement House during its days on Holyoke Street (on which my great-grandparents owned a home), and she attended events at the Freedom House as a teenager. Her memories are a major inspiration for this project. I want to thank my ancestors on both sides of my family for the many stories they passed down. I was listening. Finally, I would like to thank my late father, Marc Alan Miletsky. He was one of the first people to give me a love of reading and writing and an appreciation for history. This book is dedicated to his memory.

Notes

Preface

1. *Boston Before Busing, 1964–1974*, Northeastern University Libraries online exhibition, Boston, 2015, accessed December 27, 2021, http://dsgsites.neu.edu/desegregation.

2. Donald Brown, interview by author, 2021.

3. After attending the Ellis, Garrison, and Higginson Schools in Boston Public Schools, in the sixth grade Janey went to the Edwards Middle School in Charlestown during the second phase of desegregation busing. "As an 11-year-old girl, Kim had rocks and racial slurs thrown at her as she'd ride the bus to Charlestown each day. Later, Janey attended Reading Public Schools through the METCO program, where she was one of two Black students in her graduating class," according to the site. According to Kim Janey's now-defunct election website.

4. Renée Graham, "Yes, Boston, You Are Racist," *Boston Globe*, March 29, 2017.

5. "Boston: A Port of Entry for Enslaved Africans," Boston Middle Passage, accessed March 23, 2022, https://bostonmiddlepassage.org.

6. For many years the Union of Minority Neighborhoods has been working on a "truth and reconciliation" project around busing under the stewardship of Donna Bivens. The Boston Busing/Desegregation Project records the stories of mostly Black Americans from the school desegregation years.

7. Dr. Martin Luther King Jr., "Remaining Awake through a Great Revolution," speech given at the National Cathedral, March 31, 1968.

8. "Ten Sermons of Religion," Boston, 1854. It is possible, although difficult to prove, that Martin Luther King Jr. may have even come into contact with this quote during his time in Boston.

9. Meghan E. Irons, "Tito Jackson Found His Birth Mother; Their Family's Journey Is a Tale of Boston History," *Boston Globe*, April 14, 2021.

10. James Vaznis, "26 Boston Schools at Risk of Being Declared 'Underperforming,'" *Boston Globe*, September 17, 2017.

11. Ana Patricia Muñoz, Marlene Kim, Mariko Chang, Regine O. Jackson, Darrick Hamilton, and William A. Darity Jr. "The Color of Wealth in Boston: A Joint Publication with Duke University and the New School." Federal Reserve Bank of Boston, 2015.

Introduction

1. Ronald Formisano's *Boston against Busing: Race, Class and Ethnicity in the 1960s and 1970s* (1991) and J. Anthony Lukas's Pulitzer Prize–winning *Common Ground: A Turbulent Decade in the Lives of Three American Families* (1986) are the two most notable books in this vein.

212 Notes to Introduction

2. Audrea Jones Dunham, "Boston's 1960s Civil Rights Movement: A Look Back," accessed March 17, 2022, https://openvault.wgbh.org/exhibits/boston_civil_rights/article.

3. See Oscar Handlin, *Boston's Immigrants: A Study in Acculturation* (Cambridge, MA: Harvard University Press), 1979.

4. Lily Geismer, *Don't Blame Us: Suburban Liberals and the Transformation of the Democratic Party; Politics and Society in Twentieth-Century America* (Princeton, NJ: Princeton University Press, 2015), 13.

5. Ruth Batson, interview by Jackie Shearer, transcript, *Eyes on the Prize II*, November 8, 1988, http://digital.wustl.edu/e/eii/eiiweb/bat5427.0911.011ruthbatson.html.

6. *Brown v. Board of Education of Topeka*, 347 U.S. 483 (1954).

7. J. Anthony Lukas, *Common Ground: A Turbulent Decade in the Lives of Three American Families* (New York: Vintage Books, 1986), 232.

8. Jeanne Theoharis, *A More Beautiful and Terrible History: The Uses and Misuses of Civil Rights History* (Boston: Beacon Press, 2018), 34. See also Matthew D. Lassiter and Joseph Crespino, *The Myth of Southern Exceptionalism* (New York: Oxford University Press, 2010).

9. http://www.longroadtojustice.org/.

10. Jordan Lebeau, "When This Group of Black Mothers Locked Themselves in a Government Office, Boston Erupted in Riots," accessed December 22, 2021, https://timeline.com/when-this-group-of-black-mothers-locked-themselves-in-a-government-office-boston-erupted-in-riots-eaad1e64b92d.

11. On the variety of "race riots" during the 1960s, see Peter B. Levy, *The Great Uprising: Race Riots in Urban America during the 1960s* (Cambridge: Cambridge University Press, 2018).

12. *Boston Record American*, April 5, 1968.

13. *To Secure These Rights: A Documented History of the Negro "Freedom Movement,"* produced by Ted Mascott, WGBH, Boston, Massachusetts. Transcript located in Freedom House Papers (M16), Northeastern University Snelling Library, Archives and Special Collections, box 39, folder 1357.

14. *Morgan v. Hennigan*, 379 F. Supp. 410 (D. Mass. 1974), https://catalog.archives.gov/id/4713867.

15. J. Michael Ross and William M. Berg, *"I Respectfully Disagree with the Judge's Order": The Boston School Desegregation Controversy* (Washington, DC: University Press of America, 1981), 344.

16. Proletarian Unity League, *"It's Not the Bus": Busing and the Democratic Struggle in Boston, 1974–1975* (Boston: Proletarian Unity League, 1975).

17. Jeanne Theoharis, introduction to *Freedom North: Black Freedom Struggles Outside the South, 1940–1980*, ed. Jeanne Theoharis and Komozi Woodard (New York: Palgrave Macmillan, 2003), 2–3. In a special 2017 issue of the *Journal of Urban History* on the busing crisis, Theoharis and historian Matt Delmont write, "A new generation of historians has resoundingly challenged this dominant narrative. Fundamentally, they argue, a full history of Boston's school desegregation cannot begin in 1974 with a judge's action but must start with the longstanding pattern of segregation and inequality and the decades-long movement by blacks and Latinos that forced the city to have to address these systematic inequalities. They reject the frame of 'Boston's busing crisis' as a way to understand Boston's postwar racial history, and argue that part of the task must be to identify and investigate the mechanisms and

contemporary investments that keep these mythologies in place." Matthew Delmont and Jeanne Theoharis, "Introduction: Rethinking the Boston 'Busing Crisis,'" *Journal of Urban History* 43, no. 2 (March 2017): 191–203, https://doi.org/10.1177/0096144216688276.

18. Thomas J. Sugrue, *Sweet Land of Liberty: The Forgotten Struggle for Civil Rights in the North* (New York: Random House, 2009), xiii.

19. Patrick Jones, "Place Matters: The Indispensable Story of Civil Rights Activism beyond Dixie," in *Understanding and Teaching the Civil Rights Movement,* ed. Hasan Kwame Jeffries (University of Wisconsin Press, 2019), 109.

20. See Stephen and Paul Kendrick, *Sarah's Long Walk: The Free Blacks of Boston and How Their Struggle for Equality Changed America* (Boston: Beacon Press, 2004); Stephen David Kantrowitz, *More Than Freedom: Fighting for Black Citizenship in a White Republic, 1829–1889* (New York: Penguin Press, 2012); Leonard W. Levy and Douglas Lamar Jones, *Jim Crow in Boston: The Origin of the Separate but Equal Doctrine* (New York: Da Capo Press, 1974); Mark R. Schneider, *Boston Confronts Jim Crow, 1890–1920* (Boston: Northeastern University Press, 1997); Davison M. Douglas, *Jim Crow Moves North: The Battle over Northern School Segregation, 1865–1954* (New York: Cambridge University Press, 2005).

21. In a 2003 essay, Jeanne Theoharis stresses that racial violence in Boston did not come "out of the blue" in 1974, as the *Boston Globe* wrote at the time, but was the result of a long trail of history leading to that point. "Accounts of Boston's desegregation have focused primarily on white resistance to desegregation," she explains, "ignoring the 25 years of organizing prior to Judge Garrity's decision and the many whites who did not oppose it. While devoting ample space to white parents and their organized resistance, many authors brush over the well-coordinated, decades-long struggle that black parents went through to address racial inequalities in Boston's public schools." "For twenty-five years," Theoharis reminds us, "black activists had organized meetings, organizations, rallies, boycotts, independent busing programs, independent schools, and candidacies for public office all to draw attention to the inequalities endemic in [Boston Public Schools]." Jeanne Theoharis, "I'd Rather Go to School in the South": How Boston's School Desegregation Complicates the Civil Rights Paradigm," in *Freedom North: Black Freedom Struggles Outside the South, 1940–1980,* ed. Jeanne Theoharis and Komozi Woodard (New York: Palgrave Macmillan, 2003), 125–51.

22. Methodologically, *Before Busing* weaves together a host of secondary sources, drawing not only from Black freedom movement studies but also whiteness studies, labor history, and post–World War II political history more broadly. In addition, the manuscript puts to use a wealth of primary source material, including local and national newspapers and magazines, political and legal documents, organizational and personal records from civil rights organizations and movement participants, photographs, newsreel footage, and archival and original oral histories.

23. This fact is somewhat ironic considering that many monuments to Boston's legacy of slavery are literally "hidden in plain sight." Codman Square in Dorchester is named after John Codman, who is said to have treated his slaves so cruelly that they killed him in his home. Peter Faneuil, after whom Boston's famous Faneuil Hall is named, was involved in the slave trade, having advertised in 1738 for "a strait limbed [West Indian] Negro lad ... about the age of from 12 to fifteen years." Desrochers, Robert E. "Slave-for-Sale Advertisements and Slavery in Massachusetts, 1704–1781." *The William and Mary Quarterly* 59, no. 3 (2002): 623–64. https://doi.org/10.2307/3491467.

24. Milagros "Milly" Arbaje-Thomas became the CEO of METCO in January 2018. She is the first person of Latinx descent to helm this Black founded civil rights organization, a mainstay in the Boston school desegregation fight. Spanish-speaking students in Boston have also had their own movement against Boston's Jim Crow education, mainly centered around bilingual education. For more on this, see Milagros Gonzalez, "The impact of school desegregation and busing on the Hispanic community of Boston" (master's thesis, Boston University, 1989); Tatiana Maria Fernández Cruz, "Boston's Struggle in Black and Brown: Racial Politics, Community Development, and Grassroots Organizing, 1960–1985" (PhD diss., University of Michigan, 2017).

Chapter One

1. Christopher Columbus, *The Log of Christopher Columbus*, ed. Robert Fuson (New York: Mc-Graw Hill, 1987), 32.

2. Some may argue it was the third settlement. This account neglects the Cape Ann colony, which started in Gloucester and then grew to Salem village.

3. John Winthrop's full quote: "For we must consider that we shall be a city upon a hill. The eyes of all people are upon us."

4. Jamestown, Virginia, the first permanent British colony in North America was founded in 1607. Indentured servants sold their labor for passage to the Chesapeake. Indentures ranged anywhere from two to seven years. There was a high mortality rate, and most died before their term expired. There were Blacks and whites, and only skin color distinguished early laborers. They worked, lived, and slept together as unfree laborers. They could earn their freedom at the end of the term. The Indians were knowledgeable about East Coast survival and influenced these new arrivals, showing them how to grow food crops and tobacco and how to make clothing. See James A. Rawley, *The Transatlantic Slave Trade: A History* (New York: W. W. Norton, 1981), 346.

5. According to Lorenzo Greene, Winthrop's journal entry was "the earliest recorded account of Negro slavery in New England. . . . Negroes may have been enslaved before that time but earlier allusions to slavery are inferential." Lorenzo Greene, *The Negro in Colonial New England*, quoted in A. Leon Higginbotham, *In the Matter of Color: Race and the American Legal Process; The Colonial Period* (New York: Oxford University Press, 1978), 61.

6. John Winthrop, *The History of New England from 1630 to 1649*, ed. James Savage (New York: Arno Press, 1972), 1:278. William Pierce was the captain of the *Desire*, which sailed out of Salem, Massachusetts. Providence Isle was a Puritan settlement off the coast of Central America. As John Jennings writes, Captain William Pierce "carried a number of Indian captive slaves to the Island of Providence in the Caribbean, and returned the following year with 'some cotton, tobacco, and negroes, etc., . . . and salt from Tertugos.'" John Jennings, *Boston, Cradle of Liberty, 1630–1776* (Garden City, NY: Doubleday, 1947), 38. Winthrop's description continues, as quoted by Jennings: "Mr. James Smith with his mate Keyser were bound to Guinea to trade for negroes. But when they arrived there they met some Londoners, with whom they consorted, and the Londoners having been formerly injured by the natives (or at least pretending the same,) they invited them aboard one of their ships upon the Lord's Day, and such as came they kept prisoners, then they landed men and a murderer (a small cannon), and assaulted one of their towns and killed many of the people, but the

country coming down, they were forced to retire without any booty, divers of their men being wounded with the negroes' arrows, and one killed." Jennings, *Boston*, 38–39.

7. Higginbotham, *In the Matter of Color*, 66.

8. J. Anthony Lukas, *Common Ground: A Turbulent Decade in the Lives of Three American Families* (Vintage Books: New York, 1985), 54.

9. Jared Hardesty, *Black Lives, Native Lands, White Worlds: A History of Slavery in New England* (Amherst: Bright Leaf, 2019).

10. Massachusetts never had the number of slaves that would arrive to the Virginia colony. Lorenzo Greene states that Blacks numbered less than a thousand in 1700 and were never more than 3 percent of the total population in the eighteenth century. Lorenzo J. Greene, *The Negro in Colonial New England*, Studies in American Negro Life (New York: Atheneum, 1968), 23.

11. Samuel Maverick, who many historians acknowledge as the first slaveholder in New England, held slaves on Noddles Island, today known as East Boston. See Robert Hayden, *African Americans in Boston: More Than 350 Years* (Boston: Trustees of the Boston Public Library, 1992).

12. Higginbotham, *In the Matter of Color*, 62.

13. Higginbotham, *In the Matter of Color*, 71.

14. Parliament revoked the monopoly granted to the Royal African Company for slave trading, thereby enabling the English to engage in the slave trade legally. In 1713, England gained the Asiento from Portugal, which had given the privilege of supplying 4,800 Black people every year for thirty years to Spain's American colonies. With the region's ample "resources" in shipbuilding, seamen, and enterprise in the maritime trades, New England became one of the most active regions for the slave trade in America. See Higginbotham, *In the Matter of Color*, 63.

15. Enslaved Africans had control of their labor, demonstrating the critical relationship between slavery as an institution and labor. One looked for opportunities to have control over the labor that was contributed. See W. E. B. Du Bois's *Black Reconstruction in America* for an example in which slave labor is described in terms of labor and in which Du Bois characterizes the withdrawal of slave labor as a "general strike." Du Bois, W. E. B., *Black Reconstruction in America; an Essay Toward a History of the Part Which Black Folk Played in the Attempt to Reconstruct Democracy in America, 1860–1880* (Cleveland: World Pub. Co., 1964).

16. One example is Dylan Penningroth, *The Claims of Kinfolk: African American Property and Community in the Nineteenth-Century South* (Chapel Hill: University of North Carolina Press, 2003). See also Tera Hunter, *Bound in Wedlock: Slave and Free Black Marriage in the Nineteenth Century* (Cambridge, MA: Belknap Press of Harvard University Press, 2017).

17. As slavery became more and more limited over time, as far as Black persons in bondage were concerned, they were increasingly considered chattel. See Thomas D. Morris, *Southern Slavery and the Law, 1619–1860: Studies in Legal History* (Chapel Hill: University of North Carolina Press, 1996).

18. See Nina Sankovitch, *The Lowells of Massachusetts: An American Family* (New York: St. Martin's, 2017), 75.

19. As A. Leon Higginbotham has written, "This statement underscores the ambivalent attitude toward slavery even within the 'God-fearing' Puritan Massachusetts Bay Colony, a

point not always dealt with fully by historians and scholars." Higginbotham, *In the Matter of Color*, 61.

20. The notion of predestination—that slaves were pre-destined (ordained) to be slaves—was listed in the story of the "Curse of Ham," which had been used to popularize what was then regarded as a rather sophisticated, even commonly held theory on the origin of the races. As such, it was neither illegal nor against Christianity to own slaves. Thomas Bray, an Englishman (part of the Society for Propagation of the Gospel), helped promote the idea that where there can be no physical freedom for slaves, there should be spiritual freedom.

21. Edmund Burke, *A Vindication of Natural Society: or, A View of the Miseries and Evils arising to Mankind from every Species of Artificial Society; In a Letter to Lord **** by a Late Noble Writer*, ed. Frank N. Pagano (Indianapolis: Liberty Classics, 1982).

22. There are two kinds of rebellion that scholars discuss: "inward rebellion," through which individuals gain immediate gratification but in the end are more punished, such as with truancy, where they get punished upon return to the plantation; and "outward rebellion," which entails trying to escape slavery altogether.

23. Several factors explain this state of affairs. Due to the failure of indentured servitude and Indigenous servitude, and an ironic twist of fate in which many Africans built up an immunity to European diseases that the Indigenous population lacked, an increase in African slave labor occurred. As early as the 1490s, Africans were being used as slaves on the Canary Islands and the Azores and Majorca under the Portuguese, and only two years after Columbus's maiden voyage, the Caravel and the Lateen Sail were perfected, shortening the trip from Africa to the New World to a mere ninety days. This confluence of events earned Massachusetts and Virginia the "distinction" as the first places in the New World where the land would be cursed with racial slavery. It also made these areas sites of revolt, where African slaves repeatedly put their lives at stake in an effort to claim their freedom.

24. Greene writes, "From the evidence showing the employment of Negroes in various fields it seems evident, despite frequent assertions to the contrary, that Negroes were a valuable and essential part of New England's labor supply and that they unquestionably played a role in the commercial and industrial development of that section." Greene, *Negro in Colonial New England*, quoted in Joanne Pope Melish, *Disowning Slavery: Gradual Emancipation and "Race" in New England, 1780–1860* (Ithaca: Cornell University Press, 1998), 16.

25. It was estimated that between one-quarter to one-half of the enslaved on a given voyage did not survive the journey. As a result, it was deemed profitable to fill the ship with as many enslaved people as possible in order to maximize the number who survived the journey. Scholars estimate that between 1451 and 1870, between 9.5 million and 14.9 million Africans were brought to the New World. Demand and profitability as well as competition for commerce is what changed.

26. There was a popular belief among many Africans that one's spirit would not rest if they left their homeland. Of course, by the time they reached the ports, many had already long left their homelands, which were far away in the interior of the continent.

27. Enslaved Africans were fed twice a day, and these were the times when people were the most apt to mutiny, because everyone was on deck. As the trade picked up, men were kept below deck and women above deck. Mealtimes were unfettered—no chains.

28. There has been long debate about the migration patterns of the sharks in the Atlantic, which may have changed due to the transatlantic slave trade. See Marcus Rediker, "History

from below the Water Line: Sharks and the Atlantic Slave Trade," *Atlantic Studies* 5, no. 2 (August 2008): 285–97.

29. "In Massachusetts, where there was no staple crop, a large labor force was unnecessary; indentured servants were probably adequate. And, because the actual number of blacks in the colony was too small to prompt a fear of revolt, there seemed to be little reason for the development of a separate legal status repressive of them." Higginbotham, *In the Matter of Color*, 71. See also Winthrop D. Jordan, *The White Man's Burden: Historical Origins of Racism in the United States* (New York: Oxford University Press, 1974), 66.

30. Joanne Pope Melish, *Disowning Slavery: Gradual Emancipation and "Race" in New England, 1780–1860* (Ithaca, NY: Cornell University Press, 1998), 16.

31. The bodies of many of the first Africans who lived there are still buried in the Copp's Hill Burial Ground, dominated by the spires of Christ Church.

32. An important monument on the Boston Common, which features Crispus Attucks, commemorates not only the struggle for freedom from colonial rule but freedom from enslavement.

33. "People and Events: Crispus Attucks, c. 1723–1770," *Africans in America*, www.pbs.org /wgbh/aia/part2/2p24.html.

34. Robin D. G. Kelley and Earl Lewis, *To Make Our World Anew: A History of African Americans* (New York: Oxford University Press, 2000).

35. Harriet Beecher Stowe, introduction to *The Colored Patriots of the American Revolution: The American Negro, His History and Literature*, ed. William C. Nell (New York: Arno Press, 1968).

36. John Boyle O'Reilly, "Crispus Attucks," *Contributions in Black Studies* 13 (1995): 161–64. These later commemorations of Attucks were not the first to recognize his sacrifice. At the trial following the massacre, John Adams conceded that Attucks, whom he called "a stout mullato," had "undertaken to be the hero of the night."

37. Between 1775 and 1783, eight thousand to ten thousand Black men served on the colonial side. In Massachusetts, 572 soldiers (regular Black soldiers) served in integrated forces as boat pilots and in other roles. For Black Americans, trying to fight in the war was not easy, as George Washington had made it clear that he did not want them serving in any colonial army. Meanwhile, Massachusetts let slaves enlist in the Continental Army, and Black patriots like Peter Salem, Barzillai Lew, Prince Hall, Salem Poor, Cuff Whitmore, Cato Wood, and Col. George Middleton distinguished themselves in the battles of Bunker Hill, Lexington, Concord, and Lincoln. Despite these heroic feats, in November 1775 General George Washington maintained his policy of excluding Black soldiers. Rhode Island and Connecticut believed that neither slaves nor free Black men should serve in the Continental Army, but they changed their minds after Lord Dunmore's proclamation, which resulted in many slaves taking the opportunity to run away.

38. For more on the Black maritime tradition, see W. Jeffrey Bolster, *Black Jacks: African American Seamen in the Age of Sail* (Cambridge, MA: Harvard University Press, 1997).

39. Sidney Kaplan and Emma Nogrady Kaplan, *The Black Presence in the Era of the American Revolution* (Amherst: University of Massachusetts Press, 1989).

40. "Created Equal: How Benjamin Banneker Challenged Jefferson on Race and Freedom," Facing History and Ourselves, accessed March 23, 2022, www.facinghistory.org /nobigotry/readings/created-equal.

41. In this age of optimism and natural rights of man bloomed men and women who would hold the country up to its professed ideologies of freedom in the next generation— the ultimate indicator of freedom in the "cradle of liberty."

42. Allen Carden, *Freedom's Delay: America's Struggle for Emancipation, 1776–1865* (Knoxville: University of Tennessee Press, 2014).

43. The Declaration of Rights in the Constitution of the Commonwealth of Massachusetts is comparable to the Bill of Rights in the U.S. Constitution.

44. Commonwealth of Massachusetts v. Nathaniel Jennison (1783).

45. Van Gosse, "Fight for Black Voting Rights Precedes the Constitution," *Boston Globe*, March 12, 2015.

46. Gosse, "Fight for Black Voting." See also Van Gosse, *The First Reconstruction: Black Politics in America from the Revolution to the Civil War* (Chapel Hill: University of North Carolina Press, 2021).

47. Much later, Martin Luther King's close friend, the Reverend Michael Haynes, Pastor of Twelfth Baptist Church, in explaining Martin Luther King's admiration for the Bay State, would say, "King would never forget . . . about Boston where blacks had held the franchise long before the brutality of Selma spread passage of Voting Rights Act." "Pin His Ear to the Wisdom Post: Martin Luther King, Jr., and the School of Prophets," Exhibit, Boston University.

48. Many of the buildings George Middleton built in Boston, including the first wooden house, still stand.

49. Lerone Bennett Jr., *Before the Mayflower: A History of America* (Chicago: Johnson's, 1969).

50. Ruth Batson, *The Black Educational Movement in Boston: A Sequence of Historical Events* (Boston: School of Education, Northeastern University, 2001), 28.

51. According to James and Lois Horton, "Paul Cuffe was one of Boston's few influential black citizens of this era—a shipbuilder, a Quaker, a sea captain. Cuffe was an important supporter of African Colonization for Blacks." James Oliver Horton and Lois E. Horton, *Black Bostonians: Family Life and Community Struggle in the Antebellum North*, rev. ed. (New York: Holmes & Meier, 1999), 197. See also Martha Hodes. *The Sea Captain's Wife: A True Story of Love, Race, and War in the Nineteenth Century* (New York: W. W. Norton, 2006).

52. David Walker, *David Walker's Appeal, in Four Articles, Together with a Preamble to the Coloured Citizens of the World, but in Particular, and Very Expressly, to Those of the United States of America*, rev. ed. (New York: Hill and Wang, 1995), 7.

53. Shortly after the publication of his appeal, a bounty was put on his head.

54. Garrison burned copies of the Constitution on the front steps of the State House, haranguing it as a "pro-slavery" document. However, unlike Walker, Garrison didn't believe that blood should be spilled to end slavery.

55. Harriet H. Robinson, "Loom and Spindle, or Life amongst the Early Mill Girls" (Boston: Thomas Y. Crowell, 1898). See also Robert L. Hall, ed., *Making a Living: The Work Experience of African Americans in New England* (Boston: New England Foundation for the Humanities, 1995).

56. David Morris Potter and Don Edward Fehrenbacher, *The Impending Crisis, 1848–1861: The New American Nation Series* (New York: Harper & Row, 1976).

57. Declaration of the National Anti-Slavery Convention, 1833, https://lostmuseum.cuny .edu/archive/declaration-of-the-national-antislavery.

58. In many ways, that prediction would come true, although it would not be until much later. Lincoln, who himself believed at one point in the idea of relocating Black people to another country before he became president, would come to exemplify this idea.

59. Ousmane Power-Greene, *Against Wind and Tide: The African American Struggle against the Colonization Movement* (New York: New York University Press, 2014).

60. Manisha Sinha writes about this in her work. See Manisha Sinha, *The Slave's Cause: A History of Abolition* (New Haven, CT: Yale University Press, 2016). See also Wilson J. Moses, *Classical Black Nationalism: From the American Revolution to Marcus Garvey* (New York: New York University Press, 1996); Wilson J. Moses, *The Golden Age of Black Nationalism, 1850–1925* (Hamden, CT: Archon Books, 1978); William L. Van Deburg, *Modern Black Nationalism: From Marcus Garvey to Louis Farrakhan* (New York: New York University Press, 1997).

61. In response to the efforts of the ACS and others, Garrison decried the idea of relocating Black Americans to Africa. Rather, he and others advocated for abolition in the United States. See Power-Greene, Ousmane K., *Against Wind and Tide: The African American Struggle against the Colonization Movement* (New York: New York University Press, 2014).

62. The African Repository and Colonial Journal (1825–1850) changed its name to the African Repository from 1850–1892 and then finally to Liberia in 1892.

63. A slightly more watered-down version of this goal manifested in the American Colonization Society (ACS), founded in 1817, intended to send Black Americans to Africa as an alternative to emancipation in the United States. The ACS was a less principled form of abolitionism. It was composed primarily of slave owners as well as some "moral suasion" abolitionists, like Garrison.

64. *Liberator* 1, no. 1 (January 1831), http://www.masshist.org/database/viewer.php?old =1&item_id=1742.

65. Phyl Garland, "Too Long Have Others Spoken for Us," http://newsreel.org/guides /blackpress/toolong.htm.

66. The 55th was commanded by Norwood Penrose Hallowell; Shaw commanded the 54th until his death in battle in 1863, after which command of the 54th went to his second-in-command, Edward Needles Hallowell.

67. Historians like Steven Hahn have argued that emancipation was a response to former slaves who fled the South as the Civil War began and flooded Union camps, as well as broader military expediency.

68. John Dewey, *Democracy and Education: An Introduction to the Philosophy of Education* (New York: Macmillan, 1916).

69. Batson, *Black Educational Movement in Boston*, 27.

70. Batson, *Black Educational Movement in Boston*, 27.

71. Batson, *Black Educational Movement in Boston*, 27.

72. Russwurm, who has a fascinating backstory of his own, especially regarding his heritage, would later become involved in the American Colonization Society. Sandra Sandiford Young, "John Brown Russwurm's Dilemma: Citizenship or Emigration?," in *Prophets of Protest: Reconsidering the History of American Abolitionism*, ed. Timothy Patrick McCarthy and John Stauffer (New York: New Press: Distributed by W. W. Norton, 2006).

73. Other restrictions allow students to learn how to read and write but not to learn grammar. See Batson, *Black Educational Movement in Boston*.

74. In circumstances that proved relatively common for the time, Black abolitionists were not invited to participate in the charter meeting; the first principal actors were all white abolitionists. William Lloyd Garrison eventually led the movement to integrate the group.

74. Batson, *Black Educational Movement in Boston*, 32.

75. Batson, *Black Educational Movement in Boston*, 32.

76. Batson, *Black Educational Movement in Boston*, 32.

77. Batson, *Black Educational Movement in Boston*, 32.

78. Levy and Jones, *Jim Crow in Boston*, xxix.

79. Inspired by William Lloyd Garrison, Nell continued to lecture and organize antislavery meetings until he moved to Rochester in 1847, where he joined Frederick Douglass in publishing Douglass's newspaper, the *North Star*. He stayed involved in Boston politics through Rochester.

80. Donald M. Jacobs, *Courage and Conscience: Black and White Abolitionists in Boston* (Bloomington: Indiana University Press, 1993).

81. Batson, *Black Educational Movement in Boston*, 34.

82. Batson, *Black Educational Movement in Boston*, 34.

83. Putnam petitioned the Primary School Committee with eighty-five others. Apparently there were two petitions with the same number of signatories. "1846 Petition to Primary School Committee," June 15, 1846, Museum of African American History, www .smithcourtstories.org/assets/1846-petition-to-primary-school-committee.

84. "Opinion—Roberts," Brown Foundation, accessed December 23, 2021, https:// brownvboard.org/content/opinion-roberts?page=2.

85. Batson, *Black Educational Movement in Boston*, 35.

86. Batson, *Black Educational Movement in Boston*, 35.

87. This was based on the 1845 law. That same year, Benjamin Roberts filed a lawsuit on behalf of his daughter, Sarah Roberts. Many of the people involved in the boycott against the Smith School were also involved in the Roberts lawsuit.

88. Sarah C. Roberts v. City of Boston, 59 Mass. 198 (1850), 1.

89. Charles Sumner, *Orations and Speeches [1845–1850]* (United States: Ticknor, Reed, and Fields, 1850). See also "Equality Before the Law" 1870, www.thirteen.org/wnet/slavery /experience/education/docs6.html.

90. Richard Kluger, *Simple Justice: The History of "Brown v. Board of Education" and Black America's Struggle for Equality* (New York: Vintage Books, 1977), 75.

91. Argument of Charles Sumner, Esq., against the Constitutionality of Separate Colored Schools, in the Case of *Sarah C. Roberts v. The City of Boston*, Before the Supreme Court of Massachusetts, December 4, 1849.

92. Kluger, *Simple Justice*, 75.

93. "Brown—Opinion," Brown Foundation for Educational Equity, accessed December 23, 2021), https://brownvboard.org/content/opinion-roberts?page=4.

94. James Oliver Horton and Michele Gates Moresi, "*Roberts, Plessy,* and *Brown*: The Long, Hard Struggle against Segregation," *OAH Magazine of History* 15, no. 2 (2001): 14–16, www.jstor.org/stable/25163419.

95. Lukas, *Common Ground*, 55.

96. Stephen Kendrick and Paul Kendrick, *Sarah's Long Walk: The Free Blacks of Boston and How Their Struggle for Equality Changed America* (Boston: Beacon Press, 2004), xxiii.

97. Evelyn Brooks Higginbotham offers a course at Harvard University that delves into this history. She writes in the course description, "The legal case *Roberts v. City of Boston* emerged from the courage of the father of young Sarah Roberts and the larger Black community's protest efforts against the city's segregated public schools." See also John Hope Franklin and Evelyn Brooks Higginbotham, *From Slavery to Freedom: A History of African Americans*, 9th ed. (New York: McGraw-Hill, 2011), 111.

98. Zebulon V. Miletsky, "City of Amalgamation: Race, Marriage, Class and Color in Boston, 1890–1930" (PhD diss., University of Massachusetts Amherst, 2008).

99. Stephen Kantrowitz, *More Than Freedom: Fighting for Black Citizenship in a White Republic, 1829–1889* (New York: Penguin, 2012), 44.

Chapter Two

1. Booker T. Washington, *Up from Slavery* (New York: Penguin, 1986), 251.

2. Washington, *Up from Slavery*, 252.

3. Washington was there to celebrate the unveiling of Augustus Saint-Gaudens' monument, which took fourteen years to complete. As noted by Martin H. Blatt, "The story of the Fifty-fourth Massachusetts provides a prism for analysis of race relations from the Civil War era to the present," Martin H. Blatt, Thomas J. Brown, and Donald Yacovone, eds., *Hope and Glory: Essays on the Legacy of the 54th Massachusetts Regiment* (Amherst: University of Massachusetts Press, 2001), 2.

4. Stephen R. Fox, *The Guardian of Boston: William Monroe Trotter* (New York: Atheneum, 1970); Washington, *Up from Slavery* (New York: Penguin, 1986).

5. Shawn Leigh Alexander, *An Army of Lions: The Civil Rights Struggle before the NAACP* (Philadelphia: University of Pennsylvania Press, 2012).

6. National Afro American League (1887–1893), accessed December 26, 2021, https://blackpast.org/aah/national-afro-american-league-1887-1893.

7. These are the earliest national civil rights organizations in America.

8. Booker T. Washington, *My Larger Education; Being Chapters from My Experience* (Garden City, N.Y.: Doubleday, 1911), 120–23; *Guardian*, April 23, 1904, 4; W. M. Trotter to George A. Towns, October 28, 1903, George A. Towns Papers; Booker T. Washington and Ernest Davidson Washington, *Selected Speeches of Booker T. Washington* (Garden City, N.Y.: Doubleday, Doran & Company, 1932), 39–40; Booker T. Washington, *The Future of the American Negro* (Boston: Small, Maynard & company, 1899), 48.

9. Fox, *Guardian of Boston*, 39.

10. *Boston Guardian*, April 2, 1904, 4; *Boston Guardian*, March 19, 1904, 4; "The Industrial Threat," *Guardian* editorial enclosed with letter from Charles Alexander to Booker T. Washington, May 31, 1905, Booker T. Washington Papers.

11. Fox, *Guardian of Boston*, 41.

12. August Meier, "Toward a Reinterpretation of Booker T. Washington," *Journal of Southern History* 23, no. 2 (May 1957): 220–27.

13. It becomes essential to understand how Washington's national leadership affects that struggle—with him being a significant educator—and how that would have influenced northern cities like Boston. William Monroe Trotter's leadership not only will come to mirror the civil rights movement but also serves as a precursor to the Black Power movement.

14. Booker T. Washington to Charles William Eliot, Harvard University Archives, UAI 5.150, box 69. Also found in Louis R. Harlan, *Booker T. Washington Papers* Vol 4. (Urbana-Champaign: University of Illinois Press, 1975), 175.

15. As Stephen Fox, the principal biographer of Trotter, explains, "Three and one half months later, a thousand miles and several worlds from that Harvard commencement, Booker T. Washington stood up and made a speech at a trade exposition in Atlanta. It was a blandly phrased but desperate attempt to halt recent trends in southern race relations." Fox, *Guardian of Boston*, 19.

16. To date, the best account we have of Trotter's life is Stephen Fox's the *Guardian of Boston*. Fox's treatment of Trotter can be summarized into three significant periods: the challenge he mounted to the leadership of Booker T. Washington (1901–09), the period of his involvement in building interracial protest organizations (1910–19), and the period that Fox characterizes as the consolidation at home and the decline of Trotter's influence as a national leader (1920–34). Fox, *Guardian of Boston*.

17. They participated in a public, civic dialogue—sometimes in conflict and sometimes in agreement—regarding programs to uplift the race. Indeed, the city continued to feature prominently in these debates, serving as home to Trotter and a base of operations for Washington.

18. All three, however, shaped a generation through their philosophical clashes, many of which mirrored the earlier struggle regarding Black education during the *Roberts v. Boston* case of 1850.

19. While Du Bois would eventually come to revise his thinking on this, the notion of the Talented Tenth remains important to understanding Du Bois's evolving thoughts on education. See W. E. B. Du Bois, *The Negro Problem* (New York: James Pott, 1903).

20. It is important to state at the outset that people changed loyalties regularly during these years. At any given moment during these struggles, Du Bois, Wells, and even Trotter would find themselves working in the orbit of the primary leader of the race between 1895 and 1910: Booker T. Washington.

21. Ultimately, Washington would make it his business to undermine them, at least in the case of Wells.

22. E. L. Thornbrough, ed., *Great Lives Observed: Booker T. Washington* (New Jersey: Prentice Hall, 1969), 34.

23. Thornbrough, *Great Lives Observed*, 35.

24. Francis Jackson Garrison, the youngest son of William Lloyd Garrison and founder of the NAACP, was an ardent supporter of Washington, as was William Lloyd Garrison Jr., the eldest son and namesake of the fiery Boston abolitionist. In 1908, Garrison Jr. gave a speech in which he spoke about civil rights for Black people. Subsequently, Trotter used the piece in his newspaper to contrast Washington's line. Outraged at Trotter's misuse of his speech, Garrison Jr. fired back in a letter to Trotter that Washington was "the most remarkable living American, Black or white." Garrison Jr. went further, criticizing Trotter as elitist. "How easy for colored men with academic advantages, secure in the stronghold of anti-

slavery sentiment, to affect disdain and engage in bitter speech." Some historians contend they did not support his position on the abandonment of civil rights. See Mark R. Schneider, "The Colored American and Alexander's: Boston's Pro-Civil Rights Bookerites," *Journal of Negro History* 80, no. 4 (1995): 157–69.

25. Mark R. Schneider, *Boston Confronts Jim Crow, 1890–1920* (Boston: Northeastern University Press, 1997), 77.

26. As Mark Schneider has written, "His intellectual heritage was of New England: Puritanism, Yankee capitalists and even abolitionists all molded Washington's thought, along with the influence of Gilded Age commercialism." See Schneider, "Colored American and Alexander's, 157–69.

27. Fox notes, "Treasurer of the Business League was Gilbert C. Harris, also a Bostonian of southern background and the owner of a prosperous wig-making concern. Frank Chisholm, a Tuskegee graduate and northern field representative for the school, who lived in Cambridge. Other active black Bookerites in the area included the attorney Clifford Plummer, a manufacturing chemist named Philip J. Allston, and Peter J. Smith, a job printer and sometime handyman. Smith briefly published a newspaper to compete with the *Guardian* and was constantly seeking favors from Tuskegee." Schneider, *Boston Confronts Jim Crow*, 42.

28. Joseph Bernardo, "National Negro Business League (1900–)," BlackPast, November 26, 2008, www.blackpast.org/african-american-history/national-negro-business-league.

29. Portia was a special student, only taking three classes. She lived off-campus and suffered from extreme loneliness. "As a special student, she wasn't allowed to live on campus and roomed instead in a house on Howe Street and ate her meals with several college professors, including Katharine Lee Bates, Katharine Coman, and Emily Greene Balch. And although race was not the reason that Portia lived off campus—at the time, there were a few black students who lived in the dormitories—it is believed that she may have been subject to racism by some of the many southern white students at the school. Portia, therefore, found it difficult to make friends with her classmates. There is no doubt that this social discomfort was detrimental to her academic performance and resulted in the failure of one of her music classes, a subject at which she normally excelled." Jdorin, "Booker T. Washington," *Wellesley History: A Collection of Profiles on Historical Buildings, People, and Places* (blog), https://wellesleyhistory.wordpress.com/2013/03/07/booker-t-washington.

30. He chose Boston as the site for the first convention of the National Negro Business League in 1900 and convened several meetings in the city, some of which were attended by his children.

31. Washington concludes, "During the next half century and more, my race must continue passing through the severe American crucible. We are to be tested in our patience, our forbearance, our perseverance, our power to endure wrong, to withstand temptations, to economize, to acquire and use skill; our ability to compete, to succeed in commerce, to disregard the superficial for the real, the appearance for the substance; to be great and yet small, learned and yet simple, high and yet the servant of all. This, this is the passport to all that is best in the life of our republic, and the negro must possess it or be debarred." Booker T. Washington, *The Story of My Life and Work* (New York: Negro Universities Press, 1969), 65.

32. Schneider, *Boston Confronts Jim Crow*, 77.

33. Dan Desrochers, "A Historical Figure Hiding in Plain Sight," *Westfield News*, April 15, 2017, https://thewestfieldnews.com/historical-figure-hiding-plain-sight.

34. Fox, *Guardian of Boston*, 26.

35. Fox, *Guardian of Boston*, 46.

36. Fox, *Guardian of Boston*, 46.

37. In Trotter's mind and others', Washington carried with him some dangerous ideas, such as industrial training over liberal arts schooling and, more importantly, an accommodation to segregation and Jim Crow, which was anathema to Trotter and other inheritors of Boston's abolitionist tradition, both Black and white.

38. Fox, *Guardian of Boston*, 45.

39. Fox, *Guardian of Boston*, 45.

40. *Boston Guardian*, August 1, 1903.

41. Dick Lehr, *The Birth of a Movement: How "Birth of a Nation" Ignited the Battle for Civil Rights*, 2nd ed. (New York: Public Affairs, 2017).

42. "That Boston Riot"; *Colored American* (Washington, DC), August 22, 1903, 6.

43. *Freeman* (Indianapolis, Indiana), August 15, 1903.

44. Elliott M. Rudwick, "Race Leadership Struggle: Background of the Boston Riot of 1903," *Journal of Negro Education* 31 (1962): 16.

45. W. E. B. Du Bois, *The Autobiography of W. E. B. Dubois: A Soliloquy on Viewing My Life from the Last Decade of Its First Century* (New York: International, 1968), 380.

46. W. M. Trotter to John A. Fairlie, June 15, 1902, John Archibald Fairlie Papers; Booker T. Washington to Francis J. Garrison, May 17, 1905, Booker T. Washington Papers.

47. *Boston Guardian*, October 22, 1904, quoted in Fox, *Guardian of Boston*, 33.

48. For better or worse, Trotter would also be just as caustic in his critique of competing organizations, most notably the NAACP. At various times, when it suited his purpose, he would also collaborate with the NAACP and other broad-based organizations for social change.

49. Both of Trotter's parents were the offspring of white slave masters and their Black female slaves. See Lehr, *Birth of a Movement*.

50. Susan Gray and Bestor Cram, dirs., *Birth of a Movement: The Battle against America's First Blockbuster*, 2017, season 18, episode 7 (Arlington, VA: Public Broadcasting Service, 2017), 55 mins.

51. Carl Senna, "William Monroe Trotter: A Black Hero," *Bay State Banner*, September 24, 1966. It should be noted that Senna was faithfully chronicling Trotter's life before Fox's definitive biography was published.

52. Harvard University's first Black undergraduate, Richard T. Greener, graduated in 1870.

53. Fox, *Guardian of Boston*, 19. W. M. Trotter to John A. Fairlie, October 29, 1895, Fairlie Papers.

54. *Boston Daily Globe*, May 26, 1893, clipping in William H. Lewis folder, Harvard Archives; *Boston Guardian*, August 18, 1952, 5; *Harvard College Class of 1895: Fourth Report* (Cambridge, MA, 1910), 1999; *New York Times*, January 13, 1923, 5; Fox, *Guardian of Boston*, 19.

55. William Edward Burghardt Du Bois, "William Monroe Trotter," *Crisis* 41 no. 5 (May 1934).

56. According to historian J. A. Rogers, the business—and the inheritance that made it possible—proved so successful that Trotter became "the second wealthiest Negro in Boston." See Mabe Kountze, *A History of the Early Colored Press of Massachusetts and a Second Sketch of the "Boston Guardian*," Emory University Archives, July 10, 1967.

57. The reasons for his transformation remain elusive, but we cannot ignore the issue of mental health, which although rarely explored by scholars, likely played a role in Trotter's life.

58. *Boston Guardian*, December 28, 1918, 4; William Monroe Trotter Papers, Boston University.

59. Fox, *Guardian of Boston*, 19.

60. Melnea Cass, a trusted advocate for Black Bostonians, met William Trotter around the time of the women's suffrage movement and the passage of the Nineteenth Amendment. The militant Trotter had a lasting impact on Cass, who led several women's clubs in Boston focused on education and creating financial stability for Black families. Cass recollected what Trotter meant to the city. "Well you know Trotter," she recalled. "He was way ahead of his years I believe because he was a person who graduated from Harvard and was a member of the Phi Beta Kappa which is one of the honorary societies by rating. And when he graduated, he became so disillusioned because of the racism and the prejudice that he encountered in Boston, he decided to begin his own newspaper to gain a voice in race politics. At the time that he couldn't do his chosen field of work that he wanted which was journalism. Journalism was his calling. He couldn't get a job and pay for anything like that. And so, then he turned to real estate for a while, but that wasn't his calling. And he just felt frustrated, so he'd travel, and he'd do what he wanted. So, he established the *Guardian* in the year of 1901 and began to print it. That was the mouthpiece for freedom for equality for anything he wanted to say, and he was a highly keyed up man on integration and no discrimination on account of color, couldn't stand that. So, he went forth with his ideals, and he succeeded in writing in the paper the kind of thing that he wanted. And he worked diligently for equality for us blacks. He founded the branch of the National Equal Rights League here in Boston." "Say Brother; Senior Citizens; Melnea Cass Interview," April 25, 1974, GBH Archives, http://openvault.wgbh.org/catalog/V_5913085B57A74E3A8331EE43 BD92CAC7.

61. See Georgetta Merritt Campbell, *Extant Collections of Early Black Newspapers: A Research Guide to the Black Press, 1880–1915, with an Index to the "Boston Guardian," 1902–1903* (Troy, NY: Whiston, 1981).

62. Fox, *Guardian of Boston*, 30.

63. *Boston Guardian*, September 6, 1902; *Boston Guardian*, November 1, 1902.

64. Trotter's biography sheds light on this aspect of his personality and politics. This gender and class analysis have larger implications for thinking about Black activism in the longer-term identity of the city.

65. As Fox notes, "A final complicating factor was the nature of the *Guardian's* attack on Washington: personal, vituperative, and occasionally vicious. At its most basic it was simple name calling: Pope Washington, the Black Boss, the Benedict Arnold of the Negro race, the Exploiter of all Exploiters, the Great Traitor, the Great Divider, the miserable toady, the Imperial Caesar, the heartless and snobbish purveyor of Pharisaical moral clap-trap." Fox, *Guardian of Boston*, 39.

66. Fox, *Guardian of Boston*, 40.

67. Fox, *Guardian of Boston*, 43.

68. Du Bois, *Autobiography of W. E. B. DuBois*, 380.

69. *Boston Guardian*, December 6, 1902.

70. *Boston Guardian*, January 10, 1903.

71. Fox, *Guardian of Boston*, 43

72. Because Fortune became loyal to Booker T. Washington, Wells was primarily working in the service of Washington and had made bids for several positions within Washington's various organizations.

73. Rudwick, "Race Leadership Struggle," 16, 20.

74. *Boston Transcript*, April 25, 1899; William H. Lewis, who had gone to Harvard with Du Bois, would also eventually succumb to Washington. Although he "played the fence," bouncing at various times between Trotter, Du Bois, and Washington, he would eventually accept a DC appointment through Washington.

75. Fox, *Guardian of Boston*, 35.

76. The eternal debate between W. E. B. Du Bois and Booker T. Washington is less a study in divergent philosophical views as it is a powerful lesson in how the dissent of two extraordinary men can serve to symbolize the pitfalls, perils, and promise of an entire race. Unlike the ideological rift that enveloped Washington and Du Bois and still captivates us today, a biographical study rather than merely an ideological one defies the kind of dialectical, binary suppositions that plague most characterizations of this now famous, or infamous, ideological breach.

77. The initial impetus for the organization of a Boston NAACP chapter came about, in part, in response to an uptick in Jim Crow policies in Boston, as well as long-standing grievances among the organization's founders, which included both white progressives and Black professionals—lawyers, physicians, and others—with regard to the abuses suffered by Black citizens. Discrimination in hotels and restaurants, schools with crumbling facilities, a lack of jobs, and an inability to join any of the white unions were just some examples of the kinds of injustices befalling Black Bostonians at this time.

78. James M. McPherson, *The Abolitionist Legacy: From Reconstruction to the N.A.A.C.P.* (Princeton, NJ: Princeton University Press, 1975).

79. Robert C. Hayden, *Boston's N.A.A.C.P. History, 1910–1982* (Boston, MA: Boston Branch N.A.A.C.P., 1982).

80. Hayden, *Boston's N.A.A.C.P. History*.

81. A white lawyer born in Roxbury, Storey was a vital part of the close relationship that the Boston chapter would share with the national organization.

82. However, as late as the 1960s, books in libraries of the Boston Public Schools still bore such titles as *Ten Little Niggers* and other racial epithets. The struggle for educational justice would be long indeed.

83. Lehr, *Birth of a Movement*.

84. Hayden, *Boston's N.A.A.C.P. History*.

85. Hayden, *Boston's N.A.A.C.P. History*.

86. Fox, *Guardian of Boston*.

87. Trotter changed his mind often throughout his career. Unlike Du Bois, however, Trotter was not as effective at explaining and documenting why he had done so. The one consistent thread running through his life was a willingness to fight.

88. Ray Stannard Baker, *Following the Color Line: American Negro Citizenship in the Progressive Era* (New York: Harper Torchbook, 1964), 120; *Boston Guardian*, May 23, 1903, 4.

89. Baker, *Following the Color Line*, 120.

90. As Ida B. Wells had pointed out, while slaves were brutally maimed or punished, they were rarely killed. That changed in the period after Reconstruction, during the period called "the nadir," when Black people were killed for sport. In this period, lynchings were common. Wells famously stated, "During the slave regime the Southern white man owned the Negro, body and soul. It was to his interest to dwarf the soul and preserve the body. The slave was rarely killed. He was too valuable. But emancipation came and the vested interests of the white man in the Negro's body were lost. With freedom, a new system of intimidation came into vogue. The Negro was not only whipped, scourged, he was killed." This was quoted in "A red record" New York Public Library Digital Collections, Schomburg Center for Research in Black Culture, Manuscripts, Archives and Rare Books Division, The New York Public Library. Accessed April 28, 2022. https://digitalcollections.nypl.org/items /510d47df-8dbd-a3d9-e040-e00a18064a99; Frederick Douglass, the most prominent Black leader of the nineteenth century, wrote Wells to thank her for her vigilance in the anti-lynching campaign. See Paula Giddings, *When and Where I Enter: The Impact of Black Women on Race and Sex in America* (New York: W. Morrow, 1984).

91. Trotter married one of Du Bois's lifelong loves, Deenie. And no amount of love was lost over it. Du Bois eventually made his peace with it.

92. Fox writes, "Further exacerbating the debate was an amorphous force, later summed up in the phrase 'the Tuskegee Machine' by W. E. B. Du Bois, which made it seem to Trotter that there was a conspiracy against him and anyone else who disputed Washington's leadership. Part of this could be traced to admirers of Washington who could not understand why any Negro should quarrel with Bookerite ideas; thus, for example, it seemed to Trotter that some of the Boston daily newspapers were 'smothering all those who wished to condemn' the Tuskegeean." Du Bois, *Autobiography of W. E. B. DuBois*, 248.

93. Dubois, *Autobiography of W. E. B. DuBois*, 253.

94. *Boston Evening Transcript*, July 15, 1905, 14; Rudwick, "Race Leadership Struggle," 94–95.

95. Fox, *Guardian of Boston*, 93.

96. Niagara Movement Declaration of Principles, 1905, https://glc.yale.edu/niagaras -declaration-principles-1905.

97. Shawn Leigh Alexander, *An Army of Lions: The Civil Rights Struggle before the NAACP* (Philadelphia: University of Pennsylvania Press, 2012).

98. Henry Louis Gates, William Edward Burghardt Du Bois, *The Oxford W. E. B. Du Bois* 19 (United States: Oxford University Press, 2007), 161.

99. John Winthrop, *A Model of Christian Charity* (1630), Collections of the Massachusetts Historical Society (Boston, 1838), 3rd series 7:31–48, Massachusetts Historical Society Collections, 46–47, https://history.hanover.edu/texts/winthmod.html.

100. https://www.digitalhistory.uh.edu/disp_textbook.cfm?smtid=2&psid=3579

101. Hebrews 11:1.

102. Matthew 5:14.

103. Oliver Wendell Holmes coined the phrase "Boston State-House is the hub of the solar system" in "The Autocrat of the Breakfast-Table," *Atlantic Monthly*, April 1858.

104. Winthrop, *Model of Christian Charity*.

105. Gerald Horne, *The Apocalypse of Settler Colonialism: The Roots of Slavery, White Supremacy, and Capitalism in Seventeenth-Century North America and the Caribbean* (New York: Monthly Review Press, 2018).

106. Winthrop, *Model of Christian Charity*.

Chapter Three

1. Thomas H. O'Connor, *The Boston Irish: A Political History* (Boston: Northeastern University Press, 1995).

2. Thomas Sugrue, "It's Not the Bus: It's Us," *London Review of Books*, November 20, 2008.

3. David R. Roediger, *The Wages of Whiteness: Race and the Making of the American Working Class* (London: Verso, 1991), 133.

4. Michael Patrick MacDonald, *All Souls: A Family Story from Southie* (Boston: Beacon Press, 1999).

5. Mark R. Schneider, *Boston Confronts Jim Crow: 1890–1920* (Boston: Northeastern University Press, 1997), 184.

6. Eugene Gordon writes, "He had been arrested once before for violating a minor traffic law and held for three days like a desperate criminal, incommunicado. He knew something of the workings of Law and Order, and he was afraid." Eugene Gordon, introduction to *The Borden Case: The Struggle for Negro Rights in Boston*, by League of Struggle for Negro Rights (Boston: League of Struggle for Negro Rights, 1934), 2.

7. Gordon, introduction, 2.

8. Eben Simmons Miller, "'A New Day Is Here': The Shooting of George Borden and 1930s Civil Rights Activism in Boston," *New England Quarterly* 73, no. 1 (2000): 3–31.

9. The warrant was for three outstanding traffic violations: driving without a license, driving to endanger, and refusing to pull over.

10. Gordon, introduction, 2.

11. Gordon, introduction.

12. Elizee, Andre, Eugene Gordon Papers, New York Public Library website, April 2006.

13. *Boston Chronicle*, February 27, 1932; *Boston Chronicle*, June 25, 1932.

14. "Liberals in Boston," 1930, box 6, folder 9, Eugene Gordon Papers, 1927–1972, Manuscripts, Archives and Rare Books Division, Schomburg Center for Research in Black Culture, New York Public Library.

15. The piece ultimately did not run, and the correspondence between Gordon and the editor demonstrate a major misunderstanding. The Eugene Gordon Collection at the Schomburg explains how important the conference was in giving rise to the Non-Alignment Movement. Gordon also coauthored with Cyril Briggs a pamphlet, *The Position of Negro Women*, and lived for a time in the Soviet Union, where he worked as a reporter for the *Moscow Daily News*. He cofounded and edited the Harlem Renaissance literary magazine *Saturday Evening Quill*. Gordon also put out major features pieces in the *Pittsburgh Courier* under the title "The Thirteen Most Important Negroes in the United States," Eugene Gordon Papers, 1927–1972, Manuscripts, Archives and Rare Books Division, Schomburg Center for Research in Black Culture, New York Public Library.

16. Dan T. Carter, *Scottsboro: A Tragedy of the American South* (London: Oxford University Press, 1971); James Goodman, *Stories of Scottsboro* (New York: Pantheon Books, 1994).

17. Gordon, introduction.

18. Gordon, introduction.

19. Gordon, introduction. See also Wilson Record, *The Negro and the Communist Party* (New York: Atheneum, 1971), 107. See also, L.S.N.R., "The Borden Case: The Struggle for Negro Rights in Boston." edited by The Fighting Leadership of the League of Struggle for Negro Rights (Boston, MA: Duke University Pamphlet Collection, 1934).

20. J. Anthony Lukas tells a story in *Common Ground* about Butler Wilson to illustrate the elitism of the Boston NAACP in those years. Because Lukas does not use footnotes or citations in *Common Ground*, it is unclear whether or not the story is true or apocryphal. He writes, "In 1912, a white social worker was strolling through a black neighborhood with Butler Wilson, a prominent 'Black Brahmin' and leader of the NAACP. Arguing about the establishment of a settlement house for black youth, they passed a group of young Negroes playing craps. 'What's to become of them?' the social worker asked. 'Let them rot!' snapped Wilson." J. Anthony Lukas, *Common Ground: A Turbulent Decade in the Lives of Three American Families* (New York: Knopf, 1985), 59. According to Gerald Gill, "In a February 1951 commentary critical of an upcoming Boston-branch NAACP testimonial dinner honoring Herbert L. Jackson, president of the Malden City Council, a *Boston Chronicle* editorial writer intoned: 'Now is not time for banqueting. . . .' In particular, the paper criticized the branch for its sluggishness over the past year in not mobilizing Boston's black residents to protest against both continued segregation in public housing units throughout the city and continued residential segregation in the renting or purchasing of housing in city neighborhoods other than the South End, Roxbury and North Dorchester." Gerald Gill, "'No Time for Banqueting': African-American Protests in Boston, 1945–1955," in "Struggling Yet in Freedom's Birthplace" (unpublished manuscript), Gerald R. Gill Papers, ca. 1950s–2007, Digital Collections and Archives, Tufts University, Medford, MA. See also *Boston Chronicle*, February 24, 1951.

21. This focus on workers by communists is reflective of early Black traditions of union organizing.

22. With the exception perhaps of Trotter's National Equal Rights League, more than any other type of organization the CPUSA would come to challenge the power of groups like the Boston NAACP most severely. Tilly Teixeira and others were also allies in the struggle for racial justice.

23. This was the oldest and first all-Black union in Boston. Unlike many of the other union arrangements in the city, the Black men who served at the Vendome organized themselves, as they told the *Boston Herald* in 1890. See "Colored Men in to Stay as Waiters," *Boston Herald*, November 9, 1890.

24. See Mark R. Schneider, "The Boston NAACP and the Decline of the Abolitionist Impulse," *Massachusetts Historical Review* 1 (1999): 95–113; Schneider, *Boston Confronts Jim Crow*. See also Elizabeth Hafkin Pleck, *Black Migration and Poverty, Boston, 1865–1900* (New York: Academic Press, 1979); Stephan Thernstrom, *The Other Bostonians; Poverty and Progress in the American Metropolis, 1880–1970* (Cambridge, MA: Harvard University Press, 1973).

25. James Philip Danky and Wayne A. Wiegand, *Print Culture in a Diverse America: The History of Communication* (Urbana: University of Illinois Press, 1998), 61.

26. Alfred Baker Lewis Papers, 1944–1980, *Boston Chronicle*, March 21, 1936.

27. On further reflection, although Lewis was a member of the NAACP, the organization itself offered no formal support on behalf of the proposed bill, and it did not pass. Only

Louis Francis of the Roxbury Socialist Club testified before the committee. Although there is not a lot of information available about the Roxbury Socialist Club, it was located at 325 Harrison Avenue, according to the American Jewish Yearbook of 1932. *Boston Chronicle*, March 5, 1932.

28. Amistad Research Center, University of Illinois at Urbana-Champaign; *Boston Chronicle*, March 21, 1936.

29. *Boston Chronicle*, February 29, 1936.

30. *Boston Chronicle*, February 29, 1936.

31. *Boston Chronicle*, July 24, 1937.

32. *Boston Chronicle*, July 24, 1937.

33. *Boston Chronicle*, July 24, 1937.

34. For the inferior category, the following jobs were named: janitors; laborers; servants and waiters; stewards; hoteliers; messenger, errand, and office boys; porters (in stores); and steam railroad workers. See John Daniels, "Industrial Conditions among Negro Men in Boston," *The Negro in the Cities* (New York: Charity Organization Society of the City of New York, 1905).

35. Gerald L. Gill, "Introduction to Part V: Protest and Progress, 1900–1945," in *Making a Living: The Work Experience of African Americans in New England*, ed. Robert L. Hall (Boston: New England Foundation for the Humanities, 1995), 500.

36. Motivated by the conditions of the Great Depression, the longshoremen's union organized a strike that included both white and Black labor in 1931. See Seaton Wesley Manning, "Social-Industrial Relationships: Negro Trade Unionists in Boston" (master's diss., Boston University, 1938.

37. League of Struggle for Negro Rights, *Equality Land and Freedom: A Program for Negro Liberation* (New York: League of Struggle for Negro Rights, 1933).

38. Urban League of Eastern Massachusetts records, M139, Northeastern University Archives and Special Collections, accessed December 27, 2021, https://archivesspace.library .northeastern.edu/repositories/2/resources/905.

39. Mel King, *Chain of Change: Struggles for Black Community Development* (Boston: South End Press, 1981).

40. Adelaide M. Cromwell, *The Other Brahmins: Boston's Black Upper Class, 1750–1950* (Fayetteville: University of Arkansas Press, 1994), 143.

41. Lorraine Roses, author of many important studies on Black Bostonians, including cultural and artistic offerings, writes, "The Women's Service Club at 464 Massachusetts Avenue occupies an elegant three story town house, while the League ('558') is headquartered in a stunningly ornate Victorian mansion. Their nicknames, accordingly, are '464' and '558.'" Quoted in "A Tale of Two Womens' Organizations." http://academics.wellesley.edu /AmerStudies/BostonBlackHistory/history/tale.html.

42. Topper Carew, interview by author, 2011. Their work with community restoration and scholarships would continue. Many were helped by their programs.

43. Robert C. Hayden, *Boston's N.A.A.C.P. History, 1910–1982* (Boston, MA: Boston Branch N.A.A.C.P., 1982).

44. "Don't Buy Where You Can't Work Movement," Encyclopedia.com, accessed November 24, 2021, www.encyclopedia.com/economics/encyclopedias-almanacs-transcripts -and-maps/dont-buy-where-you-cant-work-movement.

45. James Philip Danky and Wayne A. Wiegand, *Print Culture in a Diverse America* (Urbana: University of Illinois Press, 1998), 61.

46. "No Negro Managers," *Boston Chronicle*, February 3, 1934.

47. "No Negro Managers."

48. "No Negro Managers."

49. *Boston Chronicle*, October 13, 1934.

50. In 1942, Cooper became the deputy secretary of the Urban League, after which he was promoted to executive secretary, a position he held for six years between 1948 and 1954. Later Cooper served as the first executive director of Boston's NAACP between 1954 and 1962, and chapter president of the Metropolitan Boston Chapter of the National Caucus and Center on Black Aged from 1981 to 1988.

51. *Boston Chronicle*, August 3, 1935; Danky and Wiegand, *Print Culture in a Diverse America*, 61.

52. Five Black women (including Ruth Worthy) were hired as part-time clerks at Woolworth's in Lower Roxbury. *Boston Chronicle*, December 19, 1936.

53. Gerald Gill, "'There Is No Room in Boston for Jim Crowism': Black Protest in Boston, 1935–1945," Gerald R. Gill Papers, ca. 1950s–2007, Digital Collections and Archives, Tufts University, Medford, MA.

54. The *Chronicle* was a West Indian–owned newspaper, and as such its true north pointed toward many of the issues, concerns, and belief systems of the Boston West Indian subculture.

55. Violet Showers Johnson, *The Other Black Bostonians: West Indians in Boston, 1900–1950* (Bloomington: Indiana University Press, 2006), 62; She continues, "Admittedly, the owners, editors, and reporters of the Chronicle were middle-class men. Most were professionals, such as Thaddeus Kitchener, a barrister, Uriah Murray, a doctor, and William Harrison, a Harvard graduate. . . . In spite of this socioeconomic background, their publication appealed to a broad section of the black population, which included a significant working-class audience. The reputation that West Indians had earned by then as relentless agitators was one major reason for this appeal. . . . Boston's West Indian society boasted its own firebrands. Significantly, most of them were connected with the *Chronicle*. In fact, some of them were self-proclaimed communists and in that capacity earned the trust of the working class with whom they shared the same neighborhood." Johnson, *Other Black Bostonians*, 58.

56. Violet Showers Johnson writes in Danky and Wiegand, "While focusing on worldwide issues pertaining to blacks, the *Chronicle* directed a great deal of attention at the plight of blacks in Boston and the United States. Contrary to its reputation as a haven for American blacks, Boston was in many ways inhospitable to that segment of its population throughout the first half of the twentieth century. Like Trotter's *Guardian*, the *Chronicle* devoted many efforts to protesting the blatant social, economic, and political injustice directed against blacks of that city." Danky and Wiegand, *Print Culture in a Diverse America*, 56.

57. According to Violet Showers Johnson, it was even rumored that he sometimes wrote speeches for Mayor James Michael Curley. Danky and Wiegand, *Print Culture in a Diverse America*, 64.

58. "The Communist Party of America—1921," accessed March 23, 2022, www.marxists.org/history/usa/eam/cpa/cpadownloads-1921.htm.

59. Johnson, *Other Black Bostonians*.

60. As Johnson observes, "Its Pan-African crusade, which was a constant, was most evident in the 1930s and 1940s. Several developments during this period these journalists of the global domination of blacks and, therefore, the efficacy of a Pan-African solution. The contents of the *Chronicle* in the 1930s and 1940s clearly demonstrate that its main efforts were directed at (1) highlighting the contributions of blacks around the world, with the objective of stimulating black pride, (2) tackling the problems that faced blacks in Boston and the United States, and (3) exposing the insidious nature of European and American imperialism in Africa and the Western Hemisphere." Johnson, *Other Black Bostonians.*

61. King, *Chain of Change*, 10.

62. King, *Chain of Change*, 11.

63. Gill, "'No Time for Banqueting.'"

64. "Boston Phone Company Shatters System of Public Utilities Jim-Crowing," *Boston Chronicle*, September 1, 1945.

65. As Violet Showers Johnson writes in Danky and Wiegand, "It was clear by then that a formidable structural pattern of discrimination was firmly in place. Even when the black unemployment rate dropped slightly in 1940 (from 34.0 to 30.3 percent) as a result of the employment of blacks in government projects funded by the Works Progress Administration (WPA), they still compared unfavorably with white groups." Danky and Wiegand, *Print Culture in a Diverse America*, 62.

66. Andrew Buni and Alan Rogers, *Boston, City on a Hill: An Illustrated History* (Woodland Hills, CA: Windsor, 1984).

67. Robert C. Hayden: Transcripts of Oral History Interviews with Boston African American Railroad Workers, 1977–1991, Healey Library.

68. A. Philip Randolph Papers (reel 21), box 25–26, folder: "MOWM Correspondence." See David Lucander, *Winning the War for Democracy: The March on Washington Movement, 1941–1946* (Urbana: University of Illinois Press, 2014).

69. See Hillel Levine and Lawrence Harmon, *The Death of an American Jewish Community: A Tragedy of Good Intentions* (New York: Free Press, 1992); Jim Vrabel and Bostonian Society, *When in Boston: A Time Line and Almanac* (Boston: Northeastern University Press, 2004); Jim Vrabel, *A People's History of the New Boston* (Amherst: University of Massachusetts Press, 2014); Yona Ginsberg, *Jews in a Changing Neighborhood: The Study of Mattapan* (New York: Free Press, 1975).

70. Gill, "'No Time for Banqueting.'"

71. There would be efforts to propel the Massachusetts Commission against Discrimination to take a more far-reaching stance against unemployment and against discrimination and housing in Boston and its suburbs.

Chapter Four

1. Adelaide Cromwell (The HistoryMakers A2004.243), interview by Robert Hayden, December 2, 2004, HistoryMakers Digital Archive, session 1, tape 4, story 7, "Adelaide Cromwell Talks about Her Book, *The Other Brahmins: Boston's Black Upper Class, 1750–1950.*"

2. *Pin His Ear to the Wisdom Post: Martin Luther King, Jr., and the School of Prophets*, Exhibit, Boston University.

3. Rebelling against his father's wishes that he follow him into the ministry, King Jr. had first considered a career in medicine.

4. Dissatisfied with the fundamentalist Baptist doctrines of his father, King chooses Crozer for its reputation as a bastion of liberal Protestantism. While there, he becomes uncomfortable with the view of some liberal theologians who fail to adequately recognize, in his view, the evil of social injustice.

5. One of King's most famous quotes, "The moral arc of the universe is long, but it bend toward justice," is known to have been a paraphrasing of the words of another theologian, Rev. Theodore Parker of Boston, who in one of his sermons published in 1854 wrote, "I do not pretend to understand the moral universe, the arc is a long one, my eye reaches but little ways. I cannot calculate the curve and complete the figure by experience of sight; I can divine it by conscience. But from what I see I am sure it bends towards justice." Is it possible that Martin Luther King Jr. may have learned this quote during his time in Boston? King later adapted these sentiments. "Ten Sermons of Religion," Boston, 1854.

6. Jeanne Theoharis, email message to author, November 20, 2020.

7. "New Life for Forgotten MLK Site in Camden," *New Jersey Monthly*, January 12, 2017.

8. "New Life for Forgotten MLK Site in Camden."

9. "New Life for Forgotten MLK Site in Camden."

10. "Martin Luther King, Jr.'s Roommate Reminisces," *BU Today*, Boston University, January 15, 2010, www.bu.edu/articles/2010/martin-luther-king-jr-s-roommate-reminisces.

11. Theoharis, email message to author.

12. Theoharis, email message to author.

13. "The Negro Past and Its Challenge for the Future," Negro History Week, Alpha Kappa Alpha Sorority, Twelfth Baptist Church (Boston, MA), ca. 1951–1954, OKRA: 540000-092, Morehouse College Martin Luther King, Jr. Collection: Series 2: Writings by Martin Luther King, Jr., Robert W. Woodruff Library of the Atlanta University Center.

14. *Pin His Ear to the Wisdom Post.*

15. *Pin His Ear to the Wisdom Post.*

16. *Pin His Ear to the Wisdom Post.*

17. *Pin His Ear to the Wisdom Post.*

18. *Pin His Ear to the Wisdom Post.*

19. *Pin His Ear to the Wisdom Post.*

20. A telegram in the collection of King's papers at Boston University shows the urgency with which he was called back, Boston University Special Collections.

21. *Pin His Ear to the Wisdom Post.*

22. Address of Reverend Doctor Martin Luther King, Jr., Delivered to a Joint Convention of the Two Houses of the General Court of Massachusetts on April 22, 1965.

23. "March on Roxbury; March on Roxbury," GBH Archives, September 22, 1963, http://openvault.wgbh.org/catalog/A_47A310B09A5841189161E4B8389B4072.

24. Kenneth Cooper, "Malcolm: The Boston Years," *Bay State Banner*, February 16, 2006.

25. Kenneth Cooper has reported that although Malcolm X is credited with founding Muhammad Mosque No. 11 in Roxbury and serving as its minister in 1953 and 1954, Minister Don Muhammad, the mosque's longtime leader, said those accounts are inaccurate. "He was never the minister," Don Muhammad said. "Malcolm was in Boston quite often. He did

not do so much preaching. He came to represent Mister Muhammad in public forums . . . and public gatherings." Cooper, "Malcolm."

26. At the same time, some legitimately wanted separate but equal educational institutions and were less concerned about integration. See, for example, Tomiko Brown-Nagin, *Courage to Dissent: Atlanta and the Long History of the Civil Rights Movement* (Oxford: Oxford University Press, 2011).

27. Brown-Nagin, *Courage to Dissent*.

28. In an interesting twist of fate, Houston took his classes with future Supreme Court Justice Felix Frankfurter, who called him one of the most brilliant students he'd ever taught. Frankfurter, of course, would play an instrumental role in *Brown v. Board of Education*.

29. Several cases—*Sipuel v. Board of Regents of the University of Oklahoma, Sweatt v. Painter*, and *McLaurin v. Oklahoma State Regents*—paved the way for *Brown v. Board of Education*. Ada Sipuel wanted to attend the University of Oklahoma to become a lawyer. She claimed she was entitled under the Fourteenth Amendment and its equal protection clause. The Supreme Court upheld her case, ruling that she was entitled to attend; however, it also stated that the university was not required to let her attend. In effect, the university could reject anyone it wanted. *Sweatt v. Painter* revolved around Heamon Sweatt's petition that the University of Texas's efforts to set up a Black law school was not comparable to the white law school. During the trial, Sweatt's lawyer brought evidence that showed that the university had provided a single room for Black law students, which served as a classroom, study hall, office, and so on. This was far from what was available to white students. Finally, in *McLaurin v. Oklahoma State Regents*, the university admitted George McLaurin, putting a sign along a rail that read "reserved colored." This was presumably done so that Black students could not "contaminate" books in the library. Black students were also not allowed to sit with white students in the cafeteria.

30. It should be noted that McLaurin endured all of these indignities and did eventually receive his doctorate in education.

31. One of these cases evolved from a personal incident. Lucinda Todd, a teacher, opened her own home to serve as the meeting place for the local Topeka NAACP branch. When her daughter was not allowed to play in a school concert because of her race, Todd agreed to become the first plaintiff in the Brown lawsuit.

32. J. Anthony Lukas, *Common Ground: A Turbulent Decade in the Lives of Three American Families* (New York: Knopf: Distributed by Random House, 1985), 106.

33. Leon Jones, *From Brown to Boston: Desegregation in Education, 1954–1974*, 2 vols. (Metuchen, NJ: Scarecrow Press, 1979).

34. Technically there were five questions: What are the intentions of the Fourteenth Amendment? Can the court abolish segregation in schools? Was making policy for the schools a state right? Who has the right to abolish segregation in schools? If the court has that power, should it be done slowly or quickly?

35. *Brown v. Board of Education of Topeka*, 347 U.S. 483 (1954).

36. The NAACP fought tooth and nail in the Little Rock school desegregation case. This was one of the major incidents involving violent protests against segregation and the necessity for government intervention.

37. Lukas, *Common Ground*, 231.

38. The Kennedy administration grew impatient with the state's evasion. Ross Barnett, however, while waging a fierce public war against the "tyrannical" interference of outsiders in Mississippi's affairs, was privately negotiating with Attorney General Robert Kennedy. They were able to strike a deal, and James Meredith became the first Black student to register at Ole Miss—but not without violence. Kennedy had to send in federal marshals to put down a mob that violently protested the admission of Meredith. Two people were killed, and several others were injured. Although in the end, it was effective negotiating by the Kennedy administration that gained entry for Meredith, many remained critical of Kennedy's agenda when it came to civil rights.

39. Tom Blair, "Freedom House Center Planned," *Boston Chronicle*, April 2, 1949.

40. Blair, "Freedom House Center Planned."

41. Sarah-Ann Shaw, interview by author, October 29, 2010.

42. Muriel S. and Otto P. Snowden papers, M017, Northeastern University Archives and Special Collections.

43. Gerald Gill, "'No Time for Banqueting': African-American Protests in Boston, 1945–1955," in "Struggling Yet in Freedom's Birthplace" (unpublished manuscript), Gerald R. Gill Papers, ca. 1950s–2007, Digital Collections and Archives, Tufts University, Medford, MA.

44. That same year, local activists expressed concern at the low number of African American, Jewish American, Irish American, and Italian American students admitted and enrolled in commonwealth institutions of higher education (as undergraduate, graduate, or professional degree students).

45. In 1957, E. Franklin Frazier wrote the *Black Bourgeoisie* and was accused, of being a communist. White people claimed that the Supreme Court was listening to communist sympathizers. Similar claims were made about W. E. B. Du Bois, whose passport was taken away around this time. See Gerald Gill, "Struggling Yet in Freedom's Birthplace" (unpublished manuscript), Gerald R. Gill Papers, ca. 1950s–2007, Digital Collections and Archives, Tufts University, Medford, MA.

46. Lyda S. Peters, "Reclaiming the Narrative: Black Community Activism and Boston School Desegregation History, 1960–1975" (PhD diss., Boston College, 2017).

47. As Peters writes, "Following the passage of the Civil Rights Act of 1964, the Massachusetts State Board of Education established an advisory committee to assess the racial composition of student populations in school systems throughout the Commonwealth. The advisory committee submitted a report on 'non-white' enrollment in the Commonwealth's public schools. A close examination of the 159 elementary schools in Boston in 1964 continued to show a preponderance of non-white enrollment concentrated in Black residential areas." Peters, "Reclaiming the Narrative," 4.

48. "Cloakroom Case Spotlights Deep School Issues," *Boston Globe*, May 26, 1968. See also Peters, "Reclaiming the Narrative," 6.

49. Robert Drinan, SJ—a lawyer, human rights activist, and Democratic U.S. Representative from Massachusetts from 1971 to 1981—was the first Roman Catholic priest to serve as a voting member of Congress.

50. Lenny Alkins, interview by author, November 2010.

51. Ruth Batson, letter to the editor, *Boston Globe*, 1963.

52. Jeanne Theoharis and Komozi Woodard, eds., *Groundwork: Local Black Freedom Movements in America* (New York: New York University, 2005), 23.

53. In the midst of the avalanche of criticism—both Black and white—about busing, Batson stated, "It angers me when I hear and read that black parents do not help their children—do not participate in their educational growth.... What black parents wanted was to get their children to schools where there were the best resources for education growth—smaller class sizes, up-to-date books. They wanted their children in a good school building, where there was an allocation of funds which exceeded those in the black schools; where there were sufficient books and equipment for all students. Is that too much to ask for?" Quoted in Theoharis and Woodard, eds., *Groundwork*, 23.

54. Ruth Batson, *The Black Educational Movement in Boston: A Sequence of Historical Events* (Boston: School of Education, Northeastern University, 2001), 4.

55. *To Secure These Rights: A Documented History of the Negro "Freedom Movement,"* produced by WGBH-FM, aired on February 24, 1964, transcript, p. 3, https://dsgsites.neu.edu /desegregation/wp-content/uploads/2015/04/neu_rx9140346.pdf.

56. Don West and Kenneth Cooper, *Portraits of Purpose: A Tribute to Leadership* (Boston, MA: Three Bean Press, 2014), 76.

57. West and Cooper, *Portraits of Purpose*, 76.

58. Wolff, Jeremy. *A Timeline of Boston School Desegregation, 1961–1985 with Emphasis on 1964–1976*. Northeastern University School of Law (Union of Minority Neighborhoods), 4.

59. Wolff, *A Timeline of Boston School Desegregation, 1961–1985*, 4.

60. Wolff, *A Timeline of Boston School Desegregation, 1961–1985*, 4.

61. Wolff, *A Timeline of Boston School Desegregation, 1961–1985*, 4.

62. Katherine Jones (The HistoryMakers A2004.204), interviewed by Robert Hayden, October 14, 2004, The HistoryMakers Digital Archive. Session 1, tape 3, story 8, Katherine Jones explains the reasoning behind the Metropolitan Council for Educational Opportunities program

63. Hubert Jones (panelist, Power and Protest Conference, John F. Kennedy Presidential Museum and Library, Boston, MA, October 2006).

64. Jones (panelist, Power and Protest Conference, October 2006).

65. Hubie Jones, interview by author, 2019.

66. Jones (panelist, Power and Protest Conference, October 2006).

67. Jones (panelist, Power and Protest Conference, October 2006).

68. With their immovability, the NAACP joined with other Black groups as well as white allies to begin picketing at the school committee, at its headquarters, on 15 Beacon Street.

69. Hubie Jones, interview by author, 2020.

70. Batson, *Black Educational Movement in Boston*, 4.

71. "Statement of the Press of the Boston Branch, NAACP, https://repository.library .northeastern.edu/downloads/neu:m039x538s?datastream_id=content.

72. Hubie Jones, interview by author, 2020.

73. Actually, the misunderstanding brewing this June evening was not about the right or wrong language, no data, wording or explanation that make the school committee see the problem and its responsibility for it. There were many white and Black Westonians who claimed that the school committee could see the problem, what was playing dumb in order to perpetuate the miserable status quo. Others would maintain that the committee had set a trap where the NAACP and its leaders had walked into it with their eyes wide opened, not recognizing that the committee wanted a racial confrontation to advance their political

aspirations and increase their bonding with their white constituents. The postmortems were endless. Interview with Author, Hubie Jones (2020). "Churches in Boston Panel," Power and Protest Conference, JFK Library, October, 2006.

74. Henry Hampton, Steve Fayer, and Sarah Flynn, *Voices of Freedom: An Oral History of the Civil Rights Movement from the 1950s through the 1980s* (New York: Bantam Books, 1990), 589.

75. Jones, interview, 2020.

76. Jeanne Theoharis, *A More Beautiful and Terrible History: The Uses and Misuses of Civil Rights History* (Boston: Beacon Press, 2018), 50.

77. Hampton, Fayer, and Flynn, *Voices of Freedom*, 589.

78. "Education: After Months, Divided Boston Board Is No Closer to Hiring School Chief," *New York Times*, September 5, 1990.

79. Hampton, Fayer, and Flynn, *Voices of Freedom*, 589.

80. Jones, interview, 2020.

81. *To Secure These Rights*, transcript, p. 32.

82. They also attended "Freedom Workshops" at the St. Mark's Social Center. Speakers included the Episcopal bishop of Massachusetts, Rt. Rev. Anson Phelps Stokes Jr.; the Northeast Methodist bishop, Rt. Rev. James K. Mathews, and Mr. Bill Russell.

83. Wolff, *A Timeline of Boston School Desegregation, 1961–1985*, 4.

84. Wolff, *A Timeline of Boston School Desegregation, 1961–1985*, 5.

85. Alyssa Napier, "An Experiment in Integrated Education" (unpublished paper, 2019).

86. Napier, "Experiment in Integrated Education."

87. See James Oliver Horton and Lois E. Horton, *In Hope of Liberty: Culture, Community, and Protest among Northern Free Blacks, 1700–1860* (New York: Oxford University Press, 1997), 230.

88. Through her Trotter-Fossett family lineage, Peggy is a direct descendant of Mary Hemings Bell, sister of Sally Hemings. "About," Peggy Trotter Dammond Preacely, accessed March 23, 2022, www.peggytrotterdammondpreacely.com.

89. Peggy Trotter Dammond Preacely, "It Was Also in My Blood," in *Hands on the Freedom Plow: Personal Accounts by Women in SNCC*, ed. Faith S. Holsaert et al. (Urbana: University of Illinois Press, 2010).

90. *To Secure These Rights*, transcript, 14.

91. Jones, interview, 2020.

92. Jones, interview, 2020.

93. Jones, interview, 2020.

94. Jones, interview, 2020.

95. Jones, interview, 2020.

96. Jones, interview, 2020.

97. Jones, interview, 2020.

98. Jones, interview, 2020.

99. Evelyn Brooks Higginbotham, foreword to *Freedom North: Black Freedom Struggles Outside the South, 1940–1980*, ed. Jeanne F. Theoharis and Komozi Woodard (New York: Palgrave Macmillan, 2003), x.

100. Higginbotham, foreword, x.

101. Wolff, *A Timeline of Boston School Desegregation, 1961–1985*.

102. Northern Student Movement records, box 8, folder 9, Manuscripts, Archives and Rare Books Division, Schomburg Center for Research in Black Culture, New York Public Library.

103. Robert C. Hayden, *African-Americans in Boston: More Than 350 Years* (Boston: Trustees of the Public Library of the City of Boston, 1991), 24.

104. St. Mark's Congregational Church operated until the early 1960s, when the building was demolished as a result of urban renewal. See Hayden, *African-Americans in Boston*, 24.

105. Hayden, *African-Americans in Boston*, 25.

106. Shaw, interview.

107. Shaw, interview.

108. Mel King, *Chain of Change: Struggles for Black Community Development* (Boston: South End Press, 1981), 49.

109. King, *Chain of Change*, 49.

110. King, *Chain of Change*, 49.

111. King, *Chain of Change*, 48–51.

112. King, *Chain of Change*, 49.

113. James Breeden, interview by Alyssa Napier, 2019.

114. In 1961, members of CORE picketed Sears and Roebuck and were successful in urging the department store to hire its first Black salesclerk.

115. Byron Rushing, interview by Laura Muller, John Joseph Moakley Oral History Project OH-062, November 18, 2005, John Joseph Moakley Archive and Institute, Suffolk University, Boston, MA.

116. "Churches in Boston panel." Power and Protest Conference, JFK Library, October 2006.

117. Sarah-Ann Shaw (The HistoryMakers A2007.067), interview by Larry Crowe, February 13, 2007, HistoryMakers Digital Archive, session 1, tape 4, story 1, "Sarah-Ann Shaw Describes the Agency Row in Boston, Massachusetts."

118. The Honorable Byron Rushing (The HistoryMakers A2006.013), interview by Robert Hayden, February 8, 2006, HistoryMakers Digital Archive, session 1, tape 3, story 8, "The Honorable Byron Rushing Explains His Work with CORE and the Northern Student Movement."

119. John F. Kennedy, Civil Rights Address, June 11, 1963, White House, Washington, DC.

120. "A Service for Reeb Is Held in Boston," *New York Times*, March 19, 1965.

121. "Rights Movement Gaining in Boston," *Boston Globe*, April 5, 1965.

Chapter Five

1. *Unsung*, episode 8, "Tribute to James Brown," aired February 22, 2017, on TVOne.

2. *Unsung*, episode 8, "Tribute to James Brown."

3. *Unsung*, episode 8, "Tribute to James Brown."

4. Four months later, Brown released his famous "I'm Black and I'm Proud." That song, in many ways, can be traced to what happened in Boston.

5. *The Night James Brown Saved Boston*, directed by David Leaf (Los Angeles: FreeMantleMedia, Shout! Factory, 2008), DVD.

6. *Night James Brown Saved Boston.*

7. *Night James Brown Saved Boston.*

8. *Night James Brown Saved Boston.*

9. Devorah Heitner, *Black Power TV* (Durham, NC: Duke University Press, 2013), 53.

10. *Boston Record American,* April 5, 1968.

11. "Roxbury Huddles Together to Keep Cool," *Sunday Boston Globe,* April 14, 1968.

12. Jack Tager, *Boston Riots: Three Centuries of Social Violence* (Boston: Northeastern University Press, 2001).

13. Tager, *Boston Riots.*

14. *Riots, Civil and Criminal Disorders: Hearings Before the United States Senate,* September and October 1968, Library of Congress.

15. "Roxbury Huddles Together to Keep Cool," *Sunday Boston Globe,* April 14, 1968.

16. *Night James Brown Saved Boston.*

17. *Night James Brown Saved Boston.*

18. *Night James Brown Saved Boston.*

19. *Night James Brown Saved Boston.*

20. *Night James Brown Saved Boston.*

21. *Night James Brown Saved Boston.*

22. *Night James Brown Saved Boston.*

23. *Night James Brown Saved Boston.*

24. "A Day of Mourning after the Death of Dr. King, 1968," American Experience, January 18, 2019, www.pbs.org/wgbh/americanexperience/features/lbj-mourning.

25. *Night James Brown Saved Boston.*

26. Chuck Turner, interview, February 4, 1993, *Say Brother,* episode 2319, "James Brown '68: The Politics of Soul," WGBH Educational Foundation, American Archive of Public Broadcasting, http://americanarchive.org/catalog/cpb-aacip_15-72b8h8f7.

27. *Night James Brown Saved Boston.*

28. *Night James Brown Saved Boston.*

29. *Night James Brown Saved Boston.*

30. *Night James Brown Saved Boston.*

31. When he decided to take his band to Vietnam, for example, he was fairly surprised by the reaction from the liberal progressive community, both white and Black, who said, "Association with the Vietnam War effort is an implied association with this imperialist project of the U.S." *Night James Brown Saved Boston.*

32. *Night James Brown Saved Boston.*

33. *Night James Brown Saved Boston.*

34. "Roxbury Huddles Together to Keep Cool."

35. *Night James Brown Saved Boston.*

36. *Night James Brown Saved Boston.*

37. *Night James Brown Saved Boston.*

38. Chuck Turner, interview, February 4, 1993.

39. Jim Vrabel and Bostonian Society, *When in Boston: A Time Line and Almanac* (Boston: Northeastern University Press, 2004), 335.

40. Robert Jordan, "Black Police, Schools, Businesses, Demanded at Rally," *Boston Globe,* April 9, 1968; Janet Riddell, "White, United Front, Discuss 'Principles,'" *Boston Globe,*

April 12, 1965; "Mayor White Embraces Proposals by NAACP, Turns Down Other Plans by Elliot Friedman and Alan Lupo," *Boston Globe*, April 10, 1968.

41. Tess Bundy, "'Revolutions Happen through Young People!': The Black Student Movement in the Boston Public Schools, 1968–1971," *Journal of Urban History* 43, no. 2 (March 2017): 273–93.

42. *Boston Evening Globe*, September 25, 1968.

43. Bundy, "'Revolutions Happen through Young People!'"

44. See Violet Showers Johnson, *The Other Black Bostonians: West Indians in Boston, 1900–1950* (Bloomington: Indiana University Press, 2006); Marilyn Halter, *Between Race and Ethnicity: Cape Verdean American Immigrants, 1860–1965* (Urbana: University of Illinois Press, 1993).

45. "Crisis to Crisis: Voices of a Divided City," Blackside, American Archive of Public Broadcasting, accessed December 29, 2021, http://americanarchive.org/catalog/cpb-aacip-151-2z12n4zx29.

46. For a more detailed analysis of the effects of these changes, consult Yona Ginsberg, *Jews in a Changing Neighborhood: The Study of Mattapan* (New York: Free Press, 1975). This situation created an environment of hostile racial encampment and segregated ethnic neighborhoods.

47. Lew Finfer, interview by author, 2016.

48. Karilyn Crockett, *People Before Highways: Boston Activists, Urban Planners, and a New Movement for City Making* (Amherst: University of Massachusetts Press, 2018).

49. Keeanga-Yamahtta Taylor, *Race for Profit: How Banks and the Real Estate Industry Undermined Black Homeownership* (Chapel Hill: University of North Carolina Press, 2019).

50. Audrea Jones, interview by Ollie Johnson, October 30, 1994.

51. See Donna Jean Murch, *Living for the City: Migration, Education, and the Rise of the Black Panther Party in Oakland, California* (Chapel Hill: University of North Carolina Press, 2010).

52. Jones, interview by Ollie Johnson.

53. Dan Queen, "Who Are the Black Panthers?" *Bay State Banner*, December 5, 1968.

54. See note 53 above.

55. Audrea Dunham Jones, interview by Charles S. Jones, June 15, 1997.

56. Queen, "Who Are the Black Panthers?"

57. Murch, *Living for the City*.

58. "Black Panthers Arrested at Dudley; Protest against Police Continues," *Bay State Banner*, September 11, 1969.

59. "Black Panthers Arrested at Dudley; protest against Police Continues." *Bay State Banner*, 11 September 1969.

60. "Panther Rally for Prisoners," *Bay State Banner*, November 20, 1969, 7.

61. "Panther Rally for Slain Leader," *Bay State Banner*, December 11, 1969, 1.

62. "Panther Rally for Prisoners," 7.

63. "Panther Rally for Prisoners," 7.

64. Dan Queen, "Panthers Trying to Reach All Black People," *Bay State Banner*, December 12, 1968.

65. "Panthers Rally for Huey Newton," *Bay State Banner*, February 19, 1970.

66. Charles E. Jones, *The Black Panther Party (Reconsidered)* (Baltimore: Black Classic Press, 1998).

67. Queen, "Panthers Trying to Reach All Black People."

68. "Black Leaders Speak at Boston College," *Bay State Banner*, December 11, 1969.

69. See recent scholarship on women in the Black Power movement by Ashley Farmer and Kathleen Cleaver. Ashley Farmer, "Working Toward Community Is Our Full-Time Focus: Muriel Snowden, Black Power, and the Freedom House, Roxbury, MA," *The Black Scholar* 41, no. 3 (2011): 17–25. (Accessed December 29, 2021). https://doi.org/10.5816/blackscholar.41.3 .0017; Cleaver, Kathleen, and George N. Katsiaficas. Liberation, *Imagination, and the Black Panther Party: A New Look at the Panthers and Their Legacy* (New York: Routledge, 2001).

70. The number of total membership can only be guessed at. Asked about the number of members in the party, one member replied, "Those who say don't know, those who know don't say."

71. Jones, interview by Charles S. Jones.

72. Jones, interview by Charles S. Jones.

73. Jones, interview by Charles S. Jones.

74. Margaret Tarter, "Panthers Still Alive in Dorchester," *Bay State Banner*, March 17, 1977, 19.

75. "Health Article," *Bay State Banner*, October 8, 1970.

76. Jama Lazerow, "The Black Panthers at Water's Edge: Oakland, Boston, and the New Bedford 'Riots' of 1970," in *Liberated Territory: Untold Local Perspectives on the Black Panther Party*, ed. Yohuru Williams and Jama Lazerow (Durham, NC: Duke University Press, 2008), 85–135; "Friends of the Student Non-Violent Coordinating Committee—Boston," folder 60, Freedom House, Inc., Records, M016, Archives and Special Collections, Northeastern University.

77. Anything that went beyond that goal was deemed too militant, perhaps with the exception of what organizers such as Mel King, Sadiki Kambon, the Black United Front, and others were able to accomplish in the late 1960s and 1970s.

78. Stokely Carmichael and Charles V. Hamilton, *Black Power: The Politics of Liberation in America* (New York: Random House, 1967).

79. Martha Biondi, *The Black Revolution on Campus* (Berkeley: University of California Press, 2012); Stefan M. Bradley, *Upending the Ivory Tower: Civil Rights, Black Power, and the Ivy League* (New York: New York University Press, 2018).

80. A conference was called in Boston. Robert Hall, as well as Black students from Dartmouth, Boston University, Northeastern University, and Wellesley College, joined SNCC activists in the area to organize a symposium called "Black Power and the Talented Tenth." Cleveland Sellers, Michael Thelwell, of SNCC, and a number of members of the symposium called together the privileged Black campus learners from the Northeast and people from the local community who struggled against institutional racism. Bradley, *Upending the Ivory Tower*, 336.

81. Ashley Farmer, "Working toward Community Is Our Full-Time Focus: Muriel Snowden, Black Power, and the Freedom House, Roxbury, MA," *Black Scholar* 41, no. 3 (2011): 17–25, https://doi.org/10.5816/blackscholar.41.3.0017.

Chapter Six

1. Historian Robin D. G. Kelley writes, "The generation that came of age in the '70s, '80s, and '90s has been called a lot of things: the post-soul generation, the post-civil rights generation,

the postindustrial generation. But few standing 'at the edge of history,' to use the language of the Gary Declaration, thought in terms of being 'post' anything. Rather, they entered a new period with tremendous optimism. For some, this sense of a better future came because of efforts toward racial integration. For others it was the hope for greater political and social control of their lives." Kelley is referring here to the declaration coming out of the historic Black Political Convention held in Gary, Indiana, in 1972. Robin D. G. Kelley, *Into the Fire—African Americans since 1970* (New York: Oxford University Press, 1996), 133.

2. The Gary Declaration proclaimed that "white politics" did not help Black people achieve their social and political goals; rather, to succeed, Blacks needed to work together and develop a separate agenda.

3. "(1972) Gary Declaration, National Black Political Convention," BlackPast, accessed December 29, 2021, www.blackpast.org/african-american-history/gary-declaration-national -black-political-convention-1972.

4. Paul Delaney, "The 1972 Campaign," *New York Times,* May 20, 1972.

5. *Morgan v. Hennigan,* 379 F. Supp. 410 (D. Mass. 1974), June 21, 1974, https://law.justia .com/cases/federal/district-courts/FSupp/379/410/1378130.

6. *Morgan v. Hennigan.*

7. Henry Hampton and Steve Fayer, *Voices of Freedom: An Oral History of the Civil Rights Movement from the 1950s through the 1980s* (New York: Bantam Books, 1990), 589.

8. Batson had been appointed by Lionel Lyndsay.

9. Henry Hampton, dir., *Eyes on the Prize II: America at the Racial Crossroads, 1965–1985* (Alexandria, VA: PBS Video, 1989).

10. Hampton, *Eyes on the Prize II.*

11. Hampton, *Eyes on the Prize II.*

12. Hampton, *Eyes on the Prize II.*

13. Kim Nesta Archung, interview by author, 2019.

14. Kim Nesta Archung, "From African Elephants to African Children: A Case Study of an African American Teacher's Changing Praxis" (PhD diss., Emory University, 2002).

15. Mary Gunn retired in 2017 but has continued as a volunteer. She spent many hours at school committee meetings and has worked with the administration for the last fifteen years to bring literacy services into the schools.

16. Jean McGuire, interview by author, 2021.

17. McGuire, interview.

18. McGuire, interview.

19. Shelbourne attended the Julia Ward Howe Elementary School (1970–71), then Swampscott Elementary School (1971–76). She was the only Black student in her classes; all the other students were white. As she explains, "I was forced to repeat kindergarten notwithstanding the fact that I was the only student in my kindergarten class who could read chapter books (I have an older sister four grades ahead of me; we played 'school' every day when she came home from her suburban METCO school (in Brookline) with her homework. We were not allowed to watch TV other than PBS, and then only [a] small number of programs for kids on PBS in [the] late '60s early '70s. As an adult I became a teacher in the Boston Public Schools; I taught high school Chemistry for six years before leaving teaching to become an attorney." Patrice Shelburne, "Boston Civil Rights Movement Questionnaire," by Zebulon Miletsky (2019).

20. Logan attended Philadelphia Public Schools, graduating from the Philadelphia High Schools for Girls in 1964, which at that time was a predominantly white school. She has been involved in many school desegregation projects and served as a historical consultant to Primary Source, which created a school desegregation curriculum.

21. Jonathan Kozol, *Death at an Early Age: The Destruction of the Hearts and Minds of Negro Children in the Boston Public Schools* (Boston: Houghton Mifflin, 1967), 29.

22. Philip Hart (The HistoryMakers A2017.159), interview by Randall Pinkston, August 19, 2017, HistoryMakers Digital Archive, session 1, tape 4, story 6, "Philip Hart Talks about His Role at the Federation of Boston Community Schools."

23. *Say Brother*, "There Is Always Another Way: A Mind Is a Terrible Thing to Waste; Philip Hart Discusses the History of the New School for Children and Roxbury Community College," November 23, 1979, WGBH Archives, http://openvault.wgbh.org/catalog/V _313533AF7022417CB9A6738F3B509872.

24. Philip Hart (The HistoryMakers A2017.159.

25. Judge Leslie Harris, interview by author, 2020.

26. Here is a full list of viable alternatives to Boston's public schools and some of the individuals associated with them: Roxbury Community School, St. Joseph's Community School (supported by the Archdiocese of Boston), and Paige Academy (a private school operating via tuition). Roxbury Community School: Cecilia Ware (a veteran teacher), Joyce Snowden (educational coordinator), and Michele Marrow (K–1 teacher). St. Joseph's Community School: Joyce King (acting principal) and Idella Hill (fourth grade teacher). Paige Academy: Angela Paige Cook (director); Kim Archung, Fauzia Ahmed, and Lauren Lee (teachers); and Joe Cook Jr. (administrative producer).

27. Harris, interview.

28. Juanita Wade, interview by Blackside, September 29, 1989, http://digital.wustl.edu/e /eii/eiiweb/wad5427.0586.167juanitawade.html.

29. Wade, interview.

30. Wade continues, "And parents wanted options, different options to that. So the community school movement developed very, very quickly. Parents began to take over some of the institutions that were run by the Archdiocese. . . . And parents just began to use homes for classrooms, . . . starting small, with small tuitions to get families to begin to come together and say, 'We can build an educational institution.' Many parents worked in the schools without degrees. We're talking about parents who knew child-rearing, who knew nurturing, and knew loving, were not necessarily . . . prepared . . . to understand all of the methods of instruction, but based on their willingness, . . . and strong belief that they can in fact educate their own children, participated in that educational process as teachers. And many of those parents went on to college to become educators now, professionally educated." Wade, interview.

31. Cook writes in her dissertation: "Educators and parents who have started alternative schools believe that a critical factor in determining students' intellectual and academic success is the overall social and cultural climate of the school as well as the attitude teachers and administrators have towards students, particularly inner-city Black and Latino children. Thus, students' backgrounds and needs must be linked in terms of both culture and language if they are to be educated successfully." Angela Paige Cook, "A Case Study of a Black Independent School: Reflections on Cultural Resonance in an Elementary and Pre -School Setting" (PhD diss., University of Massachusetts Boston, 2002).

32. *Say Brother*, "Paige Academy: An Alternative Education; Angela Paige Cook Comments on Standardized Testing," May 20, 1977, WGBH Archives, http://openvault.wgbh .org/catalog/V_E704B991699D401C900E608973999963.

33. Wade, interview.

34. Hampton and Fayer, *Voices of Freedom*, 592.

35. Nathaniel Jones, interview by author, 2016.

36. Jones, interview.

37. Hampton and Fayer, *Voices of Freedom*.

38. Jones, interview.

39. Jeanne Theoharis, *A More Beautiful and Terrible History: The Uses and Misuses of Civil Rights History* (Boston: Beacon Press, 2018).

40. Hampton and Fayer, *Voices of Freedom*, 589.

41. Hampton and Fayer, *Voices of Freedom*, 589.

42. Hampton and Fayer, *Voices of Freedom*, 599.

43. Hampton and Fayer, *Voices of Freedom*, 590.

44. Hampton, *Eyes on the Prize II*.

45. Hampton and Fayer, *Voices of Freedom*, 595.

46. Hampton and Fayer, *Voices of Freedom*.

47. Hampton and Fayer, *Voices of Freedom*, 594

48. Michael Patrick MacDonald, *All Souls: A Family Story from Southie* (Boston: Beacon Press, 1999), 60.

49. MacDonald, *All Souls*, 60.

50. Ruth Batson, interview by Jackie Shearer, transcript, *Eyes on the Prize II*, November 8, 1988, http://digital.wustl.edu/e/eii/eiiweb/bat5427.0911.011ruthbatson.html.

51. Facebook direct message to author, June 9, 2021.

52. Lew Finfer tells a story about a moment at this gathering. Pixie Palladino of ROAR is said to have stated, "There's no Common Ground here. All this talk about love and brotherhood. Who loves me?" Finfer recalls, "Someone called out, 'I love you Pixie!'" While humorous in many ways—and obviously meant as a moment of levity—Palladino is known to have made some of the most extreme statements of racism about Black children during the years of busing, having compared them to monkeys. How do we reconcile this kind of moment in the face of such dramatic historical contexts? I thank Lew Finfer for insights into moments like this. His eyewitness accounts, at so many key moments in this movement, are elucidating.

53. J. Anthony Lukas, "In Search of Common Ground: A Town Meeting on Race and Class in Boston" (presentation, September 28, 1985, Boston).

54. *Milliken v. Bradley*, 418 U.S. 717 (1974).

55. Lukas, "In Search of Common Ground."

56. Lew Finfer, "How a Meeting in Dorchester in 1971 Played a Role in a Judge's Busing Ruling," *Dorchester Reporter*, May 26, 2021, https://www.dotnews.com/2021/how-meeting -dorchester-1971-played-role-judges-busing-ruling.

57. Jim Vrabel, *A People's History of the New Boston* (Amherst: University of Massachusetts Press, 2014), 172.

58. Nina McCain, "Dorchester Parents Win as Craven Switches Vote," *Boston Globe*, September 22, 1971, 1.

59. Vrabel, *People's History of the New Boston*, 171.

60. Vrabel, *People's History of the New Boston*, 171–72.

61. Vrabel, *People's History of the New Boston*, 171.

62. J. Anthony Lukas, *Common Ground: A Turbulent Decade in the Lives of Three American Families* (New York: Knopf, 1985), 235. The suit had been brought by the NAACP in 1964 against the Springfield, Massachusetts, Board of Education. The case in Springfield became added into Garrity's calculus.

63. Lukas, *Common Ground*, 237.

64. Lukas, *Common Ground*, 238.

65. *Morgan v. Hennigan*, 379 F. Supp 410 (1974).

66. Lukas, *Common Ground*, 239.

67. Lew Finfer, "Busing in Boston—40 Years Later," September 3, 2014, *Boston Globe*, http://www.bostonglobe.com/opinion/2014/09/03/podium-finfer/pXARVb7Giw7AUIv LyuUG2O/story.html

68. Lukas tape-recorded more than 550 hours of interviews.

69. Theoharis and Woodard, *Groundwork*, 17.

70. Jon Hillson, "'Common Ground': Attack on Boston's Desegregation," *Militant*, November 22, 1985. See also Jon Hillson, *The Battle of Boston* (New York: Pathfinder Press, 1977).

71. Thomas I. Atkins, review of *Common Ground*, by J. Anthony Lukas, *Social Policy*, Winter 1986.

72. Tito Jackson, interview by author, June 2021.

73. Jackson, interview.

74. Jackson, interview.

75. Thomas Sugrue, "It's Not the Bus: It's Us," *London Review of Books*, November 20, 2008.

76. Sugrue, "It's Not the Bus," 401.

77. W. E. B. Du Bois, *Black Reconstruction in America: An Essay toward a History of the Part Which Black Folk Played in the Attempt to Reconstruct Democracy in America, 1860–1880* (Cleveland: World, 1964), 110.

78. King, *Chain of Change*, vii.

79. Hampton, *Eyes on the Prize II*.

80. L. W. Levy and D. L. Jones, *Jim Crow in Boston: The Origin of the Separate but Equal Doctrine* (Boston: Da Capo Press, 1974).

81. *Boston Globe*, December 31, 1974.

82. Churches in the Boston Movement Panel, Power and Protest Conference, John F. Kennedy Presidential Museum and Library, Boston, MA, October 2006.

83. Willie Mae Reid and Peter Camejo, *The Racist Offensive against Busing: The Lessons of Boston, How to Fight Back* (New York: Pathfinder, 1974).

84. Reid and Camejo, *Racist Offensive against Busing*.

Epilogue

1. See Elizabeth Hafkin Pleck, *Black Migration and Poverty: Boston, 1865–1900* (New York: Academic Press, 1979); James O. Horton and Lois E. Horton, *Black Bostonians: Family Life and Community Struggle in the Antebellum North* (New York: Holmes and Meier, 1979); Carol Buchalter Stapp, *Afro-Americans in Antebellum Boston: An Analysis of Probate Records*

(New York: Garland Press, 1993); George Levesque, *Black Boston: African-American Life and Culture in Urban America, 1750–1860* (New York: Garland, 1994).

2. James W. Loewen, *Sundown Towns: A Hidden Dimension of American Racism* (New York: New Press, 2005).

3. Leon Jones, *From Brown to Boston: Desegregation in Education, 1954–1974,* 2 vols. (Metuchen, NJ: Scarecrow Press, 1979).

4. Ironically enough, he was elected to Louise Day Hicks's old slot.

5. Jones, *From Brown to Boston,* 20.

6. See Audrea Dunham-Jones, "Boston's 1960s Civil Rights Movement: A Look Back," accessed March 23, 2022, https://openvault.wgbh.org/exhibits/boston_civil_rights/authors.

7. What are the hurdles of doing history on Northeast spaces, with their long and celebrated history of racial equality and political liberalism—the relative myths and realities of that experience? The "hidden in plain sight" nature of such racism and how that operates on the ground influences freedom movements and Black power studies of such places. Future scholars should consider the ways in which Northeast freedom movements after World War II celebrated the election of Black leaders and cultural triumphs in sports but had forms of oppression that went against that legacy.

8. "Crisis to Crisis: Voices of a Divided City," Film and Media Archive, American Archive of Public Broadcasting, accessed December 29, 2021, http://americanarchive.org/catalog /cpb-aacip-151-2z12n4zx29. See also Jason Sokol, *All Eyes Are upon Us: Race and Politics from Boston to Brooklyn* (New York: Basic Books, 2014).

9. There needs, however, to be a new wave of scholarship that details the civil rights movement in Boston and reflects the same spirit as other definitive works that have been published in the last several years on other cities, such as *Up South: Civil Rights and Black Power in Philadelphia* by Matthew Countryman, *To Stand and Fight: The Struggle for Civil Rights in Postwar New York City* by Martha Biondi, *Fighting Jim Crow in the County of Kings: The Congress of Racial Equality in Brooklyn* by Brian Purnell, *Freedom North* by Jeanne Theoharis and Komozi Woodard, *The Selma of the North* by Patrick Jones, and *Sweet Land of Liberty* by Tom Sugrue—works that have been particularly impactful in turning the tide to a renewed interest in civil rights struggles in the North.

10. Jeanne Theoharis and Komozi Woodard's work on Boston is especially instructive here, as is her scholarship on the theoretical dimensions on the northern civil rights struggle in general. This work has been a veritable call to arms that has resulted in the production of more studies of the northern urban freedom movement. This work answers both the call for more studies of the northern civil rights movement and fills the current vacuum of work on Boston. See Jeanne Theoharis and Komozi Woodard, *Freedom North: Black Freedom Struggles Outside the South, 1940–1980* (New York: Palgrave Macmillan, 2003). See also Jeanne Theoharis and Komozi Woodard, *Groundwork: Local Black Freedom Movements in America* (New York: New York University, 2005). The scholarship by Martha Biondi, Brian Purnell, Patrick Jones, and Matthew Countryman are part of a larger conversation about the northern movement and its implications for the national civil rights struggle.

11. In "'We Saved the City': Black Struggles for Educational Equality in Boston, 1960–1976," Jeanne Theoharis provides an important conceptual framework. She writes, "While scholars have sought to complicate the historiography of the movement in recent years, the dominant civil rights narrative remains that of a nonviolent movement born in

the South during the 1950s that emerged triumphant in the early 1960s but then was de-railed by the twin forces of Black Power and white backlash when it sought to move north after 1965." See also Violet Showers Johnson, *The Other Black Bostonians: West Indians in Boston, 1900–1950* (Bloomington: Indiana University Press, 2006); Marilyn Halter, *Between Race and Ethnicity: Cape Verdean American Immigrants, 1860–1965* (Urbana: University of Illinois Press, 1993).

12. Of course, it does not help that this area is now one of the most expensive and exclu-sive areas in the city of Boston, a status that only seems to enhance this period and further solidify it as the "golden age" of Boston. It's one of the reasons that many early accounts of Boston focus only on this period.

13. See Noel Ignatiev, *How the Irish Became White* (New York: Routledge, 1995).

Acknowledgments

1. Matt. 16:13–20 (NIV). It reads, "And I tell you that you are Peter, and on this rock I will build my church, and the gates of Hades will not overcome it. I will give you the 'keys of the kingdom' of heaven; whatever you bind on earth will be bound in heaven, and whatever you loose on earth will be loosed in heaven."

2. I received a scholarship in high school named after Tallulah Morgan, given by the Edwards Foundation. Both of these helped to complete my education.

3. I'd like to thank Bill Forry and Linda Dorcena-Forry for their friendship, as well as L'Mani Viney, Farouk Brown, Rui Gomes, Cory Garcia, Paulo Abu-Raya, Gibran Rivera, Saman Wickramasinghe, Nick Mounier, Rizwan Jamal, Chris Quinones, Wendy Sanchez Foulis, Massiel Medina, Rob Hines, Juan Concepcion, and Daila Gonzalez.

4. When I think about John Bracey, I can almost hear the ancestors saying: Do no harm. Do nothing to embarrass your people. We are all dignified despite what may have been done to us or to our ancestors. We are proud. We walked the earth before anyone else. There is no shame in slavery or any of the things ours people have undergone. We are bril-liant. We are human. We have nothing to be ashamed of.

5. I would also like to thank A Yẹmisi Jimoh, Toussaint Losier, Traci Parker, Nelson Stevens, Britt Rusert, Amilcar Shabazz, Bob Wolff, and Steven C. Tracy.

6. In one of those great post-panel discussions at the ASALH annual conference, Dr. Viv-ian Johnson talked about Boston being a "place of the mind." It was a razor for understand-ing some of the barriers to studying such a place.

7. Carter G. Woodson Luncheon at the Association for the Study of African American Life and History, Indianapolis, October 6, 2018.

Index

bold denotes photo

following King's assassination, 133, 138 (*see also* rebellions; riots); Harrison as architect of, 80; against host of issues, 6; against leaders who were framed, 144; nonviolent ones, 7; against segregated schooling, 111, 169; against showing of *The Birth of a Nation*, 58; targeting discrimination in education, 32; Trotter's mounting of, 11; white intransigence to, 183; against Wonder Bread, 12–13, 119, 121
Pruitts family, 163
Pullman porters, 82
Purcelle family, 163
Purnell, Brian, 8, 189
Putnam, George, 33

Quincy E. Dickerman Elementary School, 100–101

race: century-long struggles over in Boston, 1, 18, 66–67, 70, 84, 128, 150, 164, 170, 182, 183, 188, 192, 193; effect of Great Depression vision of, 71; peculiarities and paradoxes of in Boston, 85, 127; the South as constricting popular understandings of in U.S., 7; Supreme Court on separating children solely because of, 96; as used to drive wedge between white and Black workers, 75
race man, 3, 50
race relations, 7, 8, 10, 36, 75, 89, 128, 149, 183, 186, 193
race work, 52
racial borrowing, 168
racial discrimination, 1, 9, 10, 11, 13, 63, 64, 74, 90, 114, 115, 118, 182, 193
racial equality, 4, 23, 83, 97, 192
Racial Imbalance Act (Massachusetts) (1965), 6, 153–54, 172, 188
racialized slavery, 9, 16, 18–20
racial justice, 2, 6, 7, 8, 9, 12, 33, 37, 54, 76, 183, 191, 192, 193, 229n22
racial uplift, 11, 44, 59, 64, 222n17
racial violence, 13, 60, 93, 149, 167–68, 180, 182, 187, 190, 191, 193, 213n21

racism: Boston's history of, 2, 86, 103, 106, 128, 132, 145, 149, 166, 182, 188, 191, 192, 193; and class, 4, 67; CPUSA's strong stance on, 71, 73; fight against in Boston, 99; "hidden in plain sight" nature of, 246n7; the South as constricting popular understandings of in U.S., 7; student protests against, 147; Trotter's experience with, 51
rallies, 65, 111, 116, 124, 137, 144, 167, 213n21
Randolph, A. Philip, 82
Rappaport, Jerome, 140
Reagan, Ronald, 185
"Realistic Look at Race Relations, A" (MLK speech), 89
rebellions: following King's assassination, 6, 13, 127, 128, 133 (*see also* demonstrations; protests; riots); inward rebellion, 216n22; outward rebellion, 216n22
Reconstruction: busing as Boston's "Reconstruction," 180–83; in the South, 180–81
"Red Boston," 70
redlining, 82, 140. *See also* reverse redlining
Reeb, James J., 124, 125
Reed, John, 70
Reed family, 163
Reeves, Jim, 144
residential segregation/housing segregation, 67, 82, 96, 103, 140, 148, 189, 190
reverse discrimination, 185
reverse redlining, 141
Revolutionary War, Blacks in, 20–23
riots: Boston Riot, 48, 49, 56, 60; against British troops, 21; against busing, 169, 190–91; consequences of, 147, 148–49; following King's assassination, 127, 128, 129–30, 132, 133, 134, 135, 136, 140–41; race riots, 28; responses to, 140–41; riot-that-wasn't, 13; by students, 138; welfare riots (1967), 6, 13, 129, 135, 136
ROAR (Restore Our Alienated Rights), 7, 173
Roberts, Benjamin, 9–10, 34, 35, 36, 50, 220n87

Printed in the USA
CPSIA information can be obtained
at www.ICGtesting.com
CBHW022019110924
14384CB00001B/28